The Kingmaker's Women

The Kingmaker's Women

Anne Beauchamp and Her Daughters, Isabel and Anne Neville

Julia A. Hickey

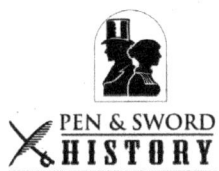

First published in Great Britain in 2023 by
Pen & Sword History
An imprint of Pen & Sword Books Limited
Yorkshire – Philadelphia

Copyright © Julia A. Hickey 2023

ISBN 978 1 39906 485 9

The right of Julia A. Hickey to be identified as
Author of this Work has been asserted by her in accordance
with the Copyright, Designs and Patents Act 1988.

A CIP catalogue record for this book is
available from the British Library

All rights reserved. No part of this book may be reproduced or
transmitted in any form or by any means, electronic or mechanical
including photocopying, recording or by any information storage and
retrieval system, without permission from the Publisher in writing.

Typeset by Mac Style
Printed in the UK by CPI Group (UK) Ltd, Croydon, CR0 4YY.

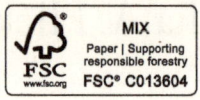

Pen & Sword Books Limited incorporates the imprints of After the
Battle, Atlas, Archaeology, Aviation, Discovery, Family History,
Fiction, History, Maritime, Military, Military Classics, Politics,
Select, Transport, True Crime, Air World, Frontline Publishing,
Leo Cooper, Remember When, Seaforth Publishing, The Praetorian
Press, Wharncliffe Local History, Wharncliffe Transport,
Wharncliffe True Crime and White Owl.

For a complete list of Pen & Sword titles please contact

PEN & SWORD BOOKS LIMITED
47 Church Street, Barnsley, South Yorkshire, S70 2AS, England
E-mail: enquiries@pen-and-sword.co.uk
Website: www.pen-and-sword.co.uk
or
PEN AND SWORD BOOKS
1950 Lawrence Rd, Havertown, PA 19083, USA
E-mail: Uspen-and-sword@casematepublishers.com
Website: www.penandswordbooks.com

Methinks truly
Bouden am I,
and that greatly.
To be content;
seeing plainly
Fortune doth wry
All contrary
from mine intent

        Anthony Woodville, 2nd Earl Rivers

Contents

Acknowledgements ix
Illustrations x
Genealogical Tables xi
Introduction xvii

Chapter 1 A Noble Family and a Troublesome One 1
Chapter 2 Childhood and Education 17
Chapter 3 Calais 39
Chapter 4 A Northern Inheritance 48
Chapter 5 The Marriage Market 57
Chapter 6 Marrying a Prince 66
Chapter 7 The Wives and Daughters of Rebels 77
Chapter 8 Anne – the Kingmaker's Bargain 86
Chapter 9 Lancastrian Princess 95
Chapter 10 From Scullery Maid to Duchess 104
Chapter 11 The Duchess of Gloucester 112
Chapter 12 The Duchess of Clarence 121
Chapter 13 Witchcraft, Murder and Treason 131
Chapter 14 The Lord Protector's Wife 139
Chapter 15 Queen Anne 146
Chapter 16 A Royal Progress 152

Chapter 17	An Enigma – Piety and Patronage	157
Chapter 18	Sudden Grief	164
Chapter 19	Christmas 1484	167
Chapter 20	Afterwards	174

Appendix
Key Dates of the Wars of the Roses — 180
Who's Who — 196
Notes — 215
Bibliography — 223
Index — 232

Acknowledgements

I have to start by thanking Beth Harding, Stefan Bobeszko and James Vaughan at Ashbourne Library, and also Fiona Raistrick and Karen Deakin at Chesterfield Library for their unstinting dedication sourcing a never-ending list of interlibrary loans. Without libraries and librarians, it would not be possible for me to access much of my reading. As Billy Connolly explains in his biography, 'libraries are your ticket to the whole world'.

I am indebted to Dr Paul Fox for his generosity in helping me to locate the position of Anne Neville's coat of arms in the north-west transept of Canterbury Cathedral; to David Harpin for information relating to heraldry; and to Janet Senior for material regarding Sheriff Hutton. Thanks to Eleri Pipien for suggesting the project and to the team at Pen and Sword for their skill, professionalism and patience: Claire Hopkins, Sarah-Beth Watkins, Laura Hirst and Lucy May. I would particularly like to thank my copy-editor Michelle Higgs for her hard work and attention to detail. Thank you for turning my dreams into reality.

My greatest debt is to Kyle who has been dragged into the fifteenth century, proofread every chapter, asked questions and remained good-humoured throughout. Without his help and support, none of this would have been possible.

Illustrations

1. Alabaster effigy of Ralph Neville, 1st Earl of Westmorland (c.1364–1425) with his two wives, Margaret Stafford and Joan Beaufort, in St Mary's Church, Staindrop, County Durham
2. Stained glass image depicting Joan Beaufort, Countess of Westmorland, in St Andrew's Church, Penrith, Cumbria
3. Gilded bronze effigy of Richard Beauchamp, 13th Earl of Warwick (1382–1439) in the Beauchamp Chapel of the Collegiate Church of St Mary, Warwick, Warwickshire
4. Bear and ragged staff in St Andrew's Church, Penrith, Cumbria
5. Anne Beauchamp, Countess of Warwick, from the *Rous Roll*
6. George, Duke of Clarence, with Duchess Isabel, the daughter of Richard Neville, from the *Rous Roll*
7. *The Earl of Warwick Submits to Queen Margaret* by James William Edmund Doyle (1864)
8. Arms of Anne Neville
9. *Richard, Duke of Gloucester, and the Lady Anne* by Edwin Austin Abbey, (oil on canvas, 1896).
10. Stained glass image depicting George, Duke of Clarence, and Isabel Neville, Cardiff Castle
11. Stained glass image depicting King Richard III and Anne Neville, Cardiff Castle
12. Church of St Mary and St Alkelda, Middleham, North Yorkshire
13. King Richard III and Edward of Middleham, Church of St Mary and St Alkelda, Middleham, North Yorkshire
14. Queen Anne, Church of St Mary and St Alkelda, Middleham, North Yorkshire
15. Middleham Castle, North Yorkshire
16. Warwick Castle, Warwickshire
17. Tewkesbury Abbey, Gloucestershire
18. Effigy thought to be Edward of Middleham, Church of St Helen and the Holy Cross, Sheriff Hutton, York
19. Unknown woman, formerly known as Margaret Pole, Countess of Salisbury

Genealogical Tables

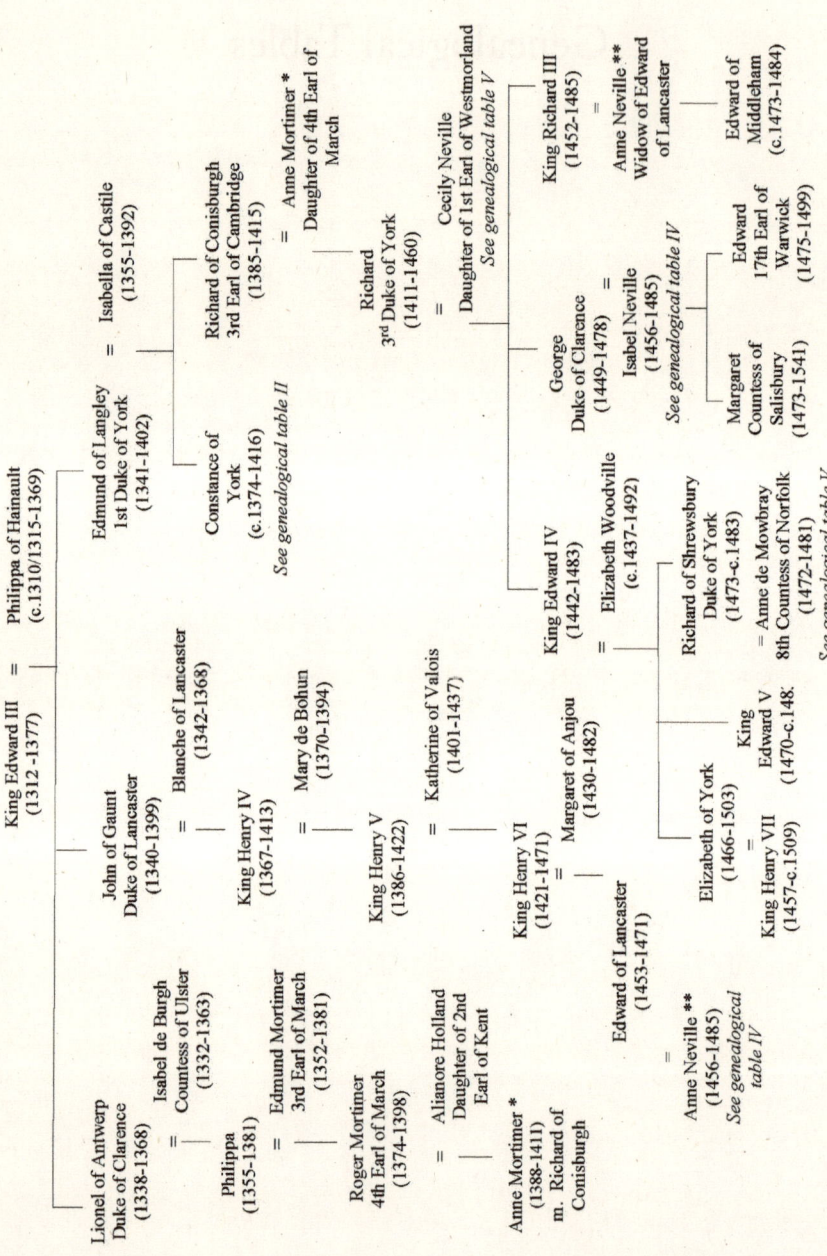

I) Simplified lines of descent from King Edward III showing the Houses of Lancaster and York.

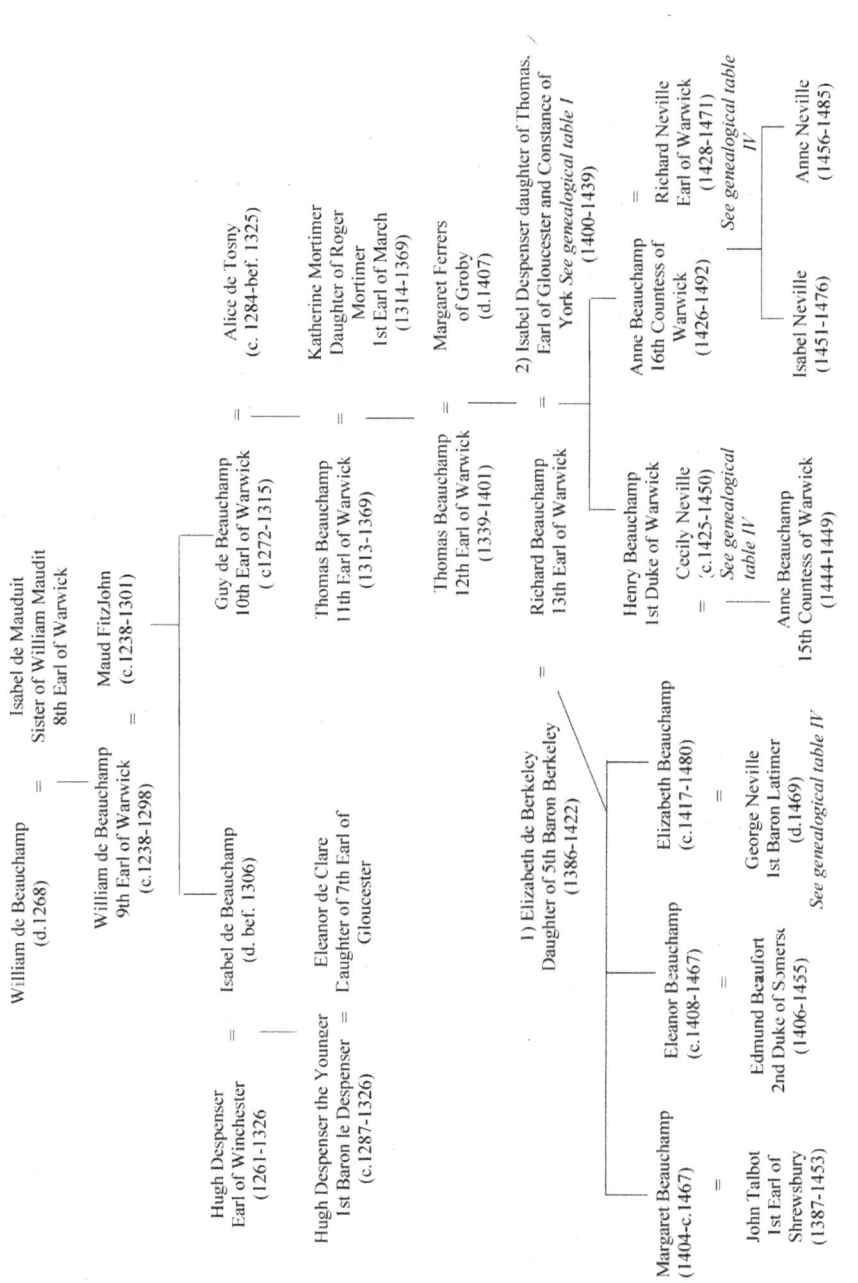

II) Simplified Beauchamp line of descent.

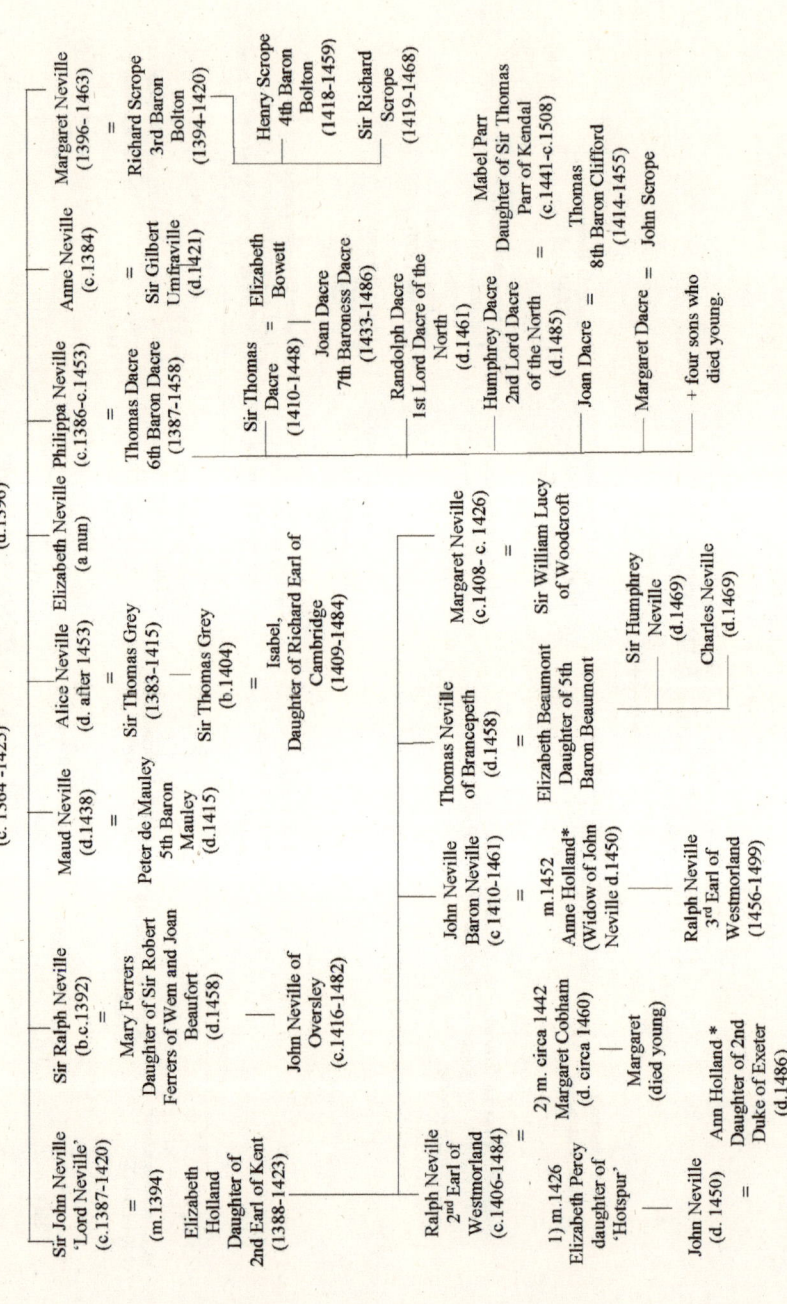

III) Neville line of descent from the first marriage of Ralph Neville, 1st Earl of Westmorland, to Margaret Stafford.

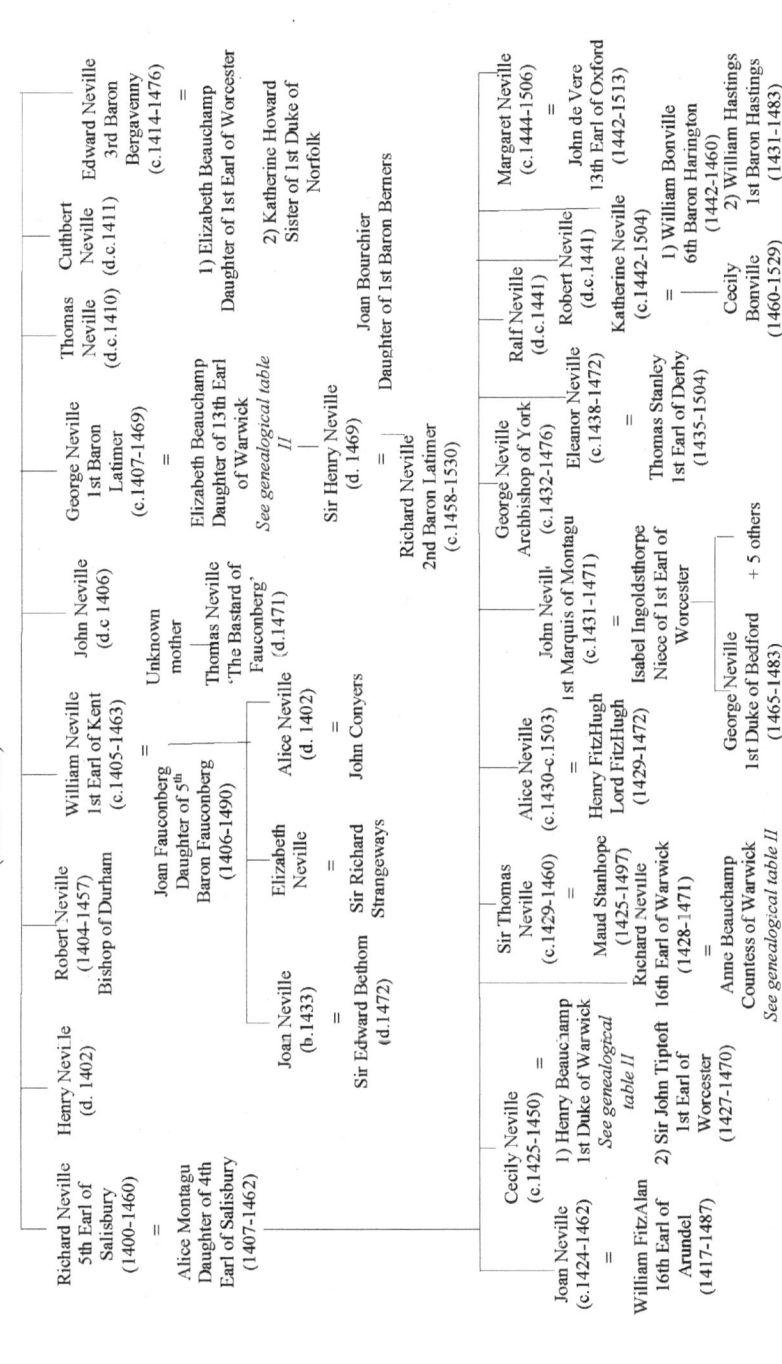

IV) Simplified male line of descent from the second marriage of Ralph Neville, 1st Earl of Westmorland, to Joan Beaufort.

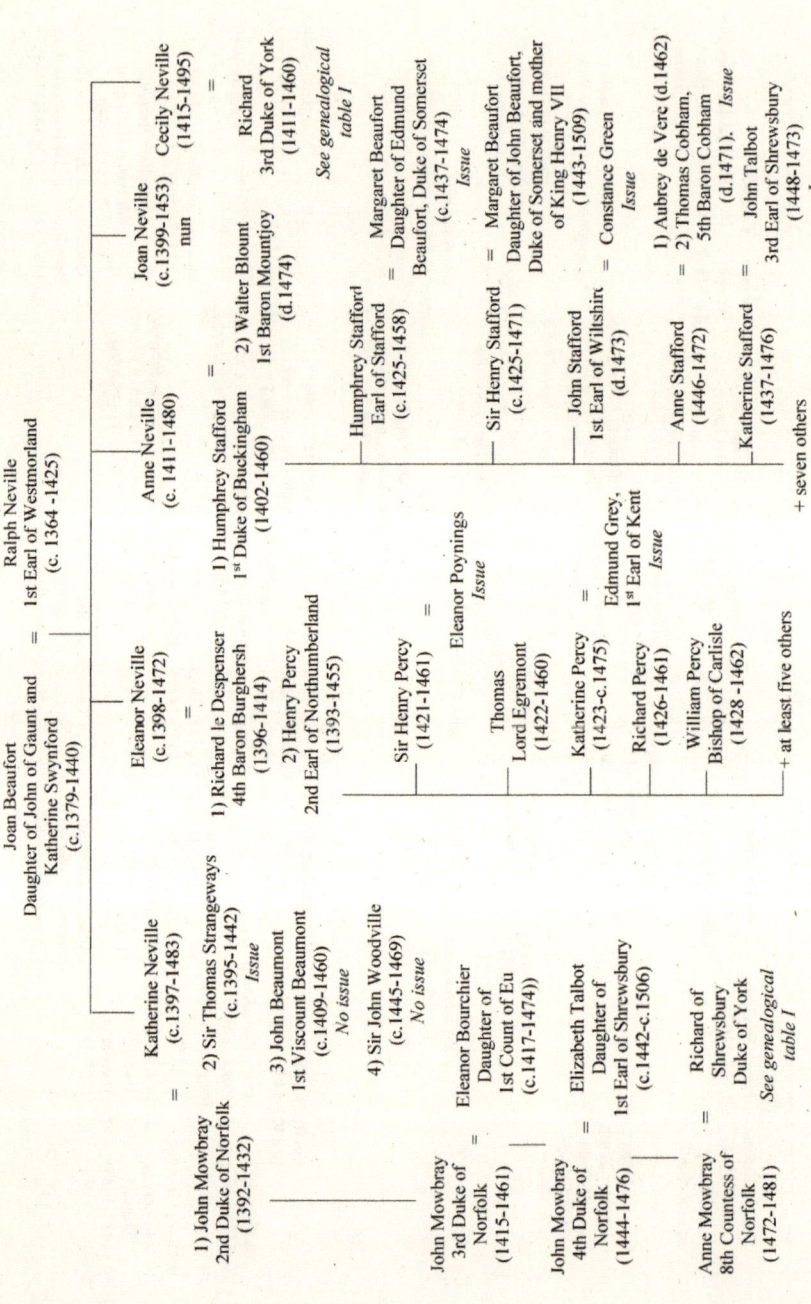

V) Simplified female line of descent from the second marriage of Ralph Neville, 1st Earl of Westmorland, to Joan Beaufort.

Introduction

Isabel and Anne Neville led brief but turbulent lives. Their father, Richard Neville, 16th Earl of Warwick by right of his wife, Anne Beauchamp, was at the heart of the conflicts of the mid-fifteenth century, earning himself the name 'Warwick the Kingmaker'. The earl was a charismatic, fearless warrior whose fortunes, and those of his family, rose and fell. Countess Anne and her children were chronicled alongside the earl in his long-played political game spanning more than twenty years, concluding only with his death on a foggy Easter morning at Barnet in 1471. By then Isabel and Anne were the currency by which their father sought to control the future of the Crown. It is impossible to write about their lives without setting them in the context of the War of the Roses and their father's influence upon it. Their identity and importance came from their roles as daughters and, later, wives of the great and the good. To understand them as individuals, it is necessary to look beyond the veil that cloaks the common life experiences of most medieval women from bride to widowhood.[1]

There is a tendency to perceive aristocratic women of the medieval era as pawns used to further the socio-political agendas of their fathers, brothers, husbands and sons while they themselves were confined to the domestic world rather than a wider political stage. Often when seeking their voices, it becomes a case of *cherchez la femme* as chroniclers tended to omit women from their accounts unless their appearance impacted on the stability of a kingdom or changed the political dynamic. If, like King Henry VI's queen Margaret of Anjou, their voices echoed too loudly within a patriarchal world, they ran the risk of being criticised as unfeminine or worse, both during their lifetimes and beyond. Margaret led armies, governed on her husband's behalf and faced down rumours of adultery, but, initially, she failed to fulfil the traditional role of a medieval queen. She had no dowry and for the first seven years of her marriage, failed to provide the kingdom with its heir. Shakespeare was able to paint Margaret as a 'foreigner, white devil, shrew, virago and vengeful fury'[2] in the three plays in which she is referenced. In time she became one of history's so-called she-wolves because of her perceived lack of femininity. Edward IV's queen, Elizabeth Woodville, fared no better during her lifetime because of her perceived humble origins; the fact that she was a widow when she married the king rather than a royal virgin; and because of her impecunious and extensive family who scrambled for preferment. Shakespeare would later emphasise her role as a bereaved mother in order to vilify King Richard III, but did not draw on contemporary criticisms of Elizabeth, perhaps recognising Tudor sensitivities on the subject. For similar reasons Henry Tudor's mother, Lady Margaret Beaufort, one of the shrewdest political operators of the Wars of the Roses is absent from his plays.

Women were supposed to be weaker than their male counterparts. The Church perceived them as responsible for original sin and therefore more likely to succumb to temptation than men. Eve tempted Adam with the apple and mankind was expelled from the Garden of Eden. The view was compounded by the medical theories of the period derived from the Greeks and transmitted through the Arab world into the West. Not only were they morally weaker than their male counterparts, but they were also regarded as physically passive, cold and much more fragile. Medieval law removed agency from women based on their perceived frailties. They were legally dependent on their male guardians whether they were fathers or brothers, unless an individual woman was granted the status of *femme sole* who could be held legally responsible for making contracts, trade in her own right and be held accountable for the payment of debts. Women who eloped with the men they loved or who were abducted and raped were subject to the same *raptus* law which showed no empathy with the woman, preferring to focus on her loss as a property theft so far as the male authority figure in her life was concerned.

Anne Beauchamp and her daughters were heiresses who inherited estates and titles. Their marriages did not legally deprive them of their inheritance, but they would have been exceptionally strong-minded, not to mention politically powerful, to keep their titles and lands to themselves. Their husbands became earls and landholders, *jure uxoris* by right of their wives, and took control of their estates. Richard Neville was transformed into a leading magnate by virtue of his marriage. Men might recognise the debt they owed their wives by working in partnership in matters of writs and charters, but they were not required to give them an administrative role in the matters which were their own birthright.

As well as inheritances, there was also the dowry that a bride took with her to her husband from her family at the time of the wedding. Anne Neville's marriage to Richard of Duke of Gloucester was unusual for a couple of their rank in that no dowry could be agreed for her. A dowry was not an inheritance; it was the property that a girl's family agreed to transfer to her new husband at the time of their marriage. In return the groom's family bestowed a dower upon the bride that became her property to control for so long as she lived, even if she was widowed or her husband was attainted of treason and lost all his possessions. Dowers and dowries were negotiated in advance of a marriage. On occasion the land that the bride's family transferred became part of her dower. Where, as was the case for Anne Neville, there was no formal agreement, common law gave one-third of a man's property to his widow for her lifetime in the event of his death before hers. This law did not apply to the widows of attainted traitors who could anticipate nothing from their husband's confiscated estates. Aristocratic women expected a jointure as well as a dower. This was land settled on both husband and wife while both were alive, but which became the property of the survivor on the death of the other, even in the case of treason. Widows who married two or three times could become extremely wealthy as their dower and jointure lands accumulated to the detriment of the heirs to their husbands' estates who had to wait for their mothers, step-mothers and even grandmothers to die before being licensed to enter their inheritance in its entirety. These women were not only wealthy, they were also independent and influential within their families.

Neither Isabel nor Anne lived long enough to have the jointures and dower rights associated with widowhood or the agency that went with them. The legal rights of their mother, the *suo jure* Countess of Warwick, were stolen from her by king and Parliament. One of the consequences of their lived experience was that they did not leave the kind of documentary trail that would help to shine a light upon their lives. Daughters and wives were expected to fulfil their familial duties without complaint. They were responsible for managing vast households, held titles in their own right and their husbands may have conferred with them as partners in their family enterprise, but they are often absent from the written record. Isabel and Anne grew up, lived and died largely unheralded in a masculine world, or so it appears at first glance. Dig deeper and the echo of women with voices demanding to be heard, including Countess Anne, can be found in court records, financial accounts, charters, wills, books commissioned by wealthy well-educated women, chantries and parish churches throughout the realm.

Aristocratic heiresses like the countess and her daughters were the means by which title and land equating to power and wealth were transmitted from family to family. It is true that marriage amongst the ruling classes and the merchant elites in the medieval period was very different to a modern marriage. Women did not have a choice as to who they would marry or an opportunity to build a relationship before the wedding. Little thought was given to the compatibility of the bride and groom. Marriages were made for political and financial benefit. Countess Anne's family arranged her wedding to Richard Neville while the couple were still children as subsidiary to the marriage of their siblings Henry Beauchamp and Cecily Neville. It was Anne's unexpected inheritance that made Richard an important magnate. She travelled with him, oversaw the management of their estates in his absence, was party to his schemes and subject to the State's wrath after his death, but history knows little of their personal feelings for one another. Her letters following the earl's death, demanding her legal rights and her determination to regain her inheritance, remain as testimony to both her education and her powerlessness.

Isabel Neville, a shadowy figure who died when she was 25, was married to King Edward's brother George, Duke of Clarence, because her father was eager to link the Neville name with that of Plantagenet. Clarence was desirous of the match because Isabel was the elder daughter of one of England's most powerful men and an heiress to vast estates. There was a distinct possibility that Warwick would topple Edward from the throne and place Clarence upon it. Yet, circumstantial evidence demonstrates that Isabel was beloved by George who was only a year older than his bride. Unlike the king, Clarence had no known mistresses or illegitimate children, he was grief-stricken by her death and he was permitted, as he desired, to be interred next to Isabel at Tewkesbury following his own execution for treason.

The idea of heiress as powerless trophy is a trope embedded into our common view of Anne Neville, thanks to Shakespeare's portrayal of her in *Richard III* as a pawn passed from Lancaster to York for the sake of her father's ambitions. Then she is manipulated into marrying Richard, Duke of Gloucester, even though she knows he is responsible for the murder of her husband and father-in-law. Anne's story, told by Shakespeare, is based on Sir Thomas More's unfinished and historically untrue *History of King Richard III* in which she features as another innocent victim of her husband's ambitions. Anne has served since Tudor times as a cypher to illustrate Richard's evils. A Victorian writer described the king as committing 'a succession of astounding crimes'[3] and that the death of his and Anne's only living child was God's vengeance for the death of his nephews. Richard remains the king of controversy while Anne lingers as a sickly pawn moved around the political gaming board by powerful men.

In reality Anne's life was an example of the changeability of fortune depicted by the popular medieval philosophy of Fortuna's wheel. History does not know if she was a woman of courage or shrewd intelligence in the way the Lady Margaret Beaufort is recognised, but John Rous who knew Anne described her as 'amiable and beauteous and in conditions full commendable and right virtuous'.[4] Evidence suggests that whatever her health might have been, she was made of the same stern stuff as Henry Tudor's mother to whom she was distantly related. Anne endured a sea battle and saw her sister Isabel give birth to a stillborn infant at sea; was married to the son of her father's bitterest enemy; made a forced march with the Lancastrian army from the south of England to Tewkesbury in 1471; was widowed after five months of marriage; and escaped the clutches of her land-hungry brother-in-law. She preferred to risk the criminals of St Martin's sanctuary near Westminster so that she could make a second marriage to the Duke of Gloucester who would fight for her portion of their mother's estates.

Ultimately Anne may have failed to provide Richard with a surviving heir and died before there could be any substantial record of her role as queen of England, but she lent her husband the Neville name which helped gain him support in the north. She might have spent the remainder of her days overseeing her household and servants in Middleham as the Duchess of Gloucester, the beloved wife of a lord respected by his people for his loyalty to the Crown, the justice he administered and the stability that his rule brought, had King Edward IV not died while his eldest son was still a child. Fortuna's wheel carried Anne to the apex of society where she chose to surround herself with Neville kinswomen familiar since childhood, including her own illegitimate half-sister, Margaret. Fate continued its abrupt revolution following Richard III's accession to the throne, carrying Anne towards an early death. The loss of her only son followed hard on the heels of a double coronation and triumphant progress to York. It was not long before Anne became so unwell that her doctors prohibited the king from sharing her bed. As winter turned into spring in March 1485, Anne died and was buried in Westminster Abbey, leaving behind only rumour, speculation and rebellion.

Her grieving widower had cause to pray for relief from 'affliction, temptation, grief, sickness and danger'.[5] It availed him nothing. Five months later Richard was dead and vanquished, buried with scant regard for ceremony, leaving Anne to be characterised as a victim rather than a woman born with a powerful name and the potential of political agency. Even more extraordinary, the circumstances surrounding the end of Isabel and Anne's brief lives were followed by accusations of murder and witchcraft. Clarence, to modern eyes at least, maddened with grief following the untimely death of Isabel, accused one of her own household of causing her death. Ankarette Twynyho, possibly a trusted midwife, fitted into an evolving stereotype of a witch and Clarence had no hesitation either in kidnapping the woman or having her judicially murdered. The concept of witchcraft was still a fluid one, but charges of witchcraft were used as a political tool against women of all walks of life. Warwick used the accusation against Jacquetta of Luxembourg, Edward IV's mother-in-law, in a bid to sway the validity of the king's marriage. Elizabeth Woodville, Edward IV's widow, would find herself facing accusations of sorcery to harm Gloucester before his coronation as King Richard III, as would Edward IV's former mistress Jane Shore who was made to do public penance for her harlotry through the streets of London. The Tudor propaganda machine turned the tables on King Richard III when he was vilified as the murderer of his nephews, a poisoner and a man of such diabolical intensity that he may have terrified his own queen, reduced to a one-dimensional prop, into an early grave.

Countess Anne lived on after her daughters. Consigned to the footnotes or forgotten by history, the *suo jure* Countess of Warwick, declared legally dead, refused to be stripped of her voice or her rights and wrote to the king, to Parliament and the aristocratic women of her acquaintance, demanding that they strive for justice on her behalf. Later she may have commissioned *The Pageants of Richard Beauchamp, Earl of Warwick* and the *Rous Roll* that depict the lives of the Earls of Warwick, the countess, and Isabel and Anne. There was no such thing as a bad Earl of Warwick in her opinion. Her power and that of her daughters lay in the land that they represented, in their kinship networks and the men they slept with. A pragmatist and political survivor, Countess Anne negotiated her return to legal life with the accession of the Tudors. When she died in 1492, she was buried next to her husband in Bisham Abbey. Anne left Isabel's surviving children, Margaret and Edward, nothing, apart from a Plantagenet legacy that would see Edward, the 17th Earl of Warwick, executed for treason in 1499 and her daughter, Margaret Pole, *suo jure* Countess of Salisbury, butchered by an inept headsman in 1541.

Countess Anne and her daughters were not the only women in their extended family to emerge onto the political stage or to suffer its consequences. Isabel and Anne's grandmother, Alice Montagu, *suo jure* Countess of Salisbury, was attainted of treason in 1459 because of her husband's support of the Yorkist cause. Cecily, Duchess of York, Warwick's aunt, was required to plea for pardon before King Henry VI during the same year before being stripped of her wealth and placed under house arrest in the custody of her elder sister Anne, Duchess of Buckingham. Isabel and Anne's own aunt Margaret Neville became the wife of an attainted traitor and was forced into sanctuary where she earned her living as a seamstress. All of them could be described as lacking in agency – married for the betterment of their families and without a right to individual legal identity. However, it was through their domestic duties as wives and mothers that they secured power and interacted with the cut and thrust of the public male domain. These women were relied upon to run estates efficiently in their husbands' absence; to give birth to the next generation and transmit land, title and wealth to those children; and to maintain social contacts and make use of familial networks in the interests of their family. Medieval chroniclers and the focus of history's lens marginalises women like Countess Anne and her daughters by imposing a distinction between the masculine public and the feminine domestic spheres. The messy reality is that the countess and her daughters lived complex and sometimes contentious lives, risking everything to protect their family's interests.

Chapter 1

A Noble Family and a Troublesome One

The arms of Anne Neville Queen of England can be found blazoned on a roof boss in the north-west transept of Canterbury Cathedral.[1] The arms are impaled, meaning that Richard's arms are on the right or the *dexter* half of the shield and Anne's are on the left or *sinister* side. On occasion, as in Canterbury, Anne used the Neville arms without difference – a white (*argent*) saltire on a red (*gules*) field displayed by inheritance from her father. Coats of arms were about identity and lineage. Status was based on blood and land. Anne and Isabel Neville's ancestry, including descent from Edward III's son, Edmund of Langley and Isabella of Castile was blazoned for the whole world to see. Anne can be identified from the arms on her mantle in Copy A of the fifteenth-century *Salisbury Rolls of Arms*[2] as well as in the *Rous Roll*.[3] Not only do the arms identify Anne and her line of descent, they also provide an insight into the status and achievements of her forefathers as well as a sense of the weight of expectations that rested on her shoulders.

In the second, differentiated, version of her arms, the *sinister* half of the blazon shows eight quarterings. Quartering simply means that the shield or lozenge is divided into equal parts for which there is no limit to the number allowed. The complexity of the differentiations reflects the total of Anne's ancestors who were permitted a coat of arms. The lineage depicted included the Beauchamp, Montagu, Monthermer, Neville, Clare and Despenser families. It tells the story of power attained through land acquisition achieved by a series of strategic marriage alliances as well as service to the monarch. John Rous was right to call Anne 'the most noble lady and princess born of royal blood of divers realms lineally descending from princes, kings, emperors, and many glorious saints'.[4]

The Beauchamps were not always as blue blooded as Rous suggested. They rose from their position as a regional landed family based in Worcestershire through a lucky marriage made in the thirteenth century by William Beauchamp to Isabel de Mauduit. Isabel's cousins Thomas de

Beaumont, the 6th Earl of Warwick, and Margaret de Beaumont, the *suo jure* 7th Countess of Warwick, both died without children. Her brother, William de Mauduit, who became the eighth earl also perished without heirs. Fortuna's wheel turned in favour of Isabel's son who inherited the earldom from his uncle. The new Beauchamp earls made judicious unions with eligible heiresses and regulated the marriages of their own daughters to prevent the dispersal of their landholdings. The political framework of the medieval period relied on the warp and weft of extended kinship networks to function, and the Beauchamp Earls of Warwick proved skilled weavers of aristocratic alliances across the next six generations. Their influence spread from the Midlands to the Marches and beyond. The outlook was bleak for daughters whose marriage settlements and inheritance rights to estates might be detrimental to the family's power and landholding rights. There was no room for sentimentality when it came to the family fortunes.

When Guy Beauchamp, the eldest son of the 11th Earl of Warwick, died in 1360 as a result of injuries sustained during the Siege of Chartres, his two young daughters, Elizabeth and Katherine, became co-heiresses to the title and its lands which were not held in tail male. Thomas, Anne Beauchamp's paternal grandfather, was the 11th earl's second son. Legally he was a collateral heir rather than a direct heir because the laws of primogeniture allowed a lineal descent to female beneficiaries, excluding land held in tail male. This simply meant that only males qualified to inherit. In the case of estates held in tail male where the direct line failed, a collateral male was able to succeed; where there was no male within the extended family, the estates identified as an entailed interest reverted to the Crown. This was not the case with much of the Beauchamp inheritance. Thomas Beauchamp, 11th Earl of Warwick, had no intention of allowing his estates or title to pass from the Beauchamp family into the hands of his granddaughters' future husbands. He decided that it would be better for the whole family that the two little girls took the veil rather than them being allowed to inherit their birthright. In addition to disposing of their availability as heiresses, he also ensured through an entail on his estates that the Church had no legal claim on any inheritance that they might have expected. Elizabeth appears to have died young but Katherine Beauchamp became a nun at the Gilbertine priory of Shouldham in Norfolk by 1369. In 1398, Katherine wrote that her profession as a nun stemmed from the need to secure the earldom and its estates[5] rather than a vocation. The priory provided a home for a number of Beauchamp women from at least the thirteenth century onwards. It was once described as 'a convenient repository for embarrassing members of the family'.[6]

Thomas Beauchamp, the 11th earl, had a formidable reputation as a warrior during the Hundred Years War playing a leading role at Crécy and Poitiers. He employed the same ruthlessness in the removal of Elizabeth and Katherine from their inheritances. He applied the same principle to the unions he made for his own children. The earl weighed the value of his daughters' dowries, the assets that went with a bride to her new husband, against any political influence that might be gained from alliances with regional families into which they married. Successive earls developed their leverage within the Midlands by offering their daughters for marriage into the local gentry. Occasionally, in addition to gaining regional leverage, fortune returned a dowry to the Beauchamp estates. The 11th earl married one of his daughters, Joan, to Ralph Basset of Drayton. Her dowry became part of Basset's estate. Crucially, he only retained a life interest in his wife's dowry until at least one child was born alive to Joan. It did not matter that the child might later die. The earl cannot have foreseen that his daughter would die without ever having children and that the land that represented Joan's dowry would return to the Beauchamp family.

The marriages of some Beauchamp daughters were used as mechanisms by which the earls extended their national interests. Maud, another of the 11th earl's daughters, was married to Roger Clifford, 5th Lord Clifford. The union developed more widespread political networks for both families as well as building upon existing kinship ties. Roger's mother was part of the powerful de Berkeley family. Sometime before 1350, the earl married Maud's younger sister Philippa to Hugh, a son of Ralph Stafford, 1st Earl of Stafford, when the boy was just eight years old. Stafford's eldest son died in 1347 and it was Hugh who became heir to the earldom. Warwick knew Hugh's father from their shared military campaigns in France and Scotland. Both men held the trust of King Edward III – they were both founding members of the Order of the Garter. Warwick became the Black Prince's guardian while Stafford was created an earl in 1350 and was such a favourite of the king that he was even excused the abduction of the heiress Margaret Audley, who became his second wife and was Hugh's mother. Marriage might have been a sacrament but political achievement relied upon being at the heart of a network of powerful connections. Philippa's eldest daughter, Margaret Stafford, would become the first wife of Ralph Neville, 1st Earl of Westmorland, demonstrating once more not only the importance of family connections when it came to arranging marriages but the 'complexities of calculation and self-interest'.[7]

Isabel and Anne Neville's ancestry reflects, on the one hand, the limited social endogamy that kept the pool of potential spouses contained within an ever more inter-related landholding elite. But on the other, it demonstrates the role of rising families and realpolitik in ensuring that the number of prospective spouses was not significantly reduced. Some of the alliances woven between families through marriage would endure across the decades; others such as the one made between the Earls of Warwick and the Clifford families would fail during the Wars of the Roses and see cousins face one another on opposite sides in some of England's bloodiest battles.

Nor were earlier generations without their own dramas and crises. The wedding of Thomas Beauchamp, the 12th earl, was arranged, like the rest of the dynasty, to enhance familial networks and acquire wealth. He married Margaret Ferrers of Groby, the daughter of William Ferrers, in order to maintain a regional alliance between the Ferrers and the Beauchamp families. Margaret's family was a cadet branch of the Ferrers Earls of Derby, William de Ferrers having received Groby from his mother who was one of three co-heiresses of Roger de Quincy, Earl of Winchester.[8] Margaret's grandmother was descended from the heiress Isabel de Verdun who was in turn a great-granddaughter of King Edward I.

Thomas Beauchamp risked his earldom and everything his family had ever attained when he rebelled against King Richard II. He was one of the five Lords Appellant who sought to separate the king from his favourites in 1387. The outcome was the humiliation of Richard, the execution of eight of his closest advisors and the dismissal of many others from court. The king bided his time, rebuilt his power and, in 1397, took his revenge against the Appellants. Warwick and two other lords were condemned of treason. One was murdered, the second was executed on the same day as he was found guilty, but the earl was spared. His sojourn as a prisoner in the Tower of London resulted in the place of his incarceration being named the Beauchamp Tower.

Margaret petitioned the king, her kinsman, for mercy on Thomas's behalf, suggesting that a marriage made for advantage resulted in affection at least. As the wife of a traitor, she was in a difficult position. The countess was entitled to her dower and jointure even if the Crown confiscated the rest of the earl's estates, but she could not claim them during her husband's lifetime. A successful petition for mercy would reduce her to poverty. The king was so angry with her entreaties that he threatened to have Margaret executed, even though she was a woman. However, Warwick's sentence was commuted to a life in exile on the Isle of Man, demonstrating the effectiveness of her arguments. The countess went on to petition the king for household items, some of her clothes and transport. The following year the king settled an annual allowance of 250 marks upon Margaret and, in 1398, she was granted a papal dispensation to live in the convent of the Poor Clares Without Aldgate. Her sister Elizabeth was a nun there and Richard II's cousin Isabel, the daughter of the murdered Duke of Gloucester, was also a resident.[9] Courage was not lacking in the distaff side of Isabel and Anne's family, nor was the capacity to step from domestic life onto the political stage when occasion demanded it.

It seemed that the turn of Fortuna's wheel had cast the Beauchamps down. The rebel earl's estates were divided in tail male amongst the king's loyal nobility with the intention of ensuring that no other overmighty magnate might spring up to challenge the monarchy in the Midlands. Amongst the beneficiaries were the king's half-brother Thomas Holland, the 1st Duke of Surrey, who held Warwick Castle. Thomas Despenser and John Lord Montagu, the new Earl of Salisbury, were given lands in Warwickshire and Worcestershire,[10] but Warwick's regional affinity was a deep-rooted one. The local gentry including John Catesby and Thomas Purfrey objected to the stripping of their own assets by Richard's men and, besides, the new lords were not so influential. Surrey was also given custody of Richard, Thomas Beauchamp's heir and his first wife, Elizabeth de Berkeley, whom he married before 1397. He was still a teenager at the time of his father's fall from power, but by some oversight he did not go to Ireland with the king as a hostage in 1398. When

Henry of Bolingbroke, the son of John of Gaunt, landed at Ravenspur on the Humber Estuary on 30 June 1399, Fortuna's wheel began to spin upward once more for the Beauchamps. The Warwick affinity rose, tore down Surrey's emblem from Warwick Castle and facilitated the return of their Beauchamp overlord from exile. By the end of August, Richard Beauchamp was a part of Henry of Bolingbroke's growing army and much, but not all, Warwick's estates were restored to him by the end of September. King Richard II was deposed on 30 September in favour of his victorious cousin Henry, who became King Henry IV despite the shaky foundations of his claim.

Kings of England were required to incorporate all manner of power players into their governments if they were to rule a harmonious kingdom. Warwick was returned to his former position and men who found favour under Richard II were also integrated into the new regime. Despite his attempts at reconciliation, Henry IV's usurpation of his cousin's throne was followed by a series of counter-rebellions. The king looked to Warwick for support and also to his own brother-in-law Ralph Neville, 1st Earl of Westmorland. Neville was part of the Lancaster affinity of Henry IV's father, John of Gaunt, and a man the king could trust. The dynamics of power were shifting and marriage alliances would be needed for the mutual benefit of the new order that emerged from King Richard II's removal.

Countess Anne's father, the 13th Earl of Warwick, married twice. As a child he was married to Elizabeth, the heiress of Thomas de Berkeley, 5th Baron Berkeley. Like the Ferrers and Beauchamp families, the de Berkeleys were related to the Despensers. The couple went on to have three daughters: Margaret, Eleanor and Elizabeth. When Elizabeth de Berkeley died in 1422, it was essential that the earl married again in the hope that a second wife produced a male heir. The earldom of Warwick and its estates were at risk of being divided between three co-heiresses. By then Richard Beauchamp was one of the most influential men in the country. His power came from his military prowess, his role in Henry V's campaigns in France, his loyalty to the Lancastrian Crown, and through his governorship of the young King Henry VI.

Richard took for his second wife Isabel Despenser, the posthumous daughter of Thomas Despenser, 1st Earl of Gloucester, who had been beheaded for treason in 1400. Her mother was Constance of York, a granddaughter of King Edward III. The union was an even more advantageous one than Richard's first marriage, bringing land, political alliances and royal connections with it. Isabel's brother Richard died in 1414 without having children, leaving Isabel as sole heiress to the family fortunes derived from the de Clare estates. A hundred years earlier, in 1314, Gilbert de Clare, 8th Earl of Gloucester, had died at the Battle of Bannockburn without heirs of his own. Eleanor de Clare, the eldest of Gilbert's three sisters, was married to Edward II's favourite Hugh Despenser the Younger[11] who received the lordship of Glamorgan as part of his wife's share. The magnificent estates that now came under Warwick's control included the lordship of Glamorgan, land in ten counties and the right to be buried amidst the Despensers in Tewkesbury Abbey. By the end of 1425 both the Despenser and the recovered Beauchamp inheritances seemed secure. Isabel bore her husband a son who they named Henry. She subsequently gave birth to a daughter, Anne, at Caversham in Oxfordshire on 13 July 1429.

The Earls of Warwick were the dominant power in the region thanks to the size of their estates and the cooperation offered by the Midlands gentry who were tied to them by blood, loyalty and the desire for patronage. The earl was able to draw on this service to further his own ends or those of the State in return for money, office and influence, all of which he had in abundance. The transactional nature of the networks that grew up around powerful magnates became known as bastard feudalism. Anne Beauchamp's father Richard continued the family tradition of extending his well-run estates during her childhood. He also built the south tower of Warwick Castle and left instructions in his will for a chapel to be created in St Mary's Church, Warwick for his tomb.

The earldom seemed destined for further riches in Countess Anne's elder brother Henry, who had succeeded to the earldom of Warwick in 1439 when he was still only 14 years old. Henry was educated alongside King Henry VI and so great was the favour shown to him that, in 1445, he was created Duke of Warwick preceded only by the Duke of Norfolk on state occasions. Rather than Henry being placed in royal wardship, the Beauchamp estates were given into the hands of eight trustees with instructions to work on behalf of the 13th earl's executors. When Henry and Anne's mother, Isabel Despenser, died at the end of the same year, her lands were also permitted to remain in the hands of trustees until the young earl came of age. It ensured that none of the Beauchamp wealth was tapped by a guardian in search of profit.

But then fate took a hand once more. The direct Beauchamp line unexpectedly faltered when Henry died in 1446, aged just 21 years, at Hanley Castle in Worcestershire. With no male heir and no immediate collateral male heir to succeed him, his infant daughter, also named Anne, became the 15th Countess of Warwick in her own right. The little girl became a ward of the Crown which granted her hand in marriage to John de la Pole, the son of Henry VI's favourite, William de la Pole, later Duke of Suffolk. Control of a large part of the child's estates passed to Suffolk at the same time. De la Pole's expectations were thwarted when, in 1449, 6-year-old Anne also died. With her death the direct line of the Beauchamp Earls of Warwick, which stretched back to 1268, ended. Without a fruitful Beauchamp bride to transmit the titles and estates to them through marriage, the de la Pole family was left with nothing.

The estates associated with the earldom of Warwick were composed of the Beauchamp inheritance, built up since the middle of the thirteenth century, and the Despenser inheritance belonging to Isabel Despenser. Isabel's two daughters, Anne Beauchamp, from her marriage to Warwick, and Elizabeth Beauchamp, from her first marriage to Warwick's cousin, Richard Beauchamp, 1st Earl of Worcester, benefited from the Despenser estates as co-heiresses. Elizabeth Beauchamp was married to Edward Neville who now became Lord of Abergavenny by right of his wife as the elder of the two half-sisters.

After Elizabeth's death in 1448, her claim passed to her only child, George, whose wardship was given into the hands of John Tiptoft in June 1449. At the time Tiptoft was recently married, in an exceptionally good match, to Cecily Neville, the widow of Henry Beauchamp, the 14th earl. No one with a claim on the estate had an interest in an *inquisition post mortem* conducting a thorough exploration of the proper title to the Despenser estates. Looking too closely might have revealed the extent to which title to part of the estate should have been escheated to the Crown in accordance with common law.[12] Instead, it was decided in 1450 that the Despenser estates should be divided equally between Isabel's grandson George Neville and her daughter Anne Beauchamp. In fact, Anne's husband, Richard Neville who had been the 16th Earl of Warwick since the 15th countess's death the previous year, took control of the whole of the Despenser inheritance. It helped that Tiptoft was part of Neville's extended family network, even though Cecily, who was Richard's sister as well as Henry Beauchamp's widow, died the same year.

When George reached his majority in 1457, he was granted his half of the estates but he was unable to enter them. They remained in the possession of Anne's husband. In 1461, following the Yorkist victory at Towton, Warwick took steps through an Act of Parliament to ensure that the Crown's claim to any of the Despenser lands which he held was dismissed. George Neville continued to fight through the courts for the right to enter his inheritance, but the law was now on Warwick's side and the whole of Isabel Despenser's estates remained in his hands until his own death in 1471.

The Beauchamp inheritance was more complicated. Richard Beauchamp, 13th Earl of Warwick, had four daughters from his two marriages: Margaret, Eleanor, Elizabeth and Anne. Their brother Henry inherited the title as the 14th earl before passing it to his own daughter Anne, who became the 15th Countess of Warwick in her own right. After her death Anne's half-sisters each expected a share of the earldom as co-heiresses, as did their husbands. John Talbot, 1st Earl of Shrewsbury, plain Baron Talbot when he married Margaret Beauchamp, the eldest of the 13th earl's daughters, anticipated becoming the next earl by right of his wife. He also looked forward to a share of the Beauchamp estates benefiting his position on the Welsh Marches and in the Midlands.

Edmund Beaufort, who became the 2nd Duke of Somerset in 1448, married Eleanor Beauchamp, the second of the sisters at the beginning of the 1430s in an unlicensed marriage following rumours of an affair with Henry VI's widow, Catherine of Valois. Parliament swiftly regulated the remarriage of queens of England when the story reached them and Beaufort, a relatively penniless younger son, looked for richer pickings elsewhere and lighted upon Eleanor.

Margaret, Eleanor and their sister Elizabeth were bypassed because unlike Anne Beauchamp, the 15th countess's aunt, they were collateral relations by half-blood only, whereas Anne, still a collateral relation, was Henry's full sister. This meant she was more closely related to her niece and regarded as more entitled to inherit the earldom than her elder half-sisters. Tensions over property rights would add an extra note to the tones of Shrewsbury and Somerset's political discord with Countess Anne's husband.

Richard Neville became the 16th Earl of Warwick *jure uxoris* or by right of his wife. He was granted licence to enter the estates that now belonged to Countess Anne because a married woman was deemed legally incapable of acting for herself. It was only with widowhood that a woman usually gained independence over the control of her dower lands and jointure. The child marriage made between Anne and Richard in 1436 had yielded unexpected dividends for the Neville family. Polydore Vergil, the Tudor chronicler, described the new earl as a virtuous young man gifted with a ready wit and good manners that made him beloved by ordinary people from Calais to the edge of Scotland. Vergil did not mention that Warwick grew up amidst the Neville's own family feud, honing his military and administrative skills under his father's watchful eye in the north of England in a society shaped by the border's own brutal codes of conduct. Countess Anne's urbane and ambitious husband knew that his only real strength and safety lay within his extended family and the number of men who would answer his call to arms.

The new Earl of Warwick's grandparents were Ralph Neville, 1st Earl of Westmorland, and his second wife, Joan Beaufort, the daughter of John of Gaunt, Duke of Lancaster, and his scandalous third duchess, Katherine Swynford. The Beaufort brood of children were all born in the 1370s outside wedlock during the couple's long-lasting affair. Gaunt only married Katherine at Lincoln in February 1396 after the death of his second wife Constanza of Castile in 1394. It was unheard of for a man as important as a duke to marry his mistress, especially as the union brought nothing with it – not wealth, title or even firm, young flesh. In January 1397 the duke's nephew, King Richard II, legitimised his four Beaufort cousins by the expedient of having a letter confirming their legitimacy read before Parliament, despite the clarity of common law which stated that children born outside wedlock remained illegitimate even if their parents subsequently married. Pope Boniface IX took similar steps in September 1396. Two years later Gaunt provided in his will for the future of his four Beaufort children.

The Neville family, firmly in the ascendant following Henry of Bolingbroke's acquisition of the throne, had previously gained regional power in the north of England across several centuries through a series of advantageous marriages. The first was the wedding of Robert FitzMaldred of Raby to Isabella, daughter and heiress of Geoffrey de

Neville, circa 1180. Isabella's son adopted his mother's name becoming 1st Baron Neville of Raby. His inheritance included Brancepeth and Sheriff Hutton. Robert's grandson Ralph married an heiress Mary FitzRanulph which secured Middleham and its estates for the Neville family. Ralph's son, also named Ralph, was so influential that when he died, he was buried in the south aisle of Durham Cathedral.

Subsequent generations of Nevilles held key regional roles including justice of the peace, royal castellanships and the wardenry of the West and East Marches. Their prominent office-holding in the north also included administration under the prince bishops and as bishops of York and Durham themselves. A formidable kinship network developed that impacted on northern power dynamics. In time a battle for precedence would develop between the Nevilles and the Percy earls of Northumberland which would have its own impact on the twists and turns of the Wars of the Roses. The Nevilles fought in the military campaigns associated with the intermittent wars against Scotland as well as the Hundred Years War. At home, they produced large broods of children who were then matched with the sons and daughters of the region's leading families to tie the local gentry more firmly into the expanding Neville affinity and, at a national level, to help consolidate their growing political influence.

John Neville, who became the 5th Baron Neville, married firstly, before 1364, a daughter of Lord Percy and secondly, by 1381, the daughter and heiress of Lord Latimer of Danby. It was he who undertook the building of Raby Castle as it would be recognised today. He arranged marriages for his children that tightened regional connections to the Dacres, Scropes, de Lucys and Cliffords. The baron was also one of John of Gaunt's lifelong retainers. His links to the Duke of Lancaster not only ensured a series of influential roles in the north including the appointment as Lord Warden of the Marches in 1378, but also secured a marital alliance between his son and heir Ralph and Gaunt's daughter Joan Beaufort in 1396. Ralph, as 6th Baron Neville, benefited from the union with the favour of both Richard II and his successor Henry IV, who became cousin and brother-in-law respectively. Close ties to the royal family paid financial and political dividends as well as elevating the Nevilles to a peerage.

In 1399 Ralph, now the 1st Earl of Westmorland, received the honour of Richmond for life as well as the lordship of Bainbridge and the Forest of Wensleydale. Much of the land granted by Henry IV to the Neville family was granted in tail male to Ralph and Joan jointly, or it was only gifted for the duration of the earl's life. Westmorland made a series of legal transactions which placed much of his pre-existing Yorkshire estates in the hands of trustees who re-enfeoffed the land back to Ralph and to Joan in tail male or alternatively directly to his sons from his second marriage.

As a younger son, Richard Neville, Anne and Isabel's paternal grandfather, ought, more rightfully, to have expected to inherit little from his father. Instead, the 2nd earl, who was descended from Westmorland's first wife Margaret Stafford, inherited his father's title but was left with only one-third of the Neville estates with the rest passing into the hands of his step-grandmother Countess Joan or her sons. The senior line might reasonably have expected a more substantial inheritance, but Joan's family emerged from the protracted squabble as the victors because, in reality, they held the upper hand. They were the de facto possessors of the contested estates and castles. Inevitably the quarrel led to a feud between the main line of the Neville family and Countess Joan's sons who were a cadet branch.

Countess Joan's family – wealthy, influential and descended from royalty – made spectacularly good marriages. Her eldest son Richard was married to Alice, the only legitimate child of Thomas Montagu, Earl of Salisbury, whose own estates included the barony of Monthermer. The girl's mother Eleanor Holland was descended from the Holland earls of Kent and was an heiress in her own right. Alice's inheritance lay to the south of the Neville hegemony. The marriage ensured that Joan's son would be an earl by right of his wife.

In 1422 William Neville, Joan's third son, was married to Joan, the heiress of Lord Fauconberg, irrelevant of the detail that she was described as 'a fool and an idiot from birth'[13] according to contemporary terminology. It was more important that a woman's property rights provided for William's future than to question Joan's capacity to consent to marriage. The union extended Neville influence into Cleveland as Skelton Castle was within Fauconberg's lordship. Nor did Joan's mental health prevent William from fathering four children upon her.

Countess Joan's second son, George, married Elizabeth Beauchamp, one of the 13th Earl of Warwick's three daughters from his first marriage. Edward Neville was married off to the earl's stepdaughter, also called

Elizabeth Beauchamp. She was the only child of Isabel Despenser's first marriage to Richard Beauchamp, 1st Earl of Worcester.

The marriages brought land and titles to the Neville family, but more importantly they secured kinship to a powerful and a long-established aristocratic line with the social cache that went alongside it. The unions were made at a time when the 13th earl was eager to ensure his ties to Henry IV's following and to strengthen an alliance with the north's family of newly prominent magnates.

Countess Joan's daughters married even more successfully than their brothers. At the age of 13, Katherine Neville married John Mowbray who would become the Duke of Norfolk. Katherine's father paid King Henry IV three thousand marks for Mowbray's wardship. In all Katherine would marry four times and she would be present at her great-niece's coronation in 1483.

Anne, the countess's third daughter born circa 1408, married Humphrey Stafford who later became Duke of Buckingham. In 1460 her husband was killed at the Battle of Northampton transforming Anne into a wealthy widow. When she made her second marriage seven years later to Walter Blount, 1st Baron Mountjoy, the terms appear to have included the right to manage her own estates demonstrating formidable business acumen.

Anne's elder sister, Eleanor, was married briefly to Richard Despenser, but was widowed by the time she was 11 years old. She was subsequently married to the Earl of Northumberland as a peace-weaver. However, the union did nothing to quell the growing hostility between the two families.

Cecily Neville, Countess Joan's youngest daughter, made the most glittering wedding of all. She was married to Richard, Duke of York, when the pair were still children. Although York's father was executed for his part in the Southampton Plot to put Edmund Mortimer, 5th Earl of March, upon the throne, he was not attainted for his treason. This meant that Richard inherited estates which would otherwise have been forfeit.

Isabel and Anne Neville's grandfather Richard Neville, Earl of Salisbury, *jure uxoris* continued the family policy of making influential child marriages. He arranged for his daughter Cecily to marry Henry Beauchamp, the heir of the 13th Earl of Warwick. Neville was so determined upon the marriage that he offered Cecily as a bride with a dowry of 4,700 marks, which was a huge amount of money and which Henry's father felt unable to refuse.[14]

Salisbury, an astute businessman as well as one of Warwick's own military commanders, took the opportunity to suggest that his own eldest son Richard, born in 1428, should marry Anne Beauchamp who was two years older than her proposed husband as part of the agreement. It was a good marriage for Anne as it would ensure that she would one day become a countess. There were advantages to a child marriage. Salisbury and Warwick were aware that in the event of their own deaths, their children would become wards of the Crown. The king was likely to sell any guardianship to the highest bidder or grant the wardship to a favourite. If that were to happen, the guardian would arrange a marriage in the interests of his own family rather than that of his wards. Both Neville and Beauchamp recognised that death was never far away, either on the battlefield, by disease or unforeseen misadventure. The marriage of their children provided an insurance against their own deaths. Even so, child marriages were relatively rare by the fifteenth century, although there are some notable exceptions including the two child marriages of Margaret Beaufort, the heiress of John Beaufort, 1st Duke of Somerset.[15]

The double marriage, recorded by the *Tewkesbury Abbey Chronicle*, was celebrated on 4 May 1436 at Abergavenny, taking the Nevilles to the heart of English political power. The location was chosen because it was the home of Joan Beauchamp, Lady Abergavenny. She was Henry and Anne's great-aunt as well as being Isabel Despenser's former mother-in-law. The celebrations started before the marriage as the two families gathered after their journeys. On the day of her wedding, Anne, aged 10, stood before the priest in a new gown with her long hair cascading down her back as befitted a virgin bride, and spoke the necessary vows for herself before her father gave her to the groom who placed a ring on his bride's finger. Her new sister-in-law Cecily was about the same age. The double wedding was followed by a Mass. Once the service was over the family sat down at a wedding feast, but there was no raucous bedding of either bride as the couples were too young to cohabit with one another. It meant that until each couple were of an age to consummate their unions, the marriages could be repudiated under canon law. Anne's groom was the youngest of all the participants, having been born on 22 November 1428. In theory the earliest that the marriage of Anne and Richard could have been consummated was at the end of 1442 when Richard turned 14 years of age. The delay in the production of Neville heirs makes it difficult to be certain when Anne began living with her husband in the fullest sense of the word.

The Church disapproved of child marriages, especially ones where a representative of the family was required to say the words of the marriage vow because the bride or groom was too young to say them. Canon law permitted children to enter into marriage as young as 7 years old, but it was more a legal agreement demonstrating an intention to marry as soon as the bride and groom reached an appropriate age. Neither Anne nor her husband had reached puberty, meaning that the vows they took were provisional and might be undone at a later date if they chose to renounce them, neither being old enough to affirm the marriage of their own free will, although Anne at 10 was old enough to know where her duty lay. Wealthy girls did not expect to marry for love. Most well-born girls married a man chosen for them by their fathers or guardians. Margaret Beaufort was promised to her guardian's son John de la Pole while she was still an infant and was married to him when she was 6 and John was 8. Margaret remained with her mother throughout and never recognised her first marriage which was dissolved in 1553 so that King Henry VI could grant Margaret's wardship, marriage and fortune to his own half-brother, Edmund Tudor, 1st Earl of Richmond.

After her wedding Anne's young husband returned to Middleham to continue his education under his father's careful tutelage. Anne also travelled with her new family to Middleham where she continued her own education as well as learning how to manage her new household from Countess Alice. The Nevilles would become her family just as Countess Isabel would become Cecily Neville's substitute mother. Isabel taught Cecily, who was of an age to join her new husband and family, how to manage Warwick Castle, care for its inhabitants and oversee the management of the estates that would one day be her husband's. Anne and Richard grew up together. It was an opportunity for a marriage based on social gain to become one of companionship, if not love.

Anne's wedding to Richard was part of a parcel of marriages which cemented an alliance between the Nevilles and the Beauchamps. Theirs was one of four unions made between 1434 and 1437. She was not a great heiress when she stood in the church at Abergavenny. Her father ensured she was sufficiently dowered, but it was Henry's bride Cecily who came to the wedding with one of the largest portions recorded throughout the medieval period. However, life was a fragile thing in the fifteenth century. Fate's twists and turns dictated that Anne's young husband became the wealthiest magnate in England. His name became synonymous with the bear and ragged staff of Warwick, while Henry Beauchamp would be largely forgotten.

Richard Beauchamp, 13th Earl of Warwick made his will before he departed for France in 1437. He died in Rouen two years later on 30 April 1439. Isabel Despenser died at the end of the same year in London. Rather than being interred in St Mary's Church, Warwick by the side of her second husband, Isabel chose to be buried in Tewkesbury Abbey next to her first husband whose two-storey tomb and chantry chapel was built in 1430. The countess's son Henry and his only child were both dead by the end of the next decade.

Richard Neville, Anne's husband, still three months short of his twenty-first birthday, was recognised as the 16th Earl of Warwick *jure uxoris* on 23 July 1449. He gained by right of his wife estates that stretched from South Wales, through the Midlands and into East Anglia and Kent. Barnard Castle in County Durham was also now added to the Neville portfolio of northern castles. It seemed that there would be no stopping the Neville family, but by 1500 the family tree had been pruned back so that all that remained from the sprawling clan were three male Neville lines. By then Countess Anne's only grandson to survive into adulthood had been executed for treason, having spent most of his life as prisoner.

Chapter 2

Childhood and Education

By 1449 Warwick and Countess Anne had been married for thirteen years. They remained childless initially because while either of them was in their minority, the marriage was unlikely to have been consummated. In most cases intercourse was postponed until husband and wife were of a suitable age, 12 for girls and 14 for boys. Often families deferred cohabitation until a young woman was more able to withstand the rigours associated with pregnancy and childbirth.

A notable exception to this rule was exemplified by Lady Margaret Beaufort who was married to King Henry VI's half-brother Edmund Tudor, 1st Earl of Richmond, on 1 November 1455. Richmond accrued all of Margaret's estates upon their marriage, but he would only retain an interest in them subject to his wife's survival and the birth of an heir. It was the existence of the child, even if it only lived for a few minutes, which allowed a husband possession of his wife's land in his own right, retaining it not only during the life of his wife but also in the event of her death. It was a restriction that most men who married heiresses faced. Richmond, desirous of Margaret's inheritance, showed a disregard for his bride's wellbeing by impregnating her while she was still 12 years old. Her only child, Henry Tudor, was born before her thirteenth birthday.

Richard Neville proved his own fertility during his teenage years sometime before 1450 when he fathered an illegitimate daughter named Margaret. Illegitimacy would have its effect on the girl's inheritance rights, but her eventual social status gives a true indication of the Neville family's regional power. Like kings of old it was enough that Warwick recognised his daughter. Her Neville bloodline made her a marketable marriage commodity within the earl's extensive sphere of influence. It is impossible to know whether Margaret's mother exercised agency or not in her relationship with Richard or whether he regarded his eldest daughter as a child born from love rather than financial interest. In later years Margaret was close to Warwick's younger daughter Anne and was present at Anne's coronation in 1483 in her own right, raising the possibility that they spent time together during their childhoods.

Although the Church may have disapproved of Richard's marital infidelity, the reality was that Margaret did not face social exclusion because of her illegitimacy. Natural children were integrated into the Neville affinity. Their loyal service could usually be guaranteed because of their lack of inheritance rights. The most well-known example of loyal service to legitimate family interests was provided by Richard's illegitimate cousin Thomas, the so-called Bastard of Fauconberg. It is more likely, then, that Margaret's existence marked her father's physical coming of age. His indiscretion may have been regarded with some indulgence since it proved his ability to beget the next generation. Countess Anne, on the other hand, would have been expected to demonstrate tolerance to the presence of another woman's child who could be held up as evidence that any failure to provide a legitimate heir lay with her rather than her husband.

Warwick learned more than wenching at Middleham. Salisbury taught his heir how to manage his tenants and command men in battle. The north was never without conflict for long. As Warden of the West Marches, it was Salisbury's job to repel Scottish invaders and cattle raiders as well as enforcing march laws which attempted to ensure the recovery of stolen property from either England or Scotland and to prosecute offences committed by the inhabitants of one country in the land of the other. Warwick learned how to negotiate with his Scottish counterparts, apply the law on agreed truce days across the border and turn the business of being a warden to his own advantage. As he grew to maturity his father gave him command of counter raids, known as 'hot trods' from the burning peat attached to a spear to signify the justification for the incursion across the border into Scotland to retrieve men's cattle and sheep. They were unruly times. In 1446 Richard was appointed joint warden by King Henry VI alongside his father. He was just 18 years old.

To Anne Beauchamp, two years older than her husband, it must have seemed that she would live out her days as the wife of a northern magnate at Middleham in the household of her mother-in-law, travelling on occasion to Sheriff Hutton, Penrith or Carlisle, or even to L'Erber, her father-in-law's London home on the banks of the Thames off Dowgate. But then her brother and niece died. She became the Countess of Warwick in her own right and Warwick Castle became her main residence until 1461.

Countess Anne became pregnant with Isabel during the Yuletide celebrations of 1450. Her longed-for pregnancy coincided with spiralling royal debts, national recession and defeat in France. Discontent turned into Cade's rebellion in the summer of 1450. The new earl remained in the background. It was his father, Salisbury, who took a lead in the politics of the period. At the end of July 1450, Anne's sister-in-law Cecily died. In light of her age and marriage to John Tiptoft two years previously, it is possible that she died as a result of complications during pregnancy or childbirth. She was buried alongside her first husband, Henry Beauchamp, Duke of Warwick, in Tewkesbury Abbey.

Isabel was born on 5 September 1451 at Warwick Castle. It is indicative of the earl's desire for legitimate heirs that we know both Isabel and Anne's dates of birth, despite the fact that they were daughters. A month before the birth Countess Anne attended a special church service to ask for God's blessing and make her confession. Afterwards she went with some ceremony to her chamber which would have been hung with tapestries to block out lights and draughts. Too much light was said to damage an expectant woman's eyes. The sight of a full moon could affect the baby and if anything startled the countess, it was thought that it would have an impact on either the child's physical or mental health. Ideally the room was warm, dark and comforting. The fire was kept burning even on the warmest August day because it was believed that the Devil might come down the chimney to feast on the unborn soul that the countess carried. For thirty days or thereabouts Anne's world contracted to the chamber, the ladies and female family members who visited her there and the gossip they shared.

When her labour started, Countess Anne may have been given a religious icon, a cross or even an amulet to hold. Trusted midwives were summoned. If a doctor was present, he would have waited outside the countess's chamber, an all-female preserve, while the midwife oversaw the countess's labour and aftercare. The author of *The Sickness of Women* described a natural birth as 'twenty pangs or less'.[1] However, since it has been estimated that one in every forty women died in childbirth throughout the medieval period and beyond, the author was perhaps too optimistic. After giving birth the midwife checked that the countess expelled the placenta; instructions for its removal ranged from a midwife using her fingernails to fumigating the new mother's vagina.[2] The *Trotula* gave advice on suturing tears. Anne's new daughter drew her first breaths and was cleaned and rubbed with salt, then her gums were smeared with honey and she was warmed in a towel before being wrapped in swaddling bands and handed to her wet nurse. Countess Anne was tended and helped into a clean loose-fitting gown and her hair was re-braided. She may have felt mixed emotions as she gazed upon the face of her infant for the first time. For Warwick, a dutiful subject of the Lancastrian regime, despite its setbacks, the birth of a daughter was likely to have been a disappointment. He needed a male heir to ensure the future of the majority of the Neville estates which were held in tail male, and that the earldom of Warwick along with his wife's estates, remained within the Neville family rather than passing into other hands.

Isabel is most likely to have spent her infancy in her nursery at Warwick Castle where her mother resided while her father began to carve out a career for himself on the national stage. Countess Anne was often at Warwick's side, but would have trusted the nursery staff appointed for the care of Isabel in her absences from Warwick Castle. Begetting a second child was a matter of urgency, yet the earl's presence was required elsewhere against a backdrop of political discord and military defeat in France.

Like the rest of England, Warwick was likely to have been appalled by the loss of Normandy following the disastrous defeat at Formigny on 15 April 1450, but he may also have felt a quiet ripple of delight. Edmund Beaufort, 2nd Duke of Somerset, was the lieutenant-general of Normandy at the time. His defeat was followed by an ignominious return to England. Somerset was married to Countess Anne's elder half-sister Eleanor and claimed lands in Wales that Warwick owned by right of his wife.

Nor was Warwick alone in his antagonism towards his brother-in-law. The rivalry between Somerset and Richard, Duke of York, who was Warwick's uncle by marriage, was of long standing. York's antipathy arose in part as a consequence of royal favour shown to Beaufort's elder brother John, 1st Duke of Somerset. York's birth and wealth lent itself to a career in public life that included a successful military command in England's French campaigns during the 1430s. In 1435, following the death of John,

Duke of Bedford, he was selected to be the king's lieutenant-general. He was appointed to a second term in office during 1440 with the promise of an annuity to fund his campaign but, as in the 1430s, much of the income to pay for men, equipment and supplies was derived from his own purse. During York's term of office, the situation in France stabilised in favour of the English with several towns in Normandy returning to English control.

York's dissatisfaction with his royal cousin intensified when his post was made largely irrelevant by the 1st Duke of Somerset's appointment to lead an expedition to Northern France in 1443 which directed resources away from York's own command. Somerset's army captured the town of La Guerche which was, unfortunately for Somerset, in neutral Brittany almost resulting in a war; levied an illegal tax in Normandy; and ended the campaign with failure in August 1443, reversing York's earlier successes. Somerset's death the following year was suspected to have been suicide. His brother Edmund succeeded as the 2nd duke and York remained without funds or royal support.

Through the influence of Margaret of Anjou and the Beaufort faction, York was made Lieutenant of Ireland in July 1447 rather than being reappointed to his post in France as he hoped. The ten-year term of office removed York's influence from both France and the court in England. *The London Chronicle* recognised that the appointment was an exile, although it was an office associated with royal heirs as well as York's own ancestors. It gave him an opportunity to pursue his own interests as a landowner in the region, but the duke did not depart for his post until 1449. In October the same year Duchess Cecily, Warwick's formidable aunt, who travelled extensively with her husband both at home and abroad, bore a son named George in Dublin to join the couple's two surviving sons, Edward, born in 1442, and Edmund, who was born the following year. The couple's youngest son Richard would be born at Fotheringhay on 2 October 1452.

During the summer of 1450 when Cade's rebellion erupted, there were some who thought that York was behind the insurgency. Cade sometimes went by the name John Mortimer leading to speculation that York, who was descended from his maternal Mortimer line from Edward III's son Lionel of Antwerp, was behind the unrest. York sent a letter to the king proclaiming his loyalty which was commented upon by *The Great*

Chronicle of London in respect of the need for justice from the king for everyone from the highest to lowest degree.[3]

By the autumn of 1450 York returned from Ireland, but continued Beaufort dominance at court and the failures of the English army in France turned York, who was King Henry VI's cousin and heir presumptive until such time as he had children of his own, into a supporter for reform and an advocate of his own political elevation for the common good. The queen, Beaufort and other influential elements of the council were convinced that York wanted the kingdom for himself rather than a share in government, and it was this view of the duke's motives that was documented by the Tudor chronicler Polydore Vergil. Conversely, York regarded Somerset's behaviour in Normandy, especially the surrender of Rouen, as verging upon treasonable. By the time Isabel Neville drew her first breath in 1451, York's marginalisation had led to a breakdown in relations with the king.

In February 1452 York refused to answer a royal summons to attend King Henry in Coventry. Instead, he sent a letter outlining his grievances and then led an army from Ludlow to London. By the beginning of March York was camped near Dartford with the royal army arrayed against him. Salisbury, who was York's brother-in-law and former military colleague, and Warwick were sent by Margaret of Anjou to negotiate a peaceful conclusion to the encounter. Neither of the earls backed the duke at that time, but during the negotiations they agreed that since the king was without children, York should be formally named as Henry's successor. They also agreed that Somerset should be arrested and made to answer for any crimes he had committed. This was achieved without Margaret of Anjou's knowledge, but once she discovered the truth, she demanded that Somerset be released and York, who had come to the king to affirm his loyalty, be arrested. Neither man was placed in custody; York was required to make a public oath of allegiance to the king at St Paul's Cathedral before being permitted to leave London and sent away once more from the seat of power.

Matters remained tense and were compounded when John Talbot, 1st Earl of Shrewsbury, took an army to Gascony in 1452 and was met in battle by King Charles VII of France on 17 July 1453. The earl was killed and the Battle of Castillon was lost. Countess Anne's half-sister Margaret lost her husband and her eldest son John who died alongside his father. England forfeited all its French territories apart from Calais and its Pale. King Henry VI suffered a mental breakdown when the news of the defeat and ensuing territorial losses arrived at his hunting lodge near Salisbury where the court had retired for the summer. It was the beginning of eighteen months in which the king 'lost his wits'.[4] For the first few months of the king's illness, the council concealed the extent of Henry's inability to govern. Final authority remained with Henry who was incapable of feeding himself or walking unaided, let alone governing his realm. There was also the problem of who would sit on the throne if the king died. He had been married to Margaret of Anjou for seven years. The queen was finally pregnant, but until she gave birth to a healthy child there was the risk of potential claimants to the throne triggering a civil war.

Isabel Neville was just 2 years old when Prince Edward was born at Westminster on 13 October 1453. The king was too ill to even acknowledge him which was a prerequisite for legitimising the succession. By then it was apparent that a regent was required to rule on Henry's behalf until he regained his wits. Margaret, not trusting York, demanded that she should be made regent during her husband's illness. In the meantime, the queen and the king's unpopular favourites, including Somerset, held sway at court. The treasury was empty, royal suppliers found themselves going unpaid and popular opinion blamed Margaret and Somerset for both the financial mismanagement and the disastrous outcome of the wars against France.

As the politics became more troubled, magnates throughout the country began to distribute their livery badges and recruit men to serve them in return for cash and favour. Warwick's accumulated wealth meant that he could put a large retinue in the field if required, as could Salisbury. Warwick's rationale for disliking Somerset was compounded when the wardship of Countess Anne's nephew George Neville was given to the duke in 1453. Warwick refused to hand over George's share of the lordship of Glamorgan to the boy's new custodian and gave orders that Cardiff Castle should prepare for a siege. The earl had no intention of yielding his influence in Wales or any other part of Countess Anne's inheritance.

The national crisis, as well as the tensions in Glamorgan, coincided with an escalation in the long-standing Neville-Percy feud. The two families had vied for power in the north for decades, but in 1453 Isabel's uncle Thomas Neville was contracted to marry Maud Stanhope, the niece and co-heiress of Ralph, Lord Cromwell. Salisbury negotiated the manor and castle at Wressle in Yorkshire as part of Maud's dowry. It was of strategic significance to the City of York and extended the sphere of the Neville family's influence, but it also lay in the East Riding which was the last remaining Yorkshire stronghold of the Percy family.

The relative importance of the Percy family in the north dwindled after the accession of Henry IV in 1400. Henry Percy was created 1st Earl of Northumberland, but he and his son 'Hotspur' concluded that they had been insufficiently rewarded for the assistance rendered to the king following his arrival at Ravenspur, as Henry of Bolingbroke, claiming only his rights as a duke of Lancaster rather than as a claimant to the throne. Their subsequent rebellion culminated in the Battle of Shrewsbury in 1404. This resulted in the loss of much of their estates and the continued rise of the Neville family who were tied by blood as well as oaths of loyalty and continued preferment to King Henry IV and his descendants. Wressle had been forfeited by the Percy family to the Crown in 1405, but they had not yet lost hope of its return in 1453. By 12 May that year, the Earl of Northumberland's second son, Lord Egremont, was distributing the Percy livery badge to his tenants within the region. The situation worsened after the Nevilles attempted to seize Lord Egremont at Topcliffe in the North Riding at the end of June.

Matters came to a head on 24 August when the Neville family and their affinity returned from attending Thomas and Maud's wedding celebrations. It is unlikely that Isabel would have been part of the wedding party. She would have remained in her nursery under the supervision of the women appointed by her parents to care for her. However, the rest of the family, including Countess Anne, were all present in their wedding finery when their retinue was attacked by Egremont and 700 men as they crossed Heworth Moor, north-east of York. The Percy family was Lancastrian in sympathy. Despite their own Beaufort antecedents, it was partly as a consequence of the regional feud that Salisbury allied himself with the Yorkists. It was evident that King Henry VI was unable to maintain order in his realm or resolve the quarrels of his magnates.

There were other ties of kinship to be considered. York was married to Salisbury's sister Cecily and in all likelihood, it was York's duchess who aided the developing alliance between her husband and Neville kin. The role of women behind the scenes may have been more significant than traditional histories of the period would suggest.[5] Countess Anne was soon to be locked into the same behind-the-scenes world as her mother-in-law and the Duchess of York. As their menfolk strutted on the political stage, women found their own approach to power while maintaining domestic stability. To a certain extent Countess Anne, and aristocratic women like her, could be likened to mobsters' wives who wielded influence over their menfolk within the frame of patriarchal social expectations. Any soft power aristocratic women employed was dependent upon their husbands' continuing influence in the wider world. By the winter of 1453 York was in control of the Royal Council, but it was only on 27 March 1454 that he was reluctantly appointed as Lord Protector ruling on behalf of his cousin. By then Somerset was locked up in the Tower.

York's change of status provided Isabel's father and grandfather with an increase of their own share of political power. Salisbury became Lord Chancellor; a judgement was delivered by York in relation to the feud with the Percys that satisfied the Neville family; and there was no further mention of handing over George Neville's portion of Glamorgan to the imprisoned duke.

York's power as protector and the Nevilles' pre-eminence lasted only until Henry regained his faculties. The *Croyland Chronicle* wrote that York faced 'serious accusations... of treason, and made him to stink in the king's nostril's even unto death'.[6] In February 1455 York lost the regency, Somerset was released from the Tower and was restored to favour. In April Queen Margaret summoned the Royal Council to meet in Leicester but excluded York and his supporters. It seemed to Salisbury, Warwick and York that the Lancastrian regime was about to take reprisals against them. A political solution seemed unlikely.

Salisbury returned to Yorkshire and gathered his troops. Armed conflict was inevitable. Three-year-old Isabel Neville might have been born into one of the most powerful families in the north of the kingdom, but as she grew from infancy towards childhood the position of the Nevilles became more perilous. Nobility and gentry were forced to decide whether they supported the queen and Somerset's rule or whether they wanted the Yorkists in power.

At home, in Warwick's absence, Countess Anne was responsible for managing their estates. Unlike Margaret Paston, the wife of an East Anglian landowner, the countess did not leave a cache of letters to provide an insight into her life and feelings as a wife, mother or landowner living during dangerous times. As early as 1448 Margaret Paston wrote to her husband John asking him to purchase 'crossbows, and windlasses to wind them with, and crossbow bolts.'[7] The same letter requested the purchase of almonds and fabric to make clothing for John's children, demonstrating the way in which women juggled their domestic roles alongside estate management and the defence of their homes. Any alarm or uncertainty Countess Anne might have felt as the political situation become more precarious can only be speculated upon.

In the meantime, Warwick still needed a son to ensure the Neville succession to his wife's title and estates. The earl was one of twelve children. His grandfather Ralph, 1st Earl of Westmorland, sired at least twenty-two legitimate children on his two wives. The blame, if it was apportioned, rested on the countess's shoulders whose duty it was to provide Warwick with heirs, even though medical texts of the period recognised that infertility was as likely to have been the man's fault as the woman's. With the passage of time Countess Anne may have found herself under increasing pressure. Amongst her prayers, she might have petitioned St Anne, the patron saint of the infertile, the Virgin Mary or Elizabeth the mother of John the Baptist to intercede on her behalf. She may have visited religious sites such as Walsingham or the shrine of St Thomas Cantelupe at Hereford which were associated with fertility. Women went there in the hope that if they demonstrated sufficient faith, they would either become pregnant or give birth to a healthy child.

Countess Anne may also have been advised by Cecily, Duchess of York. The duchess, in more peaceful times, wrote to Margaret of Anjou anticipating the discomfort of confinement. Despite her large family she had difficult deliveries and is known to have visited the shrine of the Virgin Mary in Walsingham in the hope that divine intervention would ease the pain of childbirth. It was believed that this was part of the price paid by women for Eve's original sin in tempting Adam with forbidden fruit. If being barren was a divine punishment sent by God, a large family was a blessing but not without its inherent dangers.

As well as divine intercession Countess Anne could have sought help from someone knowledgeable about herbs. *The Trotula*, comprised of three medical textbooks specialising in women's health, were written during the twelfth century in Salerno, but remained popular throughout the medieval period and beyond. Many of *The Trotula*'s treatments were based on Galen's principle of the four humours and the need for their balance. Any health problem was based on either an excess or lack of one or more humours. Women were supposed to have cold, moist bodies while men were required to be hot and dry. An excessively lubricated womb might also inhibit conception, but most theories about a woman's fertility related to the need for women to be cold and wet. *The Trotula* explained that an excess of humours was remedied by purging and that menstruation was a way of reducing excessive heat. Decisions about a woman's humours were based upon her complexion and the appearance of her urine. If the countess's uterus was too cold, it needed to be warmed and if too humid, it required cooling as too much heat would burn a man's seed.[8] Strategies aimed at increasing a woman's chance of conceiving ranged from hot baths to infusions of mint. Somewhat alarmingly the text recommended pennyroyal to stimulate the womb, whereas the herb is now known to cause abortion and organ failure. More expensive alternatives included cinnamon and cloves.[9]

After the birth of Isabel, the countess's health was poor. She was 25 when she gave birth for the first time which was considered old for a first-time mother. Medieval texts offered numerous reasons why she might have failed to become pregnant and why her health might have suffered. Concern may also have been expressed for her health because she did not conceive. If she had difficulties menstruating, she would have been encouraged to eat spicy foods, to have blood let from her big toe and to bathe in an infusion of herbs.[10] The same text advised sexual intercourse as a cure for gynaecological problems and treatment to balance the humours.

Countess Anne applied for a papal dispensation in 1453 to eat eggs and meat during Lent because she was 'weakened by former illnesses and the birth of children'.[11] There is no indication of what her ailment might have been, although it would perhaps explain the delay in becoming a mother. Nor is there a record of the countess being pregnant between the births of Isabel and Anne, but pregnancies were unpredictable during the

Middle Ages. Pregnancy remained uncertain until the baby quickened by which time a woman had carried the foetus for between seventeen and twenty-two weeks. *The Trotula* explained that miscarriage was a normal occurrence in the last trimester just as it was in the early stages of pregnancy.[12]

The text also identified that a woman's weight could be a deciding factor in whether she conceived or not – too fat or too thin decreased the chances of a pregnancy. Lent was the longest period of fasting in the medieval church calendar. Ordinarily most fifteenth-century households avoided meat on Wednesdays and Fridays. In normal circumstances Countess Anne, like all conventionally pious medieval Christians, gave up meat and dairy products, including eggs, for forty days from Shrove Tuesday until Easter. There is no indication if her doctor advised the countess to apply for a dispensation for general health reasons or whether the application was based on her need to bear a second child – especially as fish, which could be consumed, was associated with fertility.

The lack of a male heir was a strain on Countess Anne. She was aware not only of her duty as a wife, but also of the expectations of previous generations. In later life she probably commissioned *The Pageants of Richard Beauchamp, Earl of Warwick* which celebrated her father's life and chivalrous deeds. During her first years as countess, St Mary's Church rang to the sound of workmen constructing the magnificent chapel where her father was to be interred according to the instructions laid out in his will. The chapel lay at the bottom of a short flight of stairs that opened onto a marble floor beneath an airy rib-vaulted ceiling. The elaborate tomb with its gilt-bronze effigy of the 13th earl in front of the altar was created between 1447 and 1457. The countess had only to go to the chapel to be reminded of the honour of her family and its wealth, although her father would not be reinterred in his final resting place until 1475. His body remained in Rouen while construction of the chapel was completed. Countess Anne might also have paused before the high altar at the alabaster tomb of her great-grandparents to be further reminded of the deeds of the Beauchamps. Thomas Beauchamp was one of the victors of Crécy and chose to be remembered in full armour, his feet resting on his heraldic cognizance – a bear. It is difficult to know what the countess felt towards her husband, but it has been suggested that it was she who encouraged him to identify with her Beauchamp ancestors just as she herself did.

While the construction of the chapel and tomb continued, England's political situation continued to unravel. The craftsmen who crafted the fourteen weepers from latten and gilt and placed them in the niches around the sides of the 13th earl's Purbeck marble tomb chest laid aside the rivalries and grievances that tore the realm's magnates asunder and set them on the path of war. All fourteen weepers wear mantles. Countess Anne is represented in a mitred headdress and gown with a band around her waist on the north side of the chest, while her husband is depicted holding a book in his right hand on the south side. His father, Salisbury, is at the opposite end of the row of weepers. Edmund Beaufort, George Neville and John Talbot are also present, as is Humphrey Stafford, 1st Duke of Buckingham. The tranquillity on the faces of the weepers was not matched by the reality of fracturing family relationships.

Magnates and gentry were not neatly divided into two groups of protagonists supporting the red rose or the white. They were distributed by self-interest and kinship as much as resentment of Margaret of Anjou and her favourites. There was considerable political manoeuvring during the early months of 1455, although many men sought to avoid taking one side or the other. Even kin of the main protagonists including John Mowbray, 3rd Duke of Norfolk, who was Salisbury's nephew and who had good reason to hate Margaret of Anjou's court faction, was reluctant to become caught up in the power struggle.

Even so, Salisbury, York and Warwick concluded that they had no choice other than to take up arms to remove Somerset from office. They went north to recruit from amongst their tenantry and wider affinities before returning to Hertfordshire where they issued a letter protesting their loyalty to King Henry VI. York declared that it was no longer safe for him to go unarmed to the Council which Margaret summoned to meet at Leicester. The letter never reached the king. Instead, Somerset sent out commissions of array and left London with an army of his own and the king to lend weight to his cause, meeting with the Yorkists outside St Albans on 22 May 1455.

Even at that late stage with two armies facing one another, an attempt was made to negotiate in order to avoid bloodshed. York demanded that the king should hand over his unpopular councillors – including

Somerset, who was married to Countess Anne's elder half-sister Eleanor. Most of all, York wished for his complaints to be heard by the king, but his brother-in-law, the Duke of Buckingham, refused as he considered that the case should be presented when the council met at Leicester. Somerset argued that for York, Salisbury and Warwick to raise an army against the Crown was treason and gave them an order to disperse. The slow drift to civil war became an avalanche because neither side trusted the other, and York was no longer appeased by vague promises for future consideration. Buckingham warned both his brothers-in-law that they risked attainder. After three hours of fruitless discussion and with the streets of St Albans heavily barricaded, both sides withdrew to make their final preparations. The time for compromise was gone.

The First Battle of St Albans took less than an hour and Warwick's part in it won him a lasting reputation as a military leader. The *London Chronicle* recorded the deaths of the Duke of Somerset, the Earl of Northumberland and Lord Clifford[13] from amongst King Henry VI's supporters. It has been suggested that Somerset was singled out for death by his adversaries. The king himself was struck in the neck by an arrow. The experience may have triggered a second breakdown. By the end of the morning York was once again in control of both king and the country. He was appointed protector of the realm and for the next three years there was peace. However, Clifford's son swore that he would be revenged for the death of his father. Somerset's removal created a space for York and his supporters, although the duke was quick to ensure Parliament recognised that St Albans was an act against the king's evil counsellors rather than against the Crown.

With political power came other welcome news for Warwick. Countess Anne was pregnant once more. The countess delivered another girl named Anne on Friday 11 June 1456[14] at Warwick Castle. The infant would have been carefully examined and cleaned, and kept warm while her limbs were gently massaged with salt. According to medical beliefs of the time, derived from Galen, the use of honey and salt reduced excess humours.[15] The event was so momentous that Warwick did not attend Parliament, preferring to be closer at hand to his wife for the occasion. He would not have been permitted into the chamber where his wife laboured. Instead, he would have waited elsewhere, perhaps praying for both mother and child. If he prayed for a son, he was disappointed.

Soon after her birth, Anne, like Isabel before her, was carried to the Collegiate Church of St Mary's in Warwick to be baptised. In theory a baptism should have taken place within eight days of birth, but in practice most families wished to baptise their newborn child as soon as possible for fear that it might die before receiving Christian rites. Baptism was the first of the seven sacraments and it admitted Anne into the Catholic Church which in turn made salvation possible. Before baptism a child who died was destined to an eternity in limbo without ever being able to enter Heaven. After receipt of the sacrament, a child who died in infancy would be redeemed of its sins including the shadow of Adam and Eve's original sin that all humans carried with them.

On the day of the baptism, as the family party gathered in their finery, the church of St Mary's rang its bells to summon them. Anne would not have been carried to the church by either of her parents. It was traditional for either the midwife or another female to carry a girl child to its christening. Countess Anne did not attend the baptism; she remained in her chamber during her forty days of lying-in that all women who could afford it were required to undertake after birth to enable their better recovery. In addition, the Church regarded postpartum women as unclean. Childbirth and their conception were associated with corruption. Women who had given birth needed to be ritually cleansed of sin before being welcomed back into church.

Anne's family and the godparents selected for her by Warwick made their way to the church door where they were met by the priest. At the font Anne would have been given to her godmother, or proxy if her godmother could not arrive in time for the event. There is no record in Rous or elsewhere of who Anne's godparents were. As a girl it would have been normal for her to have two godmothers and one godfather. Warwick would have selected them carefully as it created a spiritual kinship between Anne and her godparents. Inevitably the politically shrewd earl used the opportunity to exploit a contact or develop an important relationship.

The person holding the infant at the font named her before handing Anne to the priest for baptism. He did this by putting salt in her mouth and immersing her in the font's water 'with great solemnity'.[16] Her godparents or their proxies made a profession of faith on Anne's behalf at the altar. No doubt Warwick provided a magnificent feast after the service in honour of his younger daughter who appears to have been named for her own mother. It was conventional either to name a child after its most senior godmother or else the godparent would have been invited to provide a name. It seems unlikely, in the circumstances, that Anne was named after the Duchess of Buckingham whose husband was a staunch Lancastrian.

In the same month that Anne was born and the peasants in the fields across Warwick's domains began the back-breaking work of haymaking, a 'blazing star'[17] appeared in the skies. It was said that the tail of the comet, which Edmund Halley later calculated to be the same one that appeared prior to the Norman Conquest in 1066, looked like a scimitar and heralded disaster. Any child in medieval Europe was born, according to the cultural mores of the time, with its fate and disposition indicated by the stars and planets. There was symmetry between the movement of the heavens and what happened on the earth below. The motion of the stars was even supposed to influence the personalities of newborn babies. The appearance of a comet in the skies was always a bad omen presaging disaster, war and the death of kings, though no one anticipated any of the misfortunes that would befall the infant being rocked to sleep in the nursery at Warwick Castle.

Countess Anne might have consulted a book of hours – a popular personal devotional text that also provided calendars, gave information to track the church year and listed new moons for the calculation of Easter and red-letter days to indicate important holy days. In addition, they provided a ready reckoner of Egyptian or unlucky days, which were regarded as inauspicious, as well as astronomical information to assist with decision-making about business, travel and medical practice such as bloodletting.

Anne's birth on 11 June narrowly missed the inauspicious 10 June – a day upon which no new project should be started. The same book provided the countess with the information that her daughter was born under the auspices of the twins, often represented by embracing lovers. Medieval philosophy looked for correspondence between people who were microcosms of the universe, which was known as the macrocosm. The most noteworthy correspondence lay in the medieval links between astrology and medicine. It was understood that this correspondence would influence Anne's health and personality. In later times John Rous would record that Anne's husband Richard was a Scorpio 'and like a Scorpion he combined a smooth front with a stinging tail.'[18] By then, the chronicler was attempting to win favour from Richard's successor Henry Tudor so Rous is not a reliable source. It was he who claimed that Duchess Cecily was pregnant for two years with Richard. In fact, Richard was born at the beginning of October – making him a Libra.

So important was astronomical interpretation that it was illegal to draw up the astronomical charts of monarchs for fear that a prediction of death would result in their demise. It was only fifteen years since Eleanor Cobham, Duchess of Gloucester, was found guilty of witchcraft because she commissioned an astrologer named Roger Bolingbroke to draw up a horoscope predicting whether she would ever become queen. It inferred a prediction for King Henry VI's life expectancy as Eleanor's husband Humphrey, Duke of Gloucester, would succeed to the throne in the event of his nephew's early death. The king was so alarmed that he commissioned a second horoscope which predicted a long life. Anne Neville, born under a sky with a comet about to make its appearance could, with the benefit of hindsight, be said to be tied to 'epochal events'[19] predicted by the heavens.

Anne's birth certainly seemed to coincide with the Neville family's accumulation of rewards for supporting York. In March 1456, as Countess Anne came to the end of her second trimester of pregnancy, Warwick's 24-year-old brother George was appointed as Bishop of Exeter, although he would not be enthroned until 1459. George was destined for the Church from childhood. He became a canon of Salisbury Cathedral in 1442 when he was still only a child. George undoubtedly owed his advance to nepotism. York was the realm's protector, and Salisbury and Warwick were both prominent in York's government. George was not alone in his advancement. Thomas Bourchier, another descendant of King Edward III and York's brother-in-law,[20] was made Archbishop of Canterbury as well as Lord Chancellor of England. But by the end of the year, disaster loomed for the Yorkist faction when Margaret of Anjou successfully dismissed York from office. Salisbury and Warwick found themselves in the political wilderness alongside him.

Countess Anne's world and that of her two daughters lay within the private sphere so remained largely unrecorded. Little is known about the childhood and education of either Isabel or Anne. Most of what can be assumed is based on the prevailing customs of the period. Both girls would have been handed into the care of a wet nurse soon after their birth. There was a medical belief that an unborn baby was fed by blood in the womb, and that after birth this blood was redirected to the mother's breasts where it reappeared as milk. If a woman were to have sex, the blood that provided the infant's sustenance would return to the womb, impacting on the quality of the milk. Physicians advised abstention if newborn infants were to thrive. It was also believed that a mother nursing her child would be unable to become pregnant.

Noblewomen were required to provide their husbands with children, preferably sons, not to nurture them. The task of breastfeeding Warwick's daughters was passed to a woman other than their mother who was known to the family, who had recently given birth herself and who had a placid temperament. There was a belief that a woman passed personality traits through her milk to the child she nursed. It was also recommended that the woman should have clear skin, look healthy and be respectable. Countess Anne, who was known to take an interest in her pregnant ladies and servants, may have had someone in mind before she took to the birthing chamber a month before either Isabel or Anne was born.

Warwick would have provided his daughters with a nursery supervised by a nurse. There would have been at least one girl called a rocker to rock the cradle and probably also to sing lullabies. Countess Anne would have taken responsibility for overseeing the education of her daughters as they grew from infancy to childhood, but they would have remained in the day-to-day care of their household and a governess. Warwick and his countess each had a separate household and travelled widely. It is impossible to know how affectionate or companiable the couple might have been, but the available evidence suggests that the countess was often by her husband's side.

Anne and Isabel's formative years were spent in the care of servants either at Warwick Castle, the garrison in Calais where their father was captain, or at one of the Neville residences in Yorkshire. Their lives were chaperoned and secluded from male company. The nursery and the countess's household would have been a female enclave. Later, the hostilities between the Houses of York and Lancaster meant that neither Isabel nor Anne ever had the opportunity to extend their education by service to the queen prior to their own marriages, and they remained in their mother's household until it was time for them to be married.

Isabel and Anne would have seen their father infrequently during their early years. Their mother would have been present more often when not at Warwick's side and oversaw their upbringing and education. Countess Anne's duty was to ensure that both her daughters were provided with the skills they needed to fulfil their roles as the wives and mothers of powerful men. The type of education aristocratic girls received varied from family to family. The countess might have drawn on texts advising parents how to rear their children. As well as learning to read they would have been taught basic mathematics. Households were divided into separate departments; kitchen, stables, pantry and chamber, for example. Expenditure for each area was recorded by a clerk so that checks could be made on outgoings and to control supplies. Countess Anne was expected to supervise her servants closely. Anne and Isabel needed to learn the difference between something that a servant might rightfully take as a perquisite and casual theft. They were skills that the sisters would need as wives and landowners in their own right. Not only would they be expected to have oversight of their own households, but they would also be responsible for the smooth running of their estates and those of their husbands in the likely absence of their spouses. Learning to write was a more specialist skill that was not taught to all aristocratic women during the fifteenth century, but since Countess Anne could write for herself there is no reason to suppose that her daughters would not have been taught penmanship.

Other domestic duties took a more practical form. Countess Anne would have required that her daughters be trained in the basics of herbalism so that they could administer care not only to their families but to their extended households. It was expected that aristocratic women would oversee the care of their servants. The countess had a reputation for caring for members of her household during childbirth. Women provided much of the day-to-day healthcare in medieval households. They were expected to be able to administer first aid and poultices and to use herbs to create remedies for a variety of illnesses.

In addition to a basic understanding of the idea of the four humours – blood, phlegm, yellow bile and black bile – Isabel and Anne learned about the need to balance humours. They were instructed in how to use the books of hours that provided guidance on the best time to let blood and from which part of the body in order to restore balance. They would have been introduced to the still room where they would have learned about preserving herbs and making pills, ointments and tonics. Well-educated women were equipped with a knowledge about the plants that cleansed, or were purgatives; and about herbs like betony, regarded as a cure for all sorts of maladies, and comfrey which treated wounds and reduced inflammation.

A household as wealthy as Warwick's had access to apothecaries and doctors, but aristocratic women were still required to have the skills necessary to 'protect and preserve their family and servants'.[21] A reputation for healing and the provision of effective care, so long as it did not teeter in the direction of witchcraft or a professional role, was an almost uniquely female way of binding an affinity together because of the obligations that came with a cure or even, in the case of the Pastons, advancing the social status of a family.[22]

As they moved towards adulthood, Isabel and Anne would have been expected to attend with their mother when ladies of the household gave birth. Rous reported that although Countess Anne only gave birth to two children, she was 'glad to be at and with women that travailed of child, full comfortable and pentious of all things that should be helping them.'[23] It would also have prepared both girls for the most fundamental duty of a woman – to become a mother and provide heirs to inherit not only their own estates but those of their husbands.

Other practical skills included embroidery and sewing. The Neville girls were expected to be accomplished needlewomen. Their aunt Margaret, the Countess of Oxford, was forced to earn a living as a seamstress during her husband's imprisonment and exile. Embroidery was used on everything from book covers to belts. Although Countess Anne and her daughters had no need to embellish their own clothes or furniture, embroidery was part of housewifery and kept well-born women from sitting idly. They were also expected to sew altar cloths and vestments to as a demonstration of personal piety.

Anne and Isabel were raised in a conventionally pious household. Rous described Countess Anne as 'a full devout Lady in God's service'.[24] From infancy onwards Anne and Isabel attended daily Mass in the family chapel. When they were at Warwick, both girls would have attended services held at the Collegiate Church of St Mary. They would have learned the *Paternoster* and the *Ave* alongside the *Credo* or *Apostles' Creed* which was a statement of belief rather than a prayer. As well as praying in Latin they would have been able to follow the services. Both girls would have been able to read some Latin, if not write it, as writing was less valuable as a life skill than reading. Isabel and Anne would also have been provided with a grounding in the French language which was an essential indication of aristocracy. Later, when Countess Anne and her children lived in Calais, both Isabel and Anne would have become even more familiar with it.

Education beginning with spiritual direction and devotional texts went hand in hand with literacy. There were different markers in the transition from infancy, to childhood and maidens who might soon be married. In an era of religious convention, as soon as the Neville girls reached an age of 'discretion', they would have been able to receive the sacrament. The prayers they learned were part of doctrinal instruction prior to confirmation. Writers dispute the age at which this might happen, but it seems to have been generally agreed that girls were perceived as being ready to embark upon adult responsibilities earlier than their male counterparts.

The Nevilles and the Beauchamps were amongst the aristocratic families associated with literary patronage during the later Middle Ages. Devout women commissioned and received richly-decorated books of hours modelled on clerical texts so that men and women could model their spiritual lives on the routines followed in monastic houses. Other popular texts included psalters and the lives of saints. One such collector was Warwick's aunt Anne, Duchess of Buckingham, whose will bequeathed books in both English and French.[25] She left some of the books in her collection to her daughter-in-law, Lady Margaret Beaufort. The duchess may also have owned a copy of Chaucer's *Troilus and Creseyde* as well as the *Romaut of the Rose*, but there is insufficient evidence for a definite confirmation. It is often through wills that ownership of books can be identified, but it would be wrong to suggest that such bequests represented the total number of books in an individual's collection. Another of Warwick's aunts, Cecily, Duchess of York, was known both for her piety and the collection of books she bequeathed to her daughters. Warwick's sister Katherine, who was married to Lord Hastings, also left books to her daughter. Later, Anne and Isabel's Neville cousins continued the tradition of bequeathing books to family members. The Beauchamp family owned several books of hours, lives of saints, missals and romances. Countess Anne's brother Henry owned the so-called *Hours of Henry Beauchamp* which was acquired by his widow's second husband, John Tiptoft. Countess Anne's half-sisters may have owned the *Canterbury Tales*. Suffice it to say that Isabel and Anne came from a family of literate women and book collectors.

If Isabel and Anne were to take their rightful place at court, they would also need to be taught manners and courtesy. They would have learned table manners from an early age as well as how to conduct themselves as daughters of the Earl of Warwick. The ability to sing, to play music and to dance were essential skills for women making their way in the social whirl of court, as were riding, hunting and archery. All children, including Isabel and Anne, would have been raised to respect their parents and to have an understanding of their position in society as well as the achievements of their forefathers. Countess Anne's father, the 13th earl, was known not only for his prowess on the battlefield and as King Henry VI's guardian but also for his patronage of John Lydgate. This poet wrote a history of the Earls of Warwick, a life of St Edmund and a poem entitled *The Fifteen Joys and Sorrows of Mary* written for Countess Anne's mother, Isabel, Lady Despenser.

The Beauchamp Pageants chronicling the life of Isabel and Anne's grandfather in fifty-five captioned drawings was made for Countess Anne. The earl is shown as a pious man at the heart of England's political life, as a warrior, ambassador and a man who could be trusted to raise a king. The work was not commissioned during Isabel and Anne's childhoods. It is thought to have been created at some time between 1483 and the countess's own death in 1492 as a testimony to her heritage and the political circumstances that denied her of her rights as the *suo jure* Countess of Warwick. It is not unreasonable, however, to suppose that the earl's granddaughters were raised to think of their grandfather as an accomplished man and a loyal servant of the Crown. During the same period, the countess would also commission the *Rous Roll* that promoted Beauchamp family history. Rous wrote that there was no such thing as a bad Earl of Warwick – a sentiment that Isabel and Anne were raised to respect.

Chapter 3

Calais

In England the situation remained tense after the end of York's second protectorate on 25 February 1456. Margaret of Anjou regarded the duke as a threat to her son's succession. It did not help that during both his protectorates, York effectively placed the queen under house arrest, or that on the day of his dismissal as protector, York and Warwick arrived at Parliament with 300 armed men. History can only speculate about Countess Anne's unease as the tension between the two factions simmered. Now, free to make a political move of her own, Margaret took her household to Tutbury and established a royal court in the Midlands close to her own allies. She began to dismiss Henry's old councillors and replace them with men loyal to her. The country looked on uneasily.

Warwick had a plan to protect himself and his family against Margaret's machinations. Following the First Battle of St Albans, the earl was appointed by York to the captaincy of Calais. In many ways Warwick was Calais's ideal captain. His personal resources represented a solution to an ongoing financial problem for the Crown. The town's fortifications needed to be maintained and its garrison paid. There were constant skirmishes with the French on the margins of the Pale. Warwick's experience as a border warden stood him in good stead, repelling the raiders on one hand and making diplomatic overtures on the other.

Other difficulties included soldiers who had not received their pay looting wool from the Calais staple merchants' warehouses on occasion. The earl recognised that the staple needed stability to function effectively. Warwick addressed the problem of looting through forced loans imposed on merchants and were repayable from customs duties.[1] Any disruption to trade also impacted on London's influential wool merchants. It was an opportunity for Warwick to extend alliances with men who would be grateful for his good lordship and to turn a profit for himself.

Most importantly, so far as Warwick was concerned, Calais provided him with a well-defended fortress where his wife and children would be safe and a large garrison of well-armed soldiers loyal to himself might be maintained. The same men might readily access Kent and London in the event of future warfare between Yorkists and Lancastrians.

Warwick took up residence in Calais as its captain on 20 April 1456 a year after his appointment, the staple merchants having agreed with Parliament that they would pay the Calais garrison's arrears and the staple loans would be repaid from the customs received at Sandwich and Southampton.[2] It is likely that Countess Anne travelled with him as the earl would still have hoped for a male heir. Isabel and Anne may have crossed the Channel at the same time or remained at Warwick in the care of their nursery staff until everything was made ready for them and their household. Certainly, by 1459, they were at Calais Castle with their parents. Nor is it known whether Countess Anne accompanied Warwick on any of his visits to London such as during the winter of 1458. Writing later, Polydore Vergil assumed that it was at Calais that the earl 'kept his wyfe and chyldren'[3] throughout the following decade. It was a more secure location than Warwick or even Middleham. The countess and her daughters would have become familiar with their new home; the markets, churches and the thirteenth-century watchtower known as the *Tour du Guet* which served as the harbour's lighthouse. As was the case at home, the presence of the bear and ragged staff insignia on the men at arms dressed in the red livery colours would have assured them of their safety.

Warwick set about controlling the Channel and recouping some of his expenses by open acts of piracy against foreign shipping. In addition to Calais the earl made use of Jersey and Guernsey as naval bases for his fleet. The Governor of the Channel Islands was John Nanfan, who served Warwick in South Wales having previously acted for Countess Anne's family. Anne's mother Isabel Despenser styled him as 'her squire' in 1423 when she appointed him as constable of Glamorgan.[4] Ports including Sandwich welcomed the earl's seagoing ventures as they were at risk of French raids, the latter having been 'robbed and dispoiled'[5] in 1457 by Pierre de Brézé, Comte de Maulévrier.

Despite his Yorkist sympathies Warwick was appointed keeper of the narrow seas for three years, permitting further acts of piracy under the pretext of guarding the Channel. The earl won popular acclaim at home when he defeated a Spanish fleet off Calais in 1458. Merchants from Genoa were no safer. English merchants can have felt nothing but delight as the earl picked off their competitors. The Lancastrian regime may have wanted to limit Warwick's authority, but they needed him and Nanfan to maintain control over the seas for them.

In March 1458 Warwick, having attended the conference which preceded it, was required to join with other supporters of York in the so-called 'love day' held in London, designed by the king to end the antagonism between supporters of York and those of Margaret and Somerset. King Henry VI walked ahead of his warring nobles to a service in St Paul's Cathedral, while they followed hand in hand with their rivals in a show of friendship. York walked with the queen; Salisbury followed with Henry Beaufort, 3rd Duke of Somerset, since the death of his father at St Albans. Smiles hid gritted teeth and the background buzz of preparation for the coming conflict.

Warwick soon returned to Calais where he resumed his unauthorised acts of piracy. In May he attacked a Castilian fleet and followed it up with an attack, in violation of an agreement made in 1456, on the Hanseatic League as their vessels passed through the Channel. The king's council summoned Warwick to appear before them to explain himself. He arrived in London with an armed retinue of men who brawled with the queen's supporters. That autumn, having been required to return to London for another council meeting, Warwick proclaimed to anyone who might listen that he narrowly avoided assassination at the hands of Somerset's thugs. While he was at the meeting in Westminster the earl's men got into a fight at the wharf-side. It was said that hostility exploded into violence when one of Warwick's retinue stood on the foot of a royal servant. The earl was caught up in the fray as he left the meeting. Accused of drawing blades, he was quick to paint himself as the victim of unprovoked aggression and withdrew to Calais before being required to answer against any charges of piracy that might be levelled against him. It is also entirely possible that Countess Anne's nephew Henry Beaufort, seeking vengeance for his father's death at St Albans, really was behind the attack, but there is insufficient evidence to draw any definitive conclusion.

Tensions between the Yorkists and Lancastrians were now at boiling point, Warwick returned to England once more when a council meeting was summoned in the Midlands, but this time he was accompanied by a large contingent of the Calais garrison led by their veteran commander, Sir Andrew Trollope. Salisbury travelled south from Middleham with his own retinue of heavily-armed men. Neither had any intention of attending the meeting, especially as word reached them that Margaret's supporters were arrayed for war. Instead, father and son arranged to meet with York at Ludlow.

Somerset was sent to intercept Warwick, but the earl evaded his opponent. *The London Chronicle* reported that Margaret of Anjou ordered an army led by Lord Audley to set upon Salisbury's smaller force. The two sides met at Blore Heath near Market Drayton. Recognising the risk Salisbury feigned a retreat to lure Audley's men into danger. During the assault that followed, Audley was killed and Warwick's father emerged victorious. He pressed on to Ludlow to join his son and brother-in-law, having deceived the Lancastrians that he was still camped nearby.

The Yorkists were outnumbered and unable to break out from the West Midlands to achieve their objective which was to reach London. On 12 October 1459, King Henry VI arrived at Ludford, adjacent to Ludlow, at the head of his army to confront the three men. The Lancastrian army was twice the size of the Yorkist force, and their leaders did not anticipate facing the king to whom York had sworn loyalty on a number of occasions since 1450. It was one thing to fight against the king's evil counsellors, but another matter entirely to oppose the realm's anointed king. An offer of pardon was made to everyone for their involvement if they changed sides, apart from York, Salisbury and Warwick. That night men deserted from the Yorkist lines. Amongst them was Warwick's captain Sir Andrew Trollope who took many of the soldiers he commanded with him into the Lancastrian ranks. He owed loyalty to Warwick, but Ludford presented a scene 'contrary to expectations'.[6]

The Yorkists could either fight, surrender or flee the country. The three men chose flight into Wales, leaving their men and banners as well as York's wife and younger children Margaret, George and Richard to take their chances with the king's mercy. Duchess Cecily and her family were taken to Coventry where she was pardoned by King Henry. Even so, they were all placed in the custody of Cecily's sister Anne, Duchess of Buckingham, whose eldest son had been killed at the First Battle of St Albans in 1455. It was, no doubt, an uncomfortable experience for all concerned.

Isabel and Anne's father went to South Wales with Salisbury and York's eldest son, Edward, Earl of March, into lands he held by right of

Countess Anne. Their intention was to sail to Ireland where York was certain of support. Instead, their ship was blown off course and Warwick returned to Calais along with Salisbury and March, having headed first to Guernsey. Fortune was on the earl's side. On 9 October Somerset was appointed to replace Warwick as Captain of Calais. The duke arrived off Calais only a few hours after Warwick's safe arrival. It was as close as Countess Anne or her daughters came to being besieged. Somerset's fleet was driven off by artillery fire so he sailed down the coast and put ashore at Guînes.

The Yorkists did not fare as well there or at Hammes, which both accepted Somerset's captaincy in part because the garrisons were owed pay.[7] The duke's men, led by Sir Andrew Trollope, set about the task of attacking the garrison at Calais. Anne Neville, who was not yet 4 years old, might have been unaware of the dangers her family faced. Isabel, at the age of 9, would have had more of an understanding of the situation. Calais, a town made for war, became a Yorkist stronghold beating off its enemies. The garrison was on active service; the sounds and smells of combat hung on the air. Fortunately, Somerset did not have sufficient men or equipment for a siege by both land and sea, especially after Warwick's men captured the fleet that carried the duke across the Channel. The earl executed any of the sailors or men he captured who reneged on their own oaths of loyalty to him. Breaking a sworn affinity to the bear and ragged staff had its consequences. Parliament attempted to forbid trade with Calais while the earl and his family were in residence to starve the Yorkists out and turn the staple merchants against them, but the people of Kent were sympathetic to the earl and very little got in the way of continuing commerce.

For Countess Anne and her women, life was more uncertain than ever. It was not a question of the countess defending bombarded battlements in the way that Margaret Paston was required to do in the absence of her husband, Sir John Paston, although aristocratic women throughout the medieval period and beyond did just that if the occasion demanded. Instead, Countess Anne was expected to oversee the care of wounded men, to manage household supplies and to demonstrate calm fortitude.

Calais was filled with extended members of Anne and Isabel's family. Together with their parents and grandfather, their great-uncle William Neville, Lord Fauconberg, who commanded Calais on Warwick's behalf, was a regular presence at the earl's table. Fauconberg, a seasoned field commander who knew York from his time in France, appeared to thrive on conflict. His natural son Thomas was an important part of Warwick's command structure. Also with them was their tall and handsome young cousin Edward, Earl of March. Later the family was joined by their grandmother Countess Alice who was forced to flee her home.

The girls saw their mother more than their father and perhaps visited extended family on occasion in England, but in Calais their sprawling, brawling, charismatic kin were condensed into a small geographic area plotting their return home and back to political power. It is impossible to know how much time any of their family spent with the little girls, or the extent to which they caught the tensions and fears of their mother or grandmother who left an unmarried daughter, Margaret, in England.

An act of attainder made against the leaders of the Yorkist faction in November 1459 involved no trial beforehand. The Crown was the victor of the confrontation at Ludford and now the Yorkists faced the penalties of defeat. Acts of attainder stripped families of their wealth and position in society. Isabel and Anne Neville became temporarily, at least, the daughters of a traitor with no worth as brides because of their penniless fugitive status and corruption of their ancestry. Women usually had no independent property rights and once their husbands were attainted, they often found it difficult to access any dower rights from the lands returned to the Crown unless they had powerful friends. The *suo jure* Countess of Warwick knew that legally none of her own freehold estates should have been confiscated as she had committed no treason. A married woman had no public role because under the law she was a *femme covert* – she was hidden in the shadows cast by her husband. The idea of coverture existed throughout a marriage and rendered women largely invisible to the law, even though a man expected his wife to provide active cooperation in the running of estates, business ventures and even treasonable plots. In reality, the law had scant regard for the wives of traitors. The countess's mother-in-law, Alice Montagu, the *suo jure* Countess of Salisbury, was not so undetectable to the vengeance of the State. Not only was she still in England prior to the encounter at Ludford Bridge but Parliament attainted her in 1459 alongside her husband and sons. Of the twenty-four people listed she was the only woman subject to attainder and forfeiture of her estates. She was accused of imagining and encompassing the king's destruction:

> the seid Aleise, at Middleham aforeseid the seid first day of August... traterously labored, abetted, procured, stered and provoked the seid duc of York, and the seid erles of Warrewyk and Salesbury, to doo the seid tresons, rebellions, gaderynges, ridynges and reryng of werre ayenst youre moost roiall persone, at the seid toune of Blore and Ludeford: to ordeyne and establissh, by the seid auctorite, that the same Aliese... for the same be reputed, taken, demed, adjugged and atteinted of high treson.[8]

It is unclear from the parliamentary roll exactly what she did to be accused of treason, or how she might have provoked her husband and sons so that she was partially to blame for the events at Blore Heath and Ludlow. More likely, the attainder was a strategy to secure her wealth. Like Warwick, Salisbury held many of his estates only by right of his wife. But if Alice was attainted to prevent Salisbury from accessing the income from his wife's estates, why was Countess Anne not similarly accused? In blaming Alice, the Lancastrians were perhaps giving Salisbury, who was more in the political background while Warwick took the lead, an opportunity to recant his Yorkist loyalties.[9] There is no reference to the Countess of Salisbury in any of the events prior to Ludford. It is possible that she travelled with Salisbury from Middleham and fled with him from Ludlow, although it is unclear why she would have chosen to travel with York rather than her immediate family. Alternatively, realising the danger in which she stood, Alice made her own way from England to Ireland at a later date with the help of families loyal to her husband and son. When Warwick went to Ireland for a conference with York the following year, the adventure was recorded by several chroniclers who also noted that when Warwick returned to Calais he was accompanied by his mother.[10]

Duchess Cecily, by contrast, was known to be present at Ludlow when her husband fled and when the town was sacked. She was granted a pardon by the king at Coventry having begged for mercy. York's attainder meant that she was ruined as the families of the other men under attainder were also stripped of their status and their possessions. Although her dower and jointure rights might have been legally hers, she was unable to access them while York was still alive. It was made impossible for her to send funds to her husband in Ireland, but the duchess was provided an annuity from the Crown which provided a 'comfortable income'[11] for the maintenance of her own and her children's expenses. Cecily, it appears, was a persuasive negotiator. Of Countess Anne, there is no word. It suited the State that she remained invisible.

For the time being, Isabel and Anne were barred from their inheritance forever. Salisbury and Warwick would never receive a royal pardon for their part in Richard of York's schemes. But the Neville family had no intention of losing Calais or forfeiting their titles and estates, despite the fact that the majority of England's magnates, including members of their own extended families, remained loyal to the House of Lancaster. Warwick used his fleet to mount naval operations in the Channel. He even sent a fleet commanded by Sir John Dynham to raid Sandwich in the early hours of a January morning in 1460. He understood that the attack was a necessity because of information laid before him by men sympathetic to his cause: Somerset was building a fleet to use against him. The vessels were destroyed as they lay at anchor.

Richard Woodville, 1st Earl Rivers, who had been instructed by the queen to assist Somerset in his campaign to take control of Calais, was captured in his bed with his wife, Jacquetta of Luxembourg. Together with their son Anthony, who had the misfortune to arrive in Sandwich on the morning of the raid, they were taken as captives back to Calais and publicly humiliated, not only for their support of Margaret of Anjou but also for Rivers' audacity in marrying Jacquetta, the widow of the Duke of Bedford, despite his comparatively low birth. The Woodvilles remained in Calais as Warwick's prisoners. They were joined by Humphrey Stafford and the new Lord Audley when bad weather forced them into the harbour at Calais rather than relieving Somerset at Guînes. Before long, both men were recruited by Warwick to his own side. In June it was Lord Fauconberg's turn to raid Sandwich, destroying the fleet that Somerset had rebuilt since January's destruction. Fauconberg remained in Sandwich afterwards. It provided a bridgehead for the return of the Nevilles to England.

Warwick said farewell to his wife and family on 26 June 1460. With the Earls of Salisbury and March and as many as 2000 men, he landed in Sandwich. Lord Audley joined them as did the papal legate, Francesco Coppini, who was also won over by Warwick's persuasiveness. Men from Kent flocked to the earl's banner which displayed St George in the hoist and the bear and ragged staff on a red (*gules*) field along with Warwick's inherited Beauchamp motto *Soulement Une* meaning 'Only One'. At Canterbury the city gates were opened and the Archbishop of Canterbury, appointed by York in 1454, gave the army his blessing. In London on 2 July, Warwick's influence amongst the merchants of the staple was so great that the capital also welcomed him, although it was suggested that the earl and his men might like to make their stay a brief one. At Southwark, Warwick was met by his brother George, the Bishop of Exeter, and other bishops. The Yorkists gave the bishops their oaths of allegiance to King Henry VI.

On 5 July, with the Tower of London under siege, Warwick set off after the Lancastrians with his brother George, Archbishop Bourchier and the papal legate to mediate with the Lancastrians. Salisbury remained behind to keep the Lancastrian garrison commanded by Lord Scales bottled up in the Tower. Five days later, Warwick's army met with the Lancastrians on the field of battle at Northampton. By the end of the day, King Henry VI was once again in the earl's custody and the Bishop of Exeter was in possession of the Great Seal. The Duke of Buckingham, Warwick's uncle by marriage, lay amongst the dead outside the king's tent as did the Neville family's old opponent, Thomas Percy, Lord Egremont. Margaret of Anjou and Prince Edward were lucky to escape into Wales where she set about rallying her supporters.

The Nevilles, led by Warwick, occupied themselves securing the country for the return of York from Ireland where he had been for eleven months. A proclamation was issued that York, Warwick and his parents were the king's loyal subjects, and their possessions were restored. There was no mention of Countess Anne, just as there was none in the attainder of the previous year. She remained invisible watching from the sidelines in Calais, even though it was the Beauchamp badge and motto on her husband's standard. *Waurin's Chronicle* recorded that Warwick returned in triumph to Calais on 7 August to collect his family who sailed to Sandwich soon after.

Chapter 4

A Northern Inheritance

Richard of York finally returned from Ireland on 9 September 1460. His retinue processed through the Marches from Chester with his bare sword and a standard bearing the royal arms carried at its head. The duke no longer wished to govern on behalf of his royal cousin – he wished to be king himself. York's claim was based on his descent from a more senior line to that of the Lancastrian monarchs. His matrilineal line was from King Edward III's second surviving son, Lionel of Antwerp, whereas King Henry VI was descended from Edward's third son to attain adulthood, John of Gaunt.

To everyone's consternation, when York arrived in London on 10 October, he strode into Parliament, made his way to the front of the gathering and laid his hand upon the empty throne, effectively claiming it for himself. It was a political miscalculation since no one, including Warwick who recognised his cousin's hubris for what it was, cheered or affirmed his actions. York was left standing by an empty throne, while everyone else waited to see what would happen next. Eventually the embarrassing scene was brought to a halt when Archbishop Bourchier asked if York would like to see the king. The duke's response was to claim Henry's Westminster chambers for himself. The grandiose gesture rather lost its effect since the king was staying in the queen's rooms at the time.

York deluded himself into believing that there was widespread support for his course. Nothing could have been further from the truth. For Warwick, an astute and able politician, the question arose as to how the blunder might be best remedied. After all, he had been governing the country since capturing the king at Northampton and York's ill-considered actions were likely to stir a hornet's nest. *Waurin's Chronicle* reported that Warwick did not spare his uncle's blushes: 'there were angry words, for the earl showed the duke how the lords and people were ill content against him because he wished to strip the king of his crown'.[1] A week later, the duke submitted his claim to the throne in writing to

Parliament. The lords discussed the matter with King Henry VI and, on 24 October 1460, the duke was finally promised through the Act of Accord that he would be king after the monarch's death.

Being almost king, but not quite, was not a good outcome for anyone. York was not the king, although Parliament conceded his claim was justified. Nor was the Act of Accord as cut and dried as the duke might have liked. It was highly unlikely that Margaret of Anjou would permit her son's rights to be ignored. Henry's queen was still at large in Wales. She sailed from there to Scotland where she elicited the support of England's old enemies. Men and arms were provided on the understanding that Prince Edward would marry a Scottish princess. In the north of England her supporters began to attack the estates of prominent Yorkists. Somerset, who was induced to leave the Calais Pale in August, travelled from Dorset to join the Lancastrians. By November the north of England was in turmoil. The Lancastrians, the Percy family and the Westmorland branch of the Neville family amongst them, took particular delight in their assaults which 'destroyed the tenants of the Duke York and the Earl of Salisbury'.[2]

Parliament was hastily dissolved; York gathered his army and left London on 9 December. He took his son Edmund, Earl of Rutland, with him as well as Isabel and Anne's grandfather. Salisbury's son, Sir Thomas Neville, was amongst his father's small retinue of retainers. He had been wounded at Blore Heath the previous year. Salisbury's intention was to recruit more men as York's army made its way along the Great North Road. Salisbury's third son John stayed in London with Warwick to ensure Yorkist control of the capital. York's eldest son Edward was sent to raise men in the Welsh Marches. From York's later response to Somerset's army at Sandal, it is evident that no one in London knew how large the Lancastrian army was becoming.

There is no documentary evidence for the location of Countess Anne or her daughters during the stormy winter months of 1460, but with Margaret of Anjou, marauding Scots and vengeful Lancastrians on the loose, it is unlikely that they would have been at Warwick Castle. It is much more probable that they were safe in the Nevilles' London residence, somewhere in Kent ready to cross the Channel if the need arose, or already back in Calais.

Winter was not a good time of year to pursue a military campaign. Sources reveal that there was heavy rainfall that year[3] and York's artillery was soon bogged down. Certainly, there is no evidence of artillery being used at the ensuing battle.[4] At Worksop, which is not on the Great North Road indicating there was a diversion, York's scouts encountered the rear of Somerset's army. There was a skirmish that saw the duke's men come off worse, but the Lancastrians continued to Pontefract while York and his men arrived at Sandal Castle, near Wakefield, on or before Christmas Eve 1460.

At about the same time, Salisbury's half-brother Lord Neville came to the duke and requested a commission of array to raise troops of his own. York granted this, believing that Lord Neville was acting on behalf of the Yorkists. *The English Chronicle*, with the benefit of hindsight, knew that John Neville was flying false colours. The two opposing commanders, garrisoned approximately 10 miles apart, agreed to a seasonal truce to last through the Christmas.

On 28 December a Lancastrian army led by Somerset and Northumberland marched on Sandal from Pontefract. They gathered outside the walls of Sandal Castle and appear to have taunted York for cowardice. *Hall's Chronicle* described a meeting held between York and Salisbury to decide whether they should fight or wait for reinforcements. The latter was part of their original plan but York, for reasons that are still not wholly apparent, decided to forego the safety of the castle walls and give battle. Waurin went so far as to say that York was tricked by Sir Andrew Trollope into leaving the castle by use of the bear and ragged staff insignia and the pretence of a body of men in service to Warwick. Historians speculate as to the real reason behind the rash nature of York's decision. It was possible that the castle lacked sufficient supplies to feed his army, or he was unaware of the true size of the Lancastrian army concealed in the woods that lay on either side of the castle.

Whatever the case, York gambled and lost. He was killed during the Battle of Wakefield and his son Rutland was slaughtered by Lord Clifford during the subsequent rout. Salisbury's son Thomas was killed during the fighting but the earl, who managed to escape the battlefield, was captured and taken to Pontefract. He might reasonably have expected to have been ransomed by his family. Instead, he was executed the following day by his enemies. York's head, adorned with a paper crown, was placed on the Micklegate Bar in York. Salisbury's head was also put on public display in a warning of the fate that awaited traitors.

The Countess of Salisbury retained her dower and jointure rights but Warwick, assuming that the Lancastrians could be halted, now inherited his father's vast estates in Yorkshire and the north-west in addition to those he already held by right of Countess Anne. As well as his own tenantry he could now call on Salisbury's former affinity of family, tenants and paid men. At a stroke the earl became the single most powerful magnate in the realm. However, he needed to act fast if he was to preserve his title, his estates and his life. Since the Act of Accord made York the rightful claimant to the throne, it followed that his eldest son inherited the right to rule. Edward was still in the Marches raising an army when news of Wakefield arrived with him. He also received information that a second Lancastrian army led by the king's half-brother, Jasper Tudor, was making its way north to join Margaret. The 18-year-old Edward engaged the enemy at Mortimer's Cross near Ludlow on 2 February 1461. His troops routed Tudor's men. The battle was followed by the execution of Owen Tudor, Henry VI's stepfather, at Hereford. The forfeiture of life in revenge for one taken earlier was becoming more common. The feud between the cousins would be washed in much more blood before the matter was finally settled.

Despite Edward's victory, the growing threat of Margaret's army of Scots and northerners led by Somerset remained. As they marched south, fear of them 'like a whirlwind from the north, and in the impulse of their fury' grew,[5] not only because of their numbers but because of stories of the 'spoil and rapine, without regard of place or person' as well as 'their unbridled and frantic rage'.[6] The Croyland Chronicler was particularly horrified at the theft of chalices and vestments, and the murder of priests. Grantham, Stamford and Peterborough were pillaged. Croyland Abbey found itself filled with refugees and set about attempting to hide both its location and its valuables from an army that the chronicler described as 'just like so many locusts'.[7]

On 12 February 1461 Warwick and his army, taking Henry VI with them, left London to confront the oncoming horde. Four days later the earl halted at St Albans, but he was poorly informed by his scouts. The Lancastrians were already at Dunstable, and Somerset was able to outflank him. At the Second Battle of St Albans, it was the Lancastrians who were victorious leaving London at the mercy of Margaret of Anjou and her army. The king changed hands once more, delegitimising Warwick's claim of loyalty to the Crown. Although Warwick escaped, panic swept the capital when news of the defeat arrived. At Baynard's Castle, Cecily, the dowager Duchess of York, grieving the loss of her husband and her son Edmund, put her younger boys George and Richard on a ship bound for the Low Countries. The family wealth was placed aboard another vessel, but she refused to flee herself and kept her daughter Margaret by her side. Nervous Londoners shut the city gates and waited anxiously.

Word began to spread that Edward was returning from the Marches with his army. Somerset and Margaret of Anjou, rather than making full use of their advantage, began to retreat northwards once more, taking King Henry VI with them. The *Croyland Chronicle* recorded that Edward 'was immediately received with unbounded joy by the clergy and all the people, and especially by the citizens of London'.[8] On 1 March 1461, George Neville, Bishop of Exeter, preached to a group of Londoners listing King Henry VI's failures, the corruption at the heart of his court and explained March's claim to the throne. This time the ground was prepared and the idea was met with popular acclaim.

Edward was proclaimed king on 4 March at St Paul's Cross. Instead of an elaborate coronation he swore that he would enforce England's laws and took his place on the King's Bench at Westminster in a symbolic act of kingship. Having negotiated a loan from London's merchants he and Warwick gathered a fresh army. On 11 March Lord Fauconberg set off for Yorkshire in pursuit of the retreating Lancastrians. Two days later the king left for Cambridge. The Croyland Chronicler regarded Edward's timely arrival in London as an example of divine intervention. More prosaically Warwick expected his own support for the Yorkists would pay dividends once the Lancastrians were vanquished.

On 28 March, having found Pontefract deserted by its Lancastrian garrison, the Yorkists advanced towards Ferrybridge where they were ambushed by Lord Clifford and Lord Neville. Salisbury's illegitimate son was killed in the encounter, but Clifford was also slain as his men fled into Dintingdale. The following morning, in a blizzard, the two armies faced one another at Towton. After a long and bloody battle, the Yorkists emerged victorious and the young king hastened back to London.

Edward's brothers George and Richard found themselves being moved from Utrecht to Bruges once news of their brother's victory arrived in Burgundy. They remained in exile until the end of April before travelling to Calais. They arrived in Canterbury on 30 May 1461. There is no written account of where Warwick's family might have been during this time, but it is not beyond the bounds of possibility that the earl arranged for his young cousins to make the final leg of their journey with his own family. By 12 June the three brothers were reunited in London. George and Richard, newly dubbed knights, were 12 and 9 respectively.

Warwick was now the most powerful and wealthiest man in the kingdom next to his newly minted royal cousin. He could expect to make glittering marriages for his daughters. Isabel Neville, at 10 years of age, was a child on the edge of marriageability. Anne, at 5, was barely past infancy. On 28 June, the date of Edward's coronation, Warwick was confirmed as the Captain of Calais. In the same year he was appointed the Constable of Dover and Warden of the Cinque Ports as well as being made the Warden of both the West and East Marches.

There were still two kings in England and it was the earl's job to subdue the Lancastrian garrisons that held fast to their strongholds in Northumberland and to prevent an invasion from Scotland. By the end of the year, Warwick was also Admiral of England. Countess Anne and her daughters travelled to Warwick Castle and then on to Middleham which now became the family's principal residence. With them was a kinswoman of the earl's named Margaret who was the daughter of Sir Lewis John. She was widowed twice in eight months. Her first husband, Sir William Lucy, was killed at Northampton. The *London Chronicle* recorded that Sir John Stafford had killed Lucy not because of their opposing political beliefs but because he was Margaret's lover. The couple married but Stafford was amongst the dead at Towton. Now Margaret's jointure from her first marriage was in doubt, and she became part of Countess Anne's household until her widow's rights could be established and a new husband found for her.

Middleham was the bustling heart of the Neville hegemony. As well as the castle there were two additional courtyards containing stables and outbuildings packed with men and animals. Neither Countess Anne nor her daughters would have been uncomfortable in their new home. Salisbury had seen to it that every suite of the family accommodation was provided with a garderobe and a roaring fire. There was even a bridge from the family range into the great hall. The keep and great hall were much changed from earlier times. It was provided with kitchens close at hand

and a large window to let in more light. It was a place to receive guests, to hold feasts and to impress visitors. At times though, when extended family members, the king and his retinue and ambassadors arrived to do business with Warwick or commissions of array were sent to the Neville tenantry, even the lodgings where the family lived must have seemed cramped and noisy. For Isabel and Anne, it was an opportunity to get to know their Neville kin. The diagonal corner turrets of Middleham's gatehouse, its forbidding machicolations and its new keyhole gunports that silently announced that Middleham was not merely a party palace signalled, for the time being at least, that they were finally safe.

Margaret of Anjou fled to Scotland with Henry and their son Edward, but Lancastrian unrest continued to rumble. Rather than return south with his cousin, Warwick remained in the north with his family. John Neville had not even attended the coronation because of the threat that a Scottish army presented to the town of Carlisle. By September Dunstanburgh and Naworth were back in the hands of King Edward IV's enemies. In October 1462 Bamburgh fell into Somerset's keeping followed by Alnwick.

For the next three years Warwick and his brother John, Lord Montagu, worked to stamp out Lancastrian opposition in Northumberland and along the borders. The earl was not without representation at court. The Bishop of Exeter became Lord Chancellor. Another kinsman, Sir James Strangeways, was appointed the new speaker of Parliament. During the Christmas of 1462 Somerset and Sir Ralph Percy were offered unconditional pardons and the reinstatement of all their estates if only they would recognise Edward as king. For the time being they bent their knees to the Yorkist king and were welcomed at court.

Christmas was the longest holiday of the medieval calendar. For a full twelve days work was set to one side, homes were decorated and a Yule log was burned through the holiday until Twelfth Night to ensure good luck for the coming year. At Middleham, the great hall hung with tapestries and evergreens, Countess Anne became Warwick's hostess welcoming men and women from across the social hierarchy to enjoy seasonal festivities and feasting. There was singing, dancing and games as well as the usual Christmas services in Middleham's chapel and raucous entertainment in the great hall. On 29 December Countess Anne and her daughters celebrated the Feast of the Holy Innocents which recalled

Herod's slaughter of children under the age of two. Gifts may have been exchanged on Christmas Day but were more likely to have been saved for 1 January. The feasting continued through the Feast of the Circumcision until Twelfth Night or Epiphany on 6 January. Mid-winter was a time for everyone, whether they were a shepherd or an earl, to take a well-earned rest. Fortune favoured those who won a seat at Warwick's table where they could indulge in fine wines and hearty food. Countess Anne ensured that any leftover food from the feast was given to the poor who waited at the gates each day. Isabel and Anne were expected to watch and learn how a great household was run.

On 15 January 1463 Warwick, his countess and, in all likelihood, Isabel and Anne were present at Bisham Abbey in Berkshire where the earl's father and brother Thomas were reinterred, having originally been buried at Pontefract. Salisbury, like Countess Anne's father, made provision for his funeral and monument in his will, but his body was in the hands of his enemies following the Battle of Wakefield and there was little time in the immediate aftermath of Towton to respect the earl's wishes.

Warwick escorted the coffins south from Pontefract on their funeral biers along with a cortège of mourners. The procession made its way slowly south, stopping overnight at convenient churches before continuing its journey. For the earl's household there was the problem of making sure there were sufficient fresh horses, that shelter and food was arranged and that the earl was sufficiently pleased with the display of mourning twinned with sumptuous pageantry. Salisbury's wife Alice, who had died about a month earlier, was also to be reburied in the Montagu family mausoleum. The men of the Neville family awaited the funeral hearses of Salisbury and Sir Thomas with George Neville, Bishop of Exeter. He, with other clerics, led the mourners in 'solemne procession'[9] behind the coffins accompanied by all Salisbury's banners and heraldic emblems, including his arms, helm and a sword, into the abbey where they were placed next to Salisbury's wife's coffin, which was attended by the women of the family.

The following day a Mass was celebrated. Both the funeral and the Mass were overseen by heralds from the College of Arms.[10] The ritual of the procession, funeral, Mass and subsequent offerings were part of a carefully choreographed narrative. Warwick, as the principal mourner, laid gold on the altar as an offering on behalf of his father. Other mourners followed in order of precedence. Amongst the nobility were the young Duke of Clarence representing the king; Lord Hastings, who was married to Warwick's sister Katherine; and Alice Chaucer, Duchess of Suffolk, and a granddaughter of the poet Geoffrey Chaucer. Alice Chaucer's third husband was the unfortunate William de la Pole who was murdered in 1450. She was also, thanks to her second marriage, Alice Montagu's stepmother. John Tiptoft, the widower of Salisbury's daughter Cecily, was also present.

The formalities of the occasion were laden with symbolism. At the end of the service Warwick's brother-in-law Hastings presented the earl with the sword that had been carried in front of Salisbury's hearse. As his father's heir Warwick would also have been formally offered Salisbury's coat of arms. The funeral ritual was much more than interring Salisbury and Countess Alice in the family mausoleum; it was about Warwick's ritual inheritance[11] and his place at the heart of the Yorkist regime. Even in death Salisbury's affiliation to the new ruling family was on display for all to see and a reminder of the sacrifice made by the Nevilles to put their kinsman on the throne. Even today, despite its poor state of preservation, the remains of a livery collar with suns and roses can be discerned about the neck of the earl's alabaster effigy at Burghfield Church where it was dragged after the dissolution of the monasteries.

Chapter 5

The Marriage Market

Countess Anne was 39 years of age and it was unlikely that she would bear another child. There would be no more Neville Earls of Warwick. The earl's hopes of securing dynastic continuity were over, even if an opportunity to remarry arose. It is uncertain whether the countess ever found herself pregnant again after Anne's conception. Her whereabouts during the difficult months following the Battle of Wakefield are unknown. Nor can we know what the countess's general health was like during the years following Anne's birth. Certainly, she would have continued to pray for a male heir until it became apparent that there would be no more children whatever steps she might take to conceive one. As Warwick reached the apex of his power, it is probable that his wife found herself dealing with the effects of menopause. Isabel and Anne were destined to be co-heiresses to their mother's patrimony, while Warwick's own Neville estates, held in tail male, would be inherited by his brother John, Lord Montagu, or his nephew George.

It is thought that the original *Salisbury Roll of Arms* was commissioned circa 1463 as part of Salisbury's funeral rites celebrating the achievements of the Montagu Earls of Salisbury.[1] Isabel and Anne's grandmother Alice was the last of the direct line. It was a timely reminder for anyone who might care to see that lineage and blood rights were all that mattered so far as the medieval world was concerned. Women might not have been able to ride to war, but the aristocratic wives depicted in the roll were blazoned and carried miniature helms. Their mantles depicted 'multiple lines of descent and alliance'[2] but it was their fathers' Montagu blood that counted for most. Courtship and marriage were the means by which land was transmitted. Isabel at 11 and Anne at nearly 7 were potentially extremely valuable brides, and Warwick intended that their Neville blood would make them the daughters of the power behind the Yorkist throne.

With Warwick basking in royal favour, he found time between Easter 1461 and his father's reinterment at the beginning of 1463, as the paterfamilias, to arrange a marriage for his widowed sister Katherine that would further enhance his own political standing with the new regime. He recognised the importance of consolidating lines of common interest. Katherine was left a widow in the aftermath of the Battle of Wakefield when her husband William Bonville was executed. Katherine, aged about 18, had an infant daughter named Cecily. William's grandfather, the 1st Baron Bonville, fought at Mortimer's Cross and at the Second Battle of St Albans. When Warwick withdrew from the field, Bonville remained to guard King Henry VI. Aside from praiseworthy distinction, the baron was promised that no harm would befall him. Queen Margaret failed to honour her husband's promise. Bonville was executed along with Sir Thomas Kyriel, who also remained to protect the unfortunate Lancastrian monarch. Katherine's infant daughter Cecily was the last of her line. At a stroke she became an heiress for both the Harrington and Bonville fortunes. The vastness of Cecily's inheritance enhanced the marriage possibilities of the young widow.

Katherine's second husband, William, Lord Hastings, was a close friend of the new king. The Hastings family were retainers of the Dukes of York; William had fought alongside Edward at Mortimer's Cross and was knighted on the battlefield.[3] Hastings' familiarity to the king would see him become one of the Midlands' most important magnates as well as Edward's Lord Chamberlain. Rumour whispered that on occasion he pimped for the king and that they even shared mistresses.

Despite Hastings' notoriety it was a good marriage for both Katherine and Warwick. Hastings and his new wife were granted Cecily's wardship as well as the enjoyment of her income during her minority. Katherine and Cecily moved from their home in Devon to one of Hastings' Leicestershire residences where Katherine raised a further two daughters and four sons. Katherine, like many other aristocratic women, was required to endure her husband's infidelities without demur. Under Hastings' guardianship Cecily's marriage would be arranged to best suit his interests, but Warwick intervened once more and arranged for the little girl's betrothal to his own nephew George Neville.

During the same month as Katherine was married to Lord Hastings, John de Vere, 12th Earl of Oxford, who avoided an active role in either politics or war during the 1450s, was executed together with his eldest son Aubrey. The executions resulted from a disclosure by a messenger in

Oxford's service. De Vere was in correspondence with Margaret of Anjou plotting the restoration of King Henry VI. Oxford's wife Elizabeth, the daughter and heiress of Sir John Howard, was also arrested but released by the end of May. King Edward granted her jointure rights as well as access to her own estates.

Warwick obtained wardship of Oxford's second son John who was now heir to the earldom in the event of its restoration. A marriage was swiftly arranged between Warwick's youngest sister Margaret and John. It was a union which showed shrewd foresight as the majority of the attainted earl's estates in East Anglia were initially granted to the king's younger brother in tail in August 1462. By the following year the lands were in the hands of George, Bishop of Exeter. John de Vere was granted royal licence to his lands as the 13th Earl of Oxford in January 1464; by the following year he was a Knight of the Bath and on occasion served as Great Chamberlain of England when Warwick was absent on other business.[4] It has been argued that the king extended the hand of friendship to the scion of a staunchly Lancastrian house because of the Neville marriage which must have appeared a guarantee for de Vere's loyalty. In all likelihood Margaret's wedding to de Vere took place before 1464. When George was translated from the bishopric of Exeter to York in 1465, Oxford was seated in a place of honour while Margaret was placed beside her sister Lady Hastings and Countess Anne.[5]

For the time being Isabel and Anne remained in Middleham where they were surrounded by extended family and by men loyal to their father. The Neville kinship network, local gentry and the wider nobility sent their sons to be raised by the Earl of Warwick at Warwick and Middleham. Amongst Warwick's household was Sir Robert Percy of Scotton whose father was loyal to the Nevilles and 8-year-old Francis, Lord Lovell, whose Lancastrian father John died at the beginning of 1465. King Edward initially kept the boy's wardship for himself, but subsequently granted Warwick the right to make Francis's marriage as well as handing him to his cousin to be educated.

Warwick might ordinarily have sought to marry Isabel or Anne to Lovell who was the most valuable of his wards. In time the boy, now the 9th Baron Lovell, would inherit a substantial estate from his paternal grandmother, but in the immediate aftermath of his father's death, all that was certain was that Lovell had inherited an inordinate amount of debt.

Instead of marrying him to one of his own children, Warwick arranged for Lovell to marry Anne FitzHugh who was the youngest daughter of his sister Alice. The earl had no intention of losing an opportunity of tying the loyalty of a Yorkshire landholder into the Neville affinity. Anne Fitzhugh's father, the 5th Baron FitzHugh of Ravensworth, was also one of the earl's most loyal supporters. It is possible that the wedding took place at Middleham a month after John Lovell's death.

Lovell remained in Middleham to be educated as a Yorkist rather than a Lancastrian. The boys and young men in Warwick's care lived together, ate together and slept together. They were regulated by a comptroller of the household whose rules they were bound to obey while they learned about warfare, weaponry and tactics. They were also expected to demonstrate good manners, to play musical instruments and to dance so it is possible that Isabel and Anne encountered them in the great hall and about errands elsewhere in the castle's precincts. They were joined in Middleham by Edward IV's brother, 12-year-old Richard, Duke of Gloucester, in 1465. The king initially arranged for his younger brothers to live with their sister Margaret at Greenwich Palace, but once George, Duke of Clarence, was old enough to assume a public responsibility, it was decided that Gloucester's education should continue under Warwick while Clarence resided chiefly at Tutbury. Warwick may have assumed that Edward placed Richard with him not just to undertake the boy's education but as a precursor to a marriage with his own youngest daughter. Anne's age and status as one of England's most eligible heiresses made her a desirable match for the youngest brother of the king. Unfortunately, while Warwick saw the appeal of such a union, the king was less convinced about any marriage between Plantagenet and Neville.

Anne and Isabel were now the daughters of the most important man in the realm apart from King Edward IV. Not only was Warwick exceptionally wealthy with a large affinity but he was popular because of his piracy and other naval adventures. He was known also for his liberality and lavish entertainments. Whenever he visited London, he was greeted by cheers. It was not surprising. *The Great Chronicle of London* recorded Warwick's famous generosity and claimed that whenever he was in residence at L'Erber, he provided six oxen for breakfast and mead was freely available to anyone who 'had any acquaintance in that house'.⁶ Any soldier who fought under his banner might go to Warwick's house and carry away as much meat as he could fit on the point of his banner. His attitude, which had the common touch, contrasted to many other magnates. The earl knew the importance of friendship, alliances and favour. He understood the significance of projecting an impression of power, strength and being the friend of kings and commoners alike.

But all was not well between Warwick and his royal cousin. Early on May Day 1464 the young king married for love, or at least for lust, without first consulting his advisers. The *Croyland Chronicle* described the union's 'immoderate haste' because it 'promoted a person sprung from a comparatively humble lineage'.⁷ Edward IV's marriage to Elizabeth Woodville, a widowed mother of two who 'had only a knight for her father'⁸ and from a Lancastrian family, surprised his council and the court. Edward's choice of consort was not for diplomacy, land or power. Polydore Vergil described the king as 'being led by blind affection'⁹ because he defied all expectations about royal brides.

It has been argued that the unanticipated match embarrassed Warwick who was negotiating a French marriage for Edward with Bona of Savoy. By itself the Woodville marriage is unlikely to have caused the breakdown in the relationship between the two cousins that Polydore Vergil ascribed to jealousy on the earl's part. It was true that Warwick favoured a French alliance. He promoted Edward's marriage to a French princess as well as French matches for Edward's sister Margaret and for his brother George. The *Warkworth Chronicle* recorded that when Warwick returned home from France he was 'greatly displeased with the King; and after that rose great dissent ever more between the King and him'.¹⁰ Warwick had no choice other than to accept Edward's choice of wife. He even escorted her on her first formal appearance as queen and acted as godfather for the couple's first child born in 1466.

In reality, 1464 was the moment when the cracks in the relationship between the king and his cousin became more noticeable and a point at which the earl's influence could be seen to wane. The king's marriage showed for all to see that Warwick had misjudged the extent to which he could dictate his cousin's policies as king. The Neville family had certainly benefited from Edward's accession. Fauconberg was created Earl of Kent. George Neville, Bishop of Exeter, held the Great Seal and became Edward's Lord Chancellor. In time he was translated from Exeter to the Archbishopric of York. Warwick benefited financially from the attainder passed against the Clifford family with the acquisition of Appleby and Brougham in Westmorland as well as Percy estates at Topcliffe and Craven.

But Warwick, already one of the wealthiest men in the kingdom, did not achieve all his goals. The king elevated only his immediate family to dukedoms. There was no dukedom for Warwick as there had been for his Beauchamp brother-in-law. It may not have mattered while the Neville family seemed all-powerful, but now the Woodvilles emerged as a political power that threatened Warwick's supremacy at court. Vergil was undoubtedly correct when he described the earl as being 'vexid in mind'.[11]

In the meantime, Warwick continued his programme of Neville wedding celebrations. He arranged for Isabel and Anne's illegitimate half-sister Margaret to marry Sir Richard Huddleston at York on 12 June 1464. Sir Richard was the eldest son of Sir John Huddleston of Millom – one of the region's leading families. His marriage to Warwick's illegitimate daughter helped to maintain Neville ties to the local gentry in the north and was probably also a reward for Sir John's service to the Neville family since '1459 and probably before'.[12] A fortnight earlier King Edward bestowed the earldom of Northumberland upon John, Lord Montagu. Edward and Warwick had travelled north to conclude a truce with the Scots so it is probable that Warwick was at Margaret's wedding for which he paid. He also dowered her with lands in Coverdale worth £6 per annum, land in Penrith and in Caldewgate, Carlisle, as well as the manors of Blennerhasset and Upmanby.[13] By 23 June the earl, having said his farewells to all his daughters who were also likely to have attended the wedding of their sister, was at Alnwick laying siege to the Lancastrian garrison there.

The Woodville marriage had other unexpected repercussions aside from the direction of foreign policy away from France in favour of Burgundy. Isabel and Anne Neville were beautiful girls in terms of fifteenth-century concepts of attractiveness, their lineage was impeccable and their prospective wealth as co-heiresses almost incomparable. Despite their desirability as heiresses, Warwick found that he forfeited opportunities to make advantageous connections because of the large numbers of ascendant

Woodvilles who sought to make ambitious marriages through their newly minted royal connections. Nor did Warwick's declining court influence help his search for suitable husbands for his daughters. The availability of eligible grooms dwindled rapidly during the eighteen months after 1464 because the marriage market was saturated by Elizabeth Woodville's sisters.

By the end of 1466 five Woodville women were married into the nobility. Earls and dukes saw the advantage of marrying their heirs into the extended royal family, Edward made generous settlements for his sisters-in-law and no one wanted to risk offending the king now that the conflict between the Houses of York and Lancaster seemed settled. Lord Maltravers, the heir to the earldom of Arundel, married Margaret Woodville while Henry Stafford, who would one day be the Duke of Buckingham, was married off to her sister Katherine. It is possible that Warwick had been considering Stafford, who was the grandson of his aunt Anne, as a potential match for one of his daughters. Anne and Eleanor Woodville married the heirs to the Earls of Essex and Kent. Their sister, Mary, was betrothed to William Herbert, the heir of the Earl of Pembroke. At the time of the betrothal Herbert was granted licence to use of the title Lord Dunster, a lordship which Warwick claimed for himself.

Pembroke also used his influence at court to secure several lucrative wardships to advance the financial and political interests of his own family. Amongst his wards was Henry Tudor, the only child of Lady Margaret Beaufort and her husband, the Earl of Richmond. Warwick may have helped his cousin win his crown, but a series of aristocratic marriages that year demonstrated that he was in danger of being precluded from further familial advancement.

Marriages within the extended Neville kinship compounded the earl's growing resentment. The Duchess of Exeter's daughter Anne Holland was promised to George Neville, the son of Lord Montagu. The duchess was the king's eldest sister and, as well as being a lucrative match, the arrangement would have tightened familial bonds between the Plantagenets and the Nevilles. Now, however, Elizabeth Woodville decided that she wanted Anne Holland to marry her own eldest son from her first marriage so she paid the duchess 4,000 marks to break the marriage contract. The queen's plans were to no avail as little Ann, niece to the king, died in 1474 but it added fuel to the fire of Warwick's resentment. There were other marriages and other insults. Warwick's aunt Katherine, the dowager Duchess of Norfolk, a woman in her sixties, was married to Sir John Woodville who was not yet 20. William of Worcester described it as a 'diabolical marriage'.[14] It gave Woodville access to Katherine's jointure from the Norfolk estates as well as those she accrued from her second and third husbands.

Warwick was extremely ambitious. Daughters, sisters and unwed nieces were a valuable advantage to a man seeking to make alliances. His attention inevitably turned to Edward's own brothers, who both spent some time under his tutelage, as potential spouses for Isabel and Anne. Edward's brother George had been created Duke of Clarence in 1461. Edward provided him with lands that had once belonged to attainted Lancastrians as well as estates from within the Duchy of Lancaster, including Tutbury which became Clarence's main residence during his early adulthood. George was at Elizabeth Woodville's coronation in 1464 in the role of Steward of England. He was 15 years old and his brother's heir, but must have recognised that his own status at court would soon be reduced if Elizabeth, who already had two sons, gave Edward a son of his own. Mancini, writing much later, stated that the duke was open in his contempt of the queen's humble beginnings as well as the fact that she was a widow.

George was not alone in his condemnation of the match if the rumours reported by the chronicles were true. It was said that on hearing of Edward's marriage to Elizabeth, the king's furious mother Cecily exclaimed 'Edward was not the offspring of her husband'.[15] The assertion, which cannot be corroborated, would be used against the king and his children by both his brothers in later years. The following year it was suggested that Clarence marry Mary of Burgundy, the young daughter of the heir to the duchy, but the proposal was soon dropped. George and Warwick became closer to one another during this period. Both were aggrieved by the turn of events.

The *Waurin Chronicle* suggests that a marriage had already been proposed between Isabel and George, but that Edward IV rejected the idea although it may have been supported by Edward and George's mother, Cecily, Duchess of York.[16] It was reported by the Milanese ambassador at the French court in April 1467 that Warwick had successfully married

Isabel to George.[17] Their source, King Louis XI, was wrongly informed. Polydore Vergil wrote afterwards that the earl did everything he could to promote the union and that the relationship between Edward and Clarence became increasingly fraught as a consequence. The king was perhaps all too aware of Warwick's power and influence so was consistent in his refusal to consider a match between Isabel and his brother, who remained heir presumptive until such time as Elizabeth Woodville gave birth to a male heir to the throne.

Chapter 6

Marrying a Prince

In September 1465 George Neville was enthroned as Archbishop of York at Cawood Castle near York. Pope Paul II translated him from Exeter in March that year to the more important see. The location was also more advantageous to the Neville clan. The enthronement was an opportunity to celebrate and for Warwick to impress a sense of his power and prestige upon his peers, family and affinity. Amongst the 6,000 or so guests were Anne and Isabel, alongside representatives of the Church and State, the extended Neville family and all their associated retinues and servants. Also present were members of York's commercial community including Sir Richard York, who was the 'mayor of the staple of Calais', as well as the sheriff for York that year.[1] Isabel, at 14, may have looked around the gathered throng and wondered with whom her father intended to match her. Anne, at 9 years old, was more likely to have been concentrating on her table manners, which included eating in moderation, not picking her teeth with her knife and waiting for her father's honoured guests to take their drink before drinking herself. Her mother also taught her daughters the importance of demureness which included neither speaking nor smiling too much.[2]

Warwick's royal guest, the 13-year-old Duke of Gloucester, was seated in a place of honour despite his youth. Seated opposite him were Anne and Isabel. Either Warwick chose to give his royal guest an opportunity for company closer his own age, or it was a ploy on the earl's part to throw his daughters in the way of the king's youngest brother. Richard's own sister Elizabeth, the Duchess of Suffolk, was placed on his right hand. The duchess was married to Alice Chaucer's eldest son by William de la Pole before 1458 when the de la Pole family were at their lowest ebb following William's murder in 1450. King Edward restored his brother-in-law, John de la Pole, to his rightful title in 1463. By the time of the feast at Cawood, the duchess had provided her husband with both an heir and a spare. She may already have been pregnant with the couple's third son.

Warwick acted in the role of steward for the occasion of the feast while Lord Montagu was the treasurer. Diners at the upper tables would expect a full choice from the dishes on offer. Guests seated lower down might expect to receive fewer choices. Isabel and Anne sat at a table laden with a mixture of sweet and savoury foods including breads, cakes, baked fruits, jellies, tarts and custards. In addition to the food the archbishop provided 300 tuns of ale, 100 tuns of wine and a pipe of hippocras,[3] the latter being a spiced wine. A printed record of the feast can be found in the Bodleian Library and in Hearne's edition of *Leland's Collectanea*. The feasting started with the bishop's enthronement and is likely to have lasted for several days. It included 400 roast swans and 104 peacocks as well as ox, mutton, pork, venison, chicken, rabbit, duck, plover, woodcock and other gamebirds. The swans and peacocks were presented at the table dressed in their feathers. The list of birds provided for the meal is shockingly extensive including herons, bitterns, curlew, sparrows and larks. Freshwater fish served during another meal which fell on a fast day, when meat was prohibited by the Church, also included porpoises and seals. The medieval world defined many aquatic mammals with fish to extend the range of their permitted diet on Wednesdays, Fridays and during Lent. It reportedly required sixty-two cooks and more than 500 scullions to serve the meals. Expensive spices and exotic ingredients such as dates made their way onto the table, all designed to show the wealth and influence of the Neville family as well as the earl's renowned generosity. Each meal concluded with a subtlety. Often made from sugar, which was an extremely expensive commodity, these confections often heralded entertainment that followed after the feasting.

One of the subtleties listed is described as a dragon. It is unclear whether the dragon was edible, but it was likely to have been constructed from marzipan and sugar which was then painted or even gilded. The dragon may even have been a reference to the Beauchamp family story about Guy of Warwick, a Saxon hero. Guy, a humble cupbearer, fell in love with Felice, the earl's daughter. He was far too low born to aspire to Felice's hand so he set off on a chivalric quest to prove himself a worthy husband. During his adventures he slayed a dragon which terrorised Northumberland. Having shown himself sufficiently worthy of Felice, Guy was allowed to marry her and they had a child. Later Guy saved England from marauding Danes. The story was retold by John Rous.

Guy's semi-mythical relationship with the Countess Anne and her daughters was evident on the Beauchamp arms – a fess[4] between six crosses crosslet.[5] Warwick, the inheritor of the Beauchamp Earls of Warwick, completed a quest to place the Yorkists on the throne. He and his brother John saved Edward's realm, especially the north, from the Lancastrians. The Battle of Hexham fought on 15 May 1464 saw the end of any substantial threat against the king from Margaret of Anjou, especially since Somerset and Lord Hungerford were both captured and executed. Aside from demonstrating the earl's wealth, the gathering at Cawood was an opportunity for Countess Anne to meet with her sisters-in-law and all her husband's extended kinship. There were family matters to be discussed and it was also an opportunity for the earl to intrigue against the man he helped place upon the throne.

By March 1466 any aspiration Warwick had for a match between Isabel and Clarence seemed on the verge of being thwarted. English ambassadors were sent to Burgundy with a view to Clarence marrying Mary, the granddaughter of the Duke of Burgundy. The overture of a match made between England and Burgundy was welcomed by the Burgundians, but they were much more interested in a union between Mary's widowed father, Charles, Count of Charolais, and Edward's sister Margaret than between George and Mary. In the summer of 1467 relations between Warwick and the king deteriorated again. According to the Croyland Chronicler the storms of January that year predicted dire events. As well as floods it noted 'a shower of blood', spectral 'horsemen and men in armour rushing through the air' and an unborn child weeping in the womb.[6] The reason was all too apparent to the chronicle's writer: 'there arose a great disagreement between that king and his kinsman, Richard, the most illustrious Earl of Warwick; which was not allayed with the shedding of the blood of many persons'.[7]

Aside from the growing ascendency of the Woodvilles, Warwick favoured a French alliance in part because of the relationship he developed with King Louis XI during his time in Calais. King Edward and his new father-in-law Earl Rivers favoured the proposed Burgundian alliance. With no matrimonial alliance between the king and Bona of Savoy possible following Edward's marriage to Elizabeth Woodville, Warwick next suggested a union with France with Edward's sister Margaret, but his designs on an Anglo-French accord were destined for failure despite the diplomatic mission that the king sent him on in June 1467. It was a lavish affair. He was even presented with the keys to Honfleur during the negotiations.

Warwick's plans began to unravel when he returned to England to discover that Edward had been entertaining a Burgundian embassy in England, led by the duke's illegitimate son Antoine, during his absence. Even worse, Warwick's brother George, the Lord Chancellor, did not attend the negotiations with Burgundy or the tournament that was part of the hospitality extended to the delegation. The queen's brother Anthony Woodville, Lord Scales since his marriage to the heiress Elizabeth Scales in 1460, represented England at the tournament. The Nevilles were conspicuous by their absence.

Edward was so angry that he visited the archbishop at his London residence and demanded the return of the Great Seal. George was replaced as Lord Chancellor by Robert Stillington, Bishop of Bath and Wells. Warwick, busy in his various roles as warden, Captain of Calais and royal ambassador, relied upon his extended family to act in his interests and without the archbishop, the earl lost a valuable interface with Edward's government. An Anglo-Burgundian alliance was agreed within the year between Edward's sister Margaret of York and Charles the Bold, Duke of Burgundy, following the death of his father. The Burgundians wished to avoid an Anglo-French alliance as it would leave King Louis XI free to conduct a campaign of territorial expansion in Burgundy. The *Croyland Chronicle* presented the argument that it was not the king's marriage which caused Warwick most dissatisfaction but the fact that Edward's foreign policy was at odds with his own. It cannot have helped that Edward was flexing his own political muscles and excluding Warwick from the decision-making process.

Warwick was not alone when he arrived back at Sandwich to the unwelcome news that the king had removed George from office. He had in his company a party of French diplomats to discuss the proposed French match. When he and the French ambassadors arrived in London, only Clarence came to greet them because the king and queen were in Windsor. The ambassadors returned home in August with nothing to show for their troubles. Clarence, who had been with the king when he dismissed the Archbishop of York from his post, was sympathetic when Warwick complained that the Woodvilles were dominant at court. According to

Waurin's Chronicle, George was quick to ask how the situation might be remedied. The answer was that Clarence should replace his brother but, on this occasion, Warwick was determined that he would not just make a king; he would ensure that he was part of the earl's immediate family.

Plague came to London that summer and its inhabitants began to flee into the countryside. Warwick travelled with his young cousins Clarence and Gloucester. By the time Gloucester arrived in Colchester, he was without his brother or cousin. The boy was welcomed by John Howard who was only recently returned from escorting the Burgundian envoys back to the Low Countries. Gloucester's itinerary included a visit to Stoke by Nayland and to pause at the shrine at Sudbury before meeting with Warwick's brother-in-law, the Earl of Oxford.[8] Warwick, having been slighted once too often by the king, took an opportunity at Cambridge to suggest to Clarence that a change in government would perhaps be a good thing for the country. The duke, ambitious on his own behalf and desirous of marriage to a wealthy heiress despite the fortune that he accrued from the estates his brother had granted him, listened with interest.

It was at this stage, according to *Waurin's Chronicle* and Polydore Vergil, that Warwick offered his eldest daughter's hand in marriage to Clarence and was accepted. It is unclear whether the duke was 'overcome'[9] by the thought of wearing his brother's crown or the chance to marry Isabel. The chronicle does not mention whether Warwick suggested that Gloucester should marry Anne or whether Richard knew that his cousin and brother were on the cusp of a plot against Edward. The latter is unlikely as Gloucester was devoted to his elder brother. Ross describes Clarence as subject to Warwick's 'wiles'[10] but as charming as George might have been, he was also extremely jealous of his elder brother and ambitious for himself. In public, Warwick had been slighted by the king he placed on the throne and humiliated in front of the French whose alliance he had cultivated since his appointment to the captaincy of Calais. He chose to return to his home at Middleham where his wife and daughters awaited him. He needed time to ensure that his scheme to marry Isabel to Clarence was successful.

Waurin's Chronicle suggests that Clarence may not have been completely circumspect following his meeting with Warwick or else the king was deeply suspicious of his politically shrewd cousin. Edward reprimanded his brothers before having them both briefly placed under arrest after discovering the direct offer of a marriage had been made, despite his earlier refusal to consider the union. Waurin, a Burgundian, was present at the tournament hosted by the king at Smithfield in 1467, but his source for the angry encounter between the brothers is unknown. There are no other sources to substantiate his narrative and he is known on occasions not to let the truth get in the way of a good story. Gloucester returned to his cousin's household to continue his education. But Clarence, on the other hand, was kept more closely under his brother's gaze. He was required to spend Christmas in Coventry with the royal court that winter.

In Middleham Warwick's next step was to apply to Pope Paul II for a dispensation permitting the marriage of Clarence to Isabel as they were related within a degree prohibited by the Church, both being descendants of Joan Beaufort and the 1st Earl of Westmorland. The marriage was politically dangerous so it was essential that the king could not invalidate it at a later date on a technicality. Warwick asked the Archbishop of York to facilitate the matter. In turn, the archbishop advised the king's proctor in Rome, Dr James Goldwell, both of the need for a dispensation and for secrecy. Isabel's marriage was not the only matter addressed behind the king's back. The bishop wished to become a cardinal.[11] It was unfortunate for him that the king discovered he aspired to a cardinal's hat and rather pointedly put forward his own candidate – George's own cousin, Thomas Bourchier, Archbishop of Canterbury, who was duly elected.

Warwick was not present in October 1467 at the Great Council at Kingston-upon-Thames when Edward's sister Margaret gave her formal consent to her proposed marriage with the Duke of Burgundy.[12] Rumour suggested that the earl refused to contribute to the dowry that the Burgundians required and which Edward could not afford to pay from his own coffers. Nonetheless Warwick was with the king when he accompanied Margaret to the shrine of Thomas Becket before she embarked at Margate. It was also noted that Lord Wenlock, Warwick's deputy in Calais, was a member of the wedding party. To all intents the earl, who the French king described as being like a father to Edward, seemed recovered from his disappointments and was reconciled to the direction that the king's foreign policy was taking. Edward might have been making his own decisions, but he wished to retain his cousin's friendship and Warwick was not excluded from government in the way that York had been ostracised by Margaret of Anjou and her favourites. Despite this, London was so awash with rumours about Warwick's enmity of Elizabeth Woodville that they were recorded by *The Great Chronicle of London*. In France there was some talk of discussions with the Earl of Warwick to restore the throne to King Henry VI. He was recaptured by the Yorkists near Clitheroe in July 1465 and had been imprisoned in the Tower ever since. At the time Warwick was able to dismiss the suspicions as false rumour, but Edward's realm was restless.

One of the reasons Edward was accepted as king in 1461 was that Londoners were tired of Margaret of Anjou and her faction's administration. Now there were fresh mutterings about the levels of taxation and the management of the realm which prompted a renewal of Lancastrian plotting followed by a surge of arrests. For a time, Lord Wenlock came under suspicion in Calais. Nor was the loyalty of Warwick's brother-in-law, the Earl of Oxford, as assured as the king might have hoped. Oxford plotted with Henry Courtenay, the brother of the Lancastrian Earl of Devon and Thomas Hungerford, whose father, Baron Hungerford, was executed in the aftermath of the Battle of Hexham in 1464. Courtenay and Hungerford were hanged, drawn and quartered for their treachery. Oxford was consigned to the Tower in November 1468 but pardoned on 15 April 1469 after turning evidence against other conspirators.

King Edward summoned his youngest brother back to court from Middleham early in 1469. Gloucester was ready to take his place in the adult world just as Clarence had done. Affairs in England remained unsettled and there was further unrest, the worst of which was described as 'a whirlwind'[13] coming from the north. The shadowy Robin of Redesdale and his supporters began complaining in the winter of 1468 that they were oppressed by taxation and levies orchestrated by the king's advisers – the Woodvilles and their faction. There were also voices raised for the return of the Percy family to their rightful title. It seemed at the time to be an extension of the ongoing pockets of sympathy for the Lancastrians. Lord Montagu, Earl of Northumberland since the Yorkist victory in 1464, set about suppressing the dissidents. It seems unlikely that the Neville affinity was behind the uprising. Montagu was rewarded with the elevation of his son George to the dukedom of Bedford, along with the suggestion that the boy would make a suitable groom for the king's daughter Elizabeth. As Montagu snuffed out the embers of rebellion in the north, the same fire caught light in Lincolnshire led by Robin of Holderness. Robin of Redesdale, Robin Mend-All or even Robin of Holderness were bi-names only one step removed from Robin Hood. It was a name used by several different groups with differing agendas. [14]

Polydore Vergil, the Tudor historian, would later claim that Warwick orchestrated the revolt in the north, but combined earlier unrest, which was subdued by the end of May 1469, with that summer's rebellion led by a captain also using the name Robin of Redesdale. Warwick, still performing the king's business and to all intents reconciled with his cousin, fermented rebellion in the name of Robin of Redesdale with his extended family and the most trusted members of his affinity. Unrest in the north was to be a diversion to distract the king from Warwick. The papal dispensation for a marriage between Isabel and Clarence was granted on 14 March 1469. All that remained was for the marriage to be celebrated.

Warwick journeyed south on official business with his family allowing the northern rebellion to bubble to the surface when it was convenient to his plans. The true identity or identities of Robin of Redesdale remain unknown, but there is sufficient circumstantial evidence to name Sir John Conyers with a degree of certainty as the leader of a band of rebels backed by Warwick for his own purposes.[15] Conyers was married to Alice Neville, the daughter of Lord Fauconberg. Also known to be involved were Warwick's nephew Sir Henry Fitzhugh and a cousin Sir Henry Neville of Latimer, the brother of Lord Latimer identified as a rebel captain by *The Great Chronicle of London*. Countess Anne may have known what her husband intended, but no woman could be taken to court to testify against her spouse nor be held responsible for what he decided. The exact whereabouts of the countess and her daughters at this time is uncertain, but it is more likely that they remained at Warwick Castle for a time while the earl continued to Calais. The king still relied on the friendship of his cousin and little realised the depth of the earl's anger or the extent to which he was prepared to disobey his monarch. Edward had little grounds for suspicion because Warwick was often present at court and, together with Lord Montagu, was a regular witness to royal charters that year.[16] The king also continued to make grants to him. There were even rumours that the Archbishop of York might be reinstated as chancellor. In April, having represented Edward at a meeting with Louis XI, Warwick asked the king for permission to return to Calais in order to conduct a naval campaign against pirates. His request was granted, as was an application to visit Charles of Burgundy and his duchess. To Edward it must have appeared that the earl had overcome his dislike of Margaret's marriage. *Waurin's Chronicle*, written with the benefit of hindsight, described Margaret's delight on seeing her cousin at Aire-sur-la-Lys and added no one would have guessed what he planned.

By 17 May Warwick was back in Sandwich with Countess Anne and both their daughters, overseeing the fitting-out of his fleet for the campaign. It is impossible to believe that the countess was unaware either of her husband's duplicity or her elder daughter's forthcoming nuptials when she ordered her trunks to be packed for her visit to Calais. Clarence arrived in Sandwich at the beginning of June. Two days later the Archbishop of York arrived in Canterbury before continuing his journey to Sandwich where he blessed a new vessel named the *Trinity* commissioned by Warwick as his flagship.[17] The whole party was joined the following week by Duchess Cecily who remained in Sandwich for the next five days. This would suggest that Cecily might also have known what her nephews and son were planning.

Warwick and Clarence remained in Kent where they were joined by Oxford who, having emerged unscathed from his incarceration in the Tower, remained actively opposed to the king. On 4 July they all paid a visit to Canterbury to pray at the shrine of Thomas Becket. By then the king had decided to deal with Robin of Redesdale himself and was in the process of gathering troops as he made his way north.

The Neville family and the Duke of Clarence sailed to Calais soon after their visit to Canterbury. Warwick had already written to his supporters in Coventry on 28 June informing them that Isabel was to marry Clarence. There was no longer any reason, aside from the lack of royal permission, why Isabel and her betrothed should not be married. Rumours of the forthcoming nuptials even reached the king's ears at Newark. Edward wrote to his brother, Warwick and the Archbishop of York asking all three to come and see him. The relationship between Warwick and the king was beyond mending, but Edward was unaware of the fact until it was too late.

On either 9 or 11 July 1469, Clarence defied his brother and married Isabel at Calais. There was nothing clandestine or furtive about the union that took place in the presence of lords, knights and gentry.[18] It was in direct contrast to the king's own secret ceremony five years previously. The event was recorded by *The Great Chronicle of London* because of its political significance. Isabel was drawn into the spotlight when the archbishop performed the ceremony, either in the castle's chapel or one of the town's fine medieval churches, joining the Nevilles to the royal family by marriage. It is unknown whether the bride or her mother were apprehensive about flouting the king's wishes. It has been suggested that Duchess Cecily, who was Isabel's godmother as well as her mother-in-law, also attended the wedding[19] but there is no definitive evidence to that effect.

There is no record of what Isabel might have thought of her husband, her elevation to the king's immediate family or the possibility that she might be queen if Clarence ever ascended to the throne. He was still Edward's heir presumptive. Her new husband was handsome, clever and charming. At 19, he was just a year older than Isabel and she had known him since childhood. Nor is there any indication of how Clarence felt about his new bride, other than the loyalty implied by the fact that he sired no known illegitimate children and by his reaction to her death.

At Newark the king discovered that the rebel army outnumbered his own. Edward retreated to Nottingham where he sent out a commission of array. Warwick's former pupil, Gloucester, was on a pilgrimage to Walsingham when he received a letter requesting help from his brother. Gloucester borrowed money and hurried to Edward's aid. In Wales, one of Edward's staunchest supporters, William Herbert, Earl of Pembroke, gathered his men, as did Humphrey Stafford in the West Country. Both armies marched north towards Nottingham, but the rebels came south bypassing the king who sent an urgent summons for reinforcement to Coventry.

Isabel's wedding was followed by five days of celebrations. They were barely concluded before Warwick and Clarence wrote a letter that contained a copy of the northern rebels' petition which launched their own rebellion. The manifesto issued by Robin of Redesdale was openly hostile to the Woodville family which had superseded King Edward's loyal supporters, by which Warwick meant himself and his family as well as those of royal blood. The document made a direct correlation between the downfall of King Henry VI, Richard II and Edward II, and indicated what might befall King Edward IV if he permitted corruption to flourish at his court. Isabel's father and new husband employed the age-old tactic of blaming the evil advisors that surrounded the monarch as a justification for their subsequent actions. Warwick once again placed himself on the side of reform, urging his supporters in Kent to join with him at Canterbury to seize control of the realm.

Chapter 7

The Wives and Daughters of Rebels

Isabel, now the Duchess of Clarence, her sister and Countess Anne remained safely in Calais while George returned with his father-in-law to Kent. The gates of Canterbury opened to them and such was Warwick's popularity in London that the mayor let the earl and his army enter the city without question. It was the earl's intention to rendezvous with his affinity who masqueraded as Robin of Redesdale's men, although he told London's mayor that he intended to meet with the king. It would soon be time for the pretence that he was loyal to his cousin to end. Unlike Richard, Duke of York, Warwick had no blood claim to England's crown, but he had come to believe that he should be the power behind the throne.

The rebels bypassed Nottingham for Derby, marching from there into the Midlands where, on 26 July 1469, they met with and defeated William Herbert, 1st Earl of Pembroke's force on its way to Nottingham at Edgecote, near Banbury. The rebels' victory, assisted by the arrival of Warwick's vanguard led by Sir William Parr[1], resulted, in part, from a quarrel between Pembroke and the new Earl of Devon over accommodation. On the morning of the battle Pembroke was without archers, leaving his troops exposed. Pembroke and his brother, Richard Herbert, were both captured and executed without trial the following day at Northampton.

King Edward, still waiting for reinforcements, did not learn of their defeat until he departed Nottingham. The king's army began to desert him and he was soon captured near Northampton by the Archbishop of York. By then Earl Rivers and two of his sons had fled into hiding, but Lord Hastings and Gloucester remained by the king's side. They were dismissed without further thought and Edward was taken to Coventry where Warwick waited. The coup d'état was complete. England was now home to not one but two imprisoned kings.

By the second week of August, King Edward IV was at Warwick Castle where Countess Anne, newly returned to England, was both hostess and jailer. It looked as though Warwick intended to rule England through Edward. Fortune turned against the Woodvilles; Earl Rivers and his son John, who was married to Warwick's aunt, Katherine Neville, Duchess of Norfolk, were both captured and executed on 12 August. The earl was not done with the Woodvilles. He sent Thomas Wake to Grafton to tell Jacquetta Woodville that her husband and son were dead. Wake also accused the grieving widow of witchcraft. He claimed that he had several figures made from lead in his possession. One, broken in the middle, represented Warwick. The other two tied together with wire represented the king bound to Jacquetta's daughter. Rather than submit to Warwick, Jacquetta placed herself in the keeping of London's mayor who began his own investigations. For the time being she and Edward's queen were safe from the earl's vengeance. Humphrey Stafford, Earl of Devon for only three months, was not so fortunate. He was killed at Bridgwater on 17 August.

Warwick, having secured the privy seal, arranged for the king to be moved in secret to Middleham where he could be more closely guarded. It took the earl into his northern stronghold and away from London which remained largely loyal to King Edward. The earl's actions also hinted that he might consider removing his cousin and starting afresh with another of York's sons. Perhaps the earl dreamed of a Neville sitting upon the throne. Certainly, it was not long after their return to England that it became apparent that Isabel was pregnant.

As the summer progressed, rumours began to circulate that Edward was the illegitimate progeny of an affair between the Duchess of York and an archer named Blaybourne. If true, it was Clarence and not Edward who was the rightful king. Warwick's involvement, or at least the belief of his fuelling the rumour mill, can be traced back to Sforza de Bettini, the Milanese ambassador in France who wrote that the earl was 'rather inventive' and also reported that Warwick's intention was for Parliament to give Clarence the crown.[2] The likely source for his news was King Louis XI who had his own interests to consider. The French were hostile to the Yorkists after their decision to form an alliance with Burgundy. Nor was the suggestion that Edward was a bastard a new one. In 1464 Cecily, on learning of her son's marriage to Elizabeth Woodville, had herself declared that he was not his father's son.[3] If confirmed by Parliament it would be Isabel Neville who was queen in place of Elizabeth Woodville.

Events did not unfold as Warwick or Clarence expected. The earl's coup was not widely popular. It has been suggested that Warwick's initial success resulted from the strength of feeling against the Woodville faction[4] rather than from a desire to overthrow Edward, who had established his rule by conciliating the Lancastrians as well as by vanquishing them. Warwick's actions were illegal. He had no right to take control of the country in the way that he did. Men like Lord Hastings, who was Warwick's brother-in-law, remained loyal to Edward. Even John, Lord Montagu, who did not have cause to hate the Woodvilles with the ferocity of Warwick, failed to come to heel as might ordinarily have been expected. He remained aloof from the whole affair concentrating on his role of Warden of the East March. In London, awash with rumour, there was rioting and the destruction of property belonging to foreign merchants. There were incidents of disturbance and civil unrest as families across the country took the opportunity to renew feuds and settle old scores. It was during this time that the Duke of Norfolk, whose grandmother was married to Sir John Woodville, the queen's youngest brother, took the opportunity that presented itself to dislodge the Paston family from Caister Castle.

There was also the danger that King Henry VI's supporters would take advantage of the instability to ferment rebellion. Sir Humphrey Neville of Brancepeth, who was descended from the 1st Earl of Westmorland's wife, Margaret Stafford, became a focus for discord. He had come to terms with the Yorkist regime in 1464 after the surrender of Bamburgh. He lived quietly, but probably became one of Robin of Redesdale's rebels because he expected to see King Henry restored. Recognising that this was not going to happen, he began a fresh insurgency of his own.

Warwick was at Sheriff Hutton when he received word of the uprising. He was unable to raise a sufficient force of his own to counter his Lancastrian kinsman because he was powerless to issue an effective commission of array. The realm's magnates and gentry refused to obey him. Even his own extended kinship network was slow in coming to Warwick's assistance on this occasion. Lord Montagu continued in his loyalty to Edward who was his king. Warwick, who had no wish to see a resurgence of the Lancastrians, was forced to release King Edward at the beginning of September. It was either that or put Clarence on the throne, but that would have resulted in a complete breakdown of law and order.

It was only when the king went to York that a force was gathered to quash Sir Humphrey's rebellion. From York the king went to Pontefract. A nominal reconciliation was arranged between the cousins, but the atmosphere remained tense even after Sir Humphrey Neville's rising was suppressed and he was executed. Edward summoned Gloucester and other men whose loyalty he could rely upon to Pontefract and began to reconsolidate his power. The king, always affable in Warwick's company, returned to London leaving the earl without his prize.

Warwick and his family remained in the Midlands or the north with their armed retinues. Clarence was invited back to court with Isabel by the end of October 1469. Somehow fortune slowed the turn of her wheel against the earl. For the time being Isabel and Anne were still the daughters of the Lord of the North, but Edward began to strip the family of its power. At court Neville appointees were replaced. Both Clarence and Warwick were omitted from commissions of array. Nor did Warwick benefit from the death of the Earl of Pembroke as he might have expected, even if he did initially help himself to Pembroke's role of chief justice in South Wales. Edward had no intention of permitting his cousin to become the power broker for Wales as well as the north of England. Instead, he appointed Gloucester whose loyalty was unquestioned to administer the region on his behalf. That Christmas Warwick came to court for the festivities having received assurances of the king's goodwill. It is likely that his countess and younger daughter were with him. Afterwards, according to *Waurin's Chronicle*, it is thought that the whole family, including Clarence and Isabel, travelled to the earl's 'western estates' while the king went to Canterbury where he prayed at the shrine of Thomas Becket.

Without any real influence at court, and fearing the queen's vengeance for the death of her father and brother, Warwick took advantage of the Welles family feud with Sir Thomas Burgh, the king's Master of Horse, to launch a fresh insurrection. Historians are divided as to whether Warwick orchestrated an assault led by Richard, Lord Welles, who was the earl's second cousin as well as an avowed Lancastrian, on Sir Thomas's property, or whether he took advantage of an opportunity that presented itself.[5] Burgh's belongings were looted and his manor burned to the ground. The king, on hearing of the outrage, summoned Welles and his brother-in-law Sir Thomas Dymmock to London to answer for their attack. Both men claimed sanctuary in Westminster rather than comply. They were lured from safety by the promise of a pardon.

Meanwhile, Lord Welles' son, Sir Robert Welles, in receipt of orders from Warwick, gathered his troops in Lincolnshire and on 4 March 1470, issued a summons to the men of the county to join him in resisting King Edward. Welles claimed the king was coming north to punish the men who supported Robin of Redesdale's rebellion the previous year, despite the general pardon that had been issued. The real intention of the men behind the rising was to put Clarence on the throne. As unrest spread, the voices of Lancastrians demanding the return of King Henry VI began to be heard. The king marched from London at the beginning of March to suppress the uprising, having finally granted Warwick a commission of array to raise men in Warwickshire to join him in restoring order in Lincolnshire.

The earl's real intention when he set off to the Midlands was to trap the king between Welles' men and his own. It is unclear where Countess Anne and her younger daughter were at this time. It is certain that Isabel was not with her father or husband. On 4 March, Clarence visited his mother at Baynard's Castle. At that time, he intimated that he intended to travel westward to join Isabel.[6] It is possible, given Isabel's pregnancy, that Countess Anne had remained with both her daughters in the West Country rather than return to London or Warwickshire. While the earl schemed, the king threatened to execute Sir Robert Welles' father and uncle if Robert did not submit. This resulted in Robert turning back from his intended rendezvous with Warwick and Clarence. Even worse, the earl discovered too late that he could not raise an army large enough to vanquish Edward. He failed to learn the lesson of the summer that England required a king rather than a kingmaker. Even Coventry, where Warwick made his headquarters, sent its quota of men to join the king.

King Edward moved to intercept Welles' army on the Great North Road close to Stamford on 12 March 1470. The two armies drew up opposite one another but before battle was joined, the king, ignoring his previous offer of a pardon, ordered that Lord Welles and Sir Thomas Dymmock should be executed in full sight of both armies. The battle that followed was a short one ending in a rout with the rebels discarding their liveries as they ran – resulting in the battle becoming known as Losecoat during the nineteenth century rather than the Battle of Empingham after its location. Sir Robert Welles was executed a week later having named Warwick and Clarence as the 'chief provokers'[7] of rebellion.

Warwick, his wife and their daughters were now fugitives. Lord Montagu did not join his brother's rebellion but nor did he respond to Edward's call for assistance. By the end of March Lord Montagu was Earl of Northumberland no more. Instead, Edward created him Marquis of Montagu and granted him estates belonging to the Courtenay Earls of Devon. In June the wardenry of the West March fell into the hands of Henry Percy. The Neville stranglehold on the north was at an end.

Warwick and Clarence's army dwindled as they travelled north to Chesterfield whose lordship was in the earl's hands. While they were there, they sent messengers asking for a safe conduct from the king. Their request was denied. Recognising that pretending innocence was no longer an option, Warwick crossed the Pennines to Manchester having been promised the support of Thomas, Lord Stanley. When this was not forthcoming, he and Clarence headed to Bristol with a price on their heads. Warwick or Clarence may have entrusted goods to William Spenser, who was accused of treason when he became Mayor of Bristol in 1479. It was alleged by John Wilkins, a prisoner in Newgate, that Spenser retained property worth £400 belonging to the duke and a further £300 worth of goods that belonged to the earl.[8]

Isabel, staying at the bishop's palace in Exeter, was heavily pregnant with her first child. She was joined on 3 April 1470 by her father and husband. The pair had pushed their men and animals to the limit. The news that they were to pack and leave as soon as possible must have been met with alarm, not only because of the turn of events that tilted fortune's wheel so disastrously but because Isabel was preparing for the birth of her child. Childbirth was dangerous at the best of times. The countess's sister-in-law Cecily lived only 15 months after her second marriage to John Tiptoft. She probably died during childbirth, as did Tiptoft's second wife Elizabeth. The women may even have recalled twice-widowed Margaret Lucy who found shelter in the countess's household after Towton. A third marriage had been made for her to Thomas Wake, but the young woman died in 1466 probably due to complications in childbirth. Her infant son died soon after his mother. Birth ran close to death in the medieval period for both mother and child.

In normal times, an aristocratic medieval woman whose pregnancy had reached the stage where she wore her dress unlaced because of her swelling belly was encouraged to avoid excessive movement or extreme emotions. Galen specifically instructed that women should avoid being frightened for fear of miscarriage. Medical opinion believed that pregnant women should be calm and happy to maintain a balance to their humours. Sharp movements associated with travel were also discouraged, but now it seemed that Isabel could not be left behind. Warwick remained in Exeter for five days before travelling to Dartmouth where he was able to gather a fleet of ships which were speedily outfitted. Countess Anne, Isabel, Anne and 'a great number of their retinue'[9] boarded the vessels to take them to safety. Commines described Anne as 'a child' when she fled England and explained that the earl took the precaution of giving instructions to his 'private friends'[10] before his flight.

Warwick's flagship, the *Trinity*, was at Southampton. He sent a number of vessels under the command of Sir Geoffrey Gate to reclaim his ship and any other vessel which might be in the harbour. Anthony Woodville, Earl Rivers since the execution of his father, commanded the port and was waiting for them. He beat off Warwick's fleet and captured Gate as well as many of the earl's fleet and men. Gate was spared execution, but many others were not so fortunate. John Tiptoft[11] ordered that after hanging, the executed men should be impaled as a warning against rebellion. His actions earned him the nickname 'Butcher of England'. The brutality of his actions ended a long friendship between Warwick and Worcester. They were brothers-in-law who both rose to prominence under the administration of Richard of York, and Tiptoft was one of Salisbury's principal mourners in 1463.

Warwick was still Captain of Calais. The countess and her daughters must have felt some relief when they received the news that the end of their journey was in sight on 16 April. They hoped that Calais would once again provide the safe haven it had offered in 1459. At that time the garrison was loyal to its captain rather than its king. Warwick was still careful to ensure that key posts were given to his own men, but the family were to be disappointed in their expectations. The guns of Calais opened fire on Warwick's fleet. The earl was not the only one who remembered their flight after the rout of Ludford Bridge in 1459. King Edward had taken the precaution of sending a message to Calais, forbidding the garrison to admit the earl. On this occasion the earl arrived too late. Just when it seemed as though it could become no worse, Isabel went into labour.

Warwick withdrew his fleet out of range, dropped anchor and demanded to parley. The earl's own lieutenant, John Wenlock, arrived with a delegation. He confirmed that the loyalty of the garrison was divided. He explained that he was playing a double game. He remained true to Warwick, but nonetheless refused to grant him or his family access to Calais. Besides, he added, the port was a trap. Warwick would be safer in France. According to Commines, Wenlock would restore Calais to its captain when the time was right. The Duke of Burgundy, who took a close interest in English affairs, believed otherwise and rewarded him well for refusing to admit the earl.[12]

Assurances of loyalty were no solace to Isabel who faced a difficult first birth in a cramped cabin without the comforts or support aristocratic women could usually expect. There was no clean bed linen, beneficial herbs, relaxing oils or soothing tonics – just the terrifying reality of giving birth at sea. The only people to help deliver the child were her mother and younger sister. Countess Anne and her daughters are likely to have offered up prayers to both the Virgin Mary and to St Margaret who was the patron saint of childbirth. Countess Anne relied on her knowledge of childbirth which included the repetition of benedictions or even eating or drinking words regarded as holy written on a strip of paper. It would have been impossible to employ more elaborate rituals. Warwick begged for help for his daughter, and Wenlock sent two flagons of wine to the labouring woman before Warwick's fleet began to withdraw.

Isabel gave birth to a stillborn infant who was buried at sea. Prayers were said as the little body was consigned to the waves. When Rous came to write his genealogy of the Earls of Warwick, he was unable to add whether Isabel's child was a son or a daughter.[13] Without baptism an infant was destined for an eternity in limbo. Medieval Christians believed that babies were born in original sin and until they received baptism, they remained burdened by that sin. Midwives were permitted to baptise infants who were unlikely to survive birth or were feared to be stillborn, even if they were only partly born. Priests ensured that the women who delivered children within their communities knew the correct form of words so that if the life of the child was lost, its soul was not. Even Countess Anne was permitted to perform a baptism to save the soul of her firstborn grandchild.

Chapter 8

Anne – the Kingmaker's Bargain

With his womenfolk below deck, Warwick resorted to open piracy. He was joined by a small fleet of vessels under the command of his cousin Thomas Neville, the Bastard of Fauconberg. Together they attacked and captured Burgundian, Spanish, Hanseatic and even English shipping. Finally, the earl sailed to Honfleur; he had been given the key to the port in 1467, where the family sought asylum on 1 May 1470. King Louis offered hospitality to Warwick's wife and two daughters, but it seems that Warwick liked his family close at hand. They were at Valognes near Barfleur on 8 July.[1] For the time being at least, Isabel and Anne's lives of privilege were curtailed. Fortune's wheel turned against them. Their father had rebelled against the monarchy once too often. It must have seemed that there was no way back, even if he did count the French king amongst his friends.

The Burgundians complained that Warwick used French ports to commit piracy in contravention of the Treaty of Péronne signed in 1468. King Louis XI was unperturbed. He saw an opportunity to strike at both England and Burgundy. The refuge he offered the earl and his family came at a price: he demanded that Warwick come to terms with Margaret of Anjou in the name of King Henry VI who remained a captive in the Tower of London. Louis saw the unlikely coalition as an opportunity to gain an ally against the Burgundians in the event of King Edward IV being toppled from his throne. As early as the beginning of June, the Milanese ambassador in France advised his master that it was certain that Louis and Warwick 'will arrange a marriage between a daughter of the earl and the Prince of Wales'.[2] However, it should be added that in the previous months, he reported that Edward and Warwick were in accord over a plan to invade France and also supplied false news that the English king was slain during a battle.

Neither Warwick nor Margaret of Anjou found the suggestion of an alliance palatable, but it was evident to both parties that the pact was a necessity. Warwick would never again be a dominant political power while Edward was king, and men like Jasper Tudor and Oxford, who were loyal Lancastrians, recognised that the chance of King Henry VI being restored to the throne was remote unless Warwick added his political weight to their own. Louis XI acted as an intermediary, meeting with Warwick and Clarence who left their families in Normandy. On 22 July Warwick arrived at Angers. He was in the company of Oxford who received a warm welcome from the Lancastrian queen because 'he and his friends had suffered much... for King Henry's quarrels'.[3] The Milanese ambassador Sforza di Bettini reported that, by contrast, Margaret kept Warwick on his knees for more than twenty minutes while he apologised for his Yorkist credentials.

By then the earl's attention had shifted from Isabel to his younger daughter as a potential queen of England. It seems that the possibility of an alliance between Lancaster and Warwick had been suggested by the French as early as 1467. Queen Margaret's chancellor, Sir John Fortescue, first proposed a union between Warwick's daughter Anne and Prince Edward sometime after May 1469.[4] It is impossible to know what Anne, Isabel or their mother thought about Warwick's political about-turn or the ensuing negotiations which included 14-year-old Anne's marriage to Edward of Lancaster who was now 17 years old and determined upon the destruction of the House of York. It did not matter that Anne did not know Edward or that she would be entering a household with reason to hate the name Neville. Warwick's ambitions were more important than the happiness of his youngest child. If Isabel was now unlikely to wear a crown, it seemed possible that Anne would become a Lancastrian queen. No doubt he once again contemplated the enticing possibility of a Neville grandson sitting upon the throne.

Wedlock was an inescapable duty for Anne, who would have been raised to defer to her father's wishes, even if the match was fraught with danger rather than securing her future. Marriage alliances were sought to benefit the wider family rather than to satisfy the desires of the couple at the altar. Anne was older than her mother and many of her aunts had been on the occasion of their betrothals and weddings. On 25 July 1470 Anne's betrothal to Prince Edward of Lancaster was celebrated in Angers Cathedral. The *Croyland Chronicle* described the 'reconcilement'[5] of the two opposing factions and the 'espousals contracted between the said prince and the lady Anne'⁶, which included Warwick and Margaret of Anjou swearing an oath of assurance to one another on a fragment of the true cross. A week later the two families and their retinues departed Angers for Normandy where Anne and Edward's marriage was to take place. It was an uncomfortable moment for Isabel and Clarence. The agreement with the House of Lancaster meant that Clarence was required to renounce his claim to the throne. In return, he received the promise of lands; the dukedom of York; and the promise that should King Henry VI and his son Edward of Westminster die without heirs, that he would succeed to the throne. It left him no better placed than he was before he sided with Warwick against his brother. The earl prepared his followers for his political volte-face with a manifesto that explained the rationale for his actions at Angers.

Warwick was initially unable to advance the union with Lancaster further as Margaret was determined that the marriage would not be fulfilled until the earl had won the kingdom back for Lancaster. In addition, Anne was related within the prohibited degree to Prince Edward. For the earl, his daughter's wedding was part contract with the Lancastrian regime and part tool for future Neville aggrandisement, but marriage was also a sacrament that was subject to the Church's laws. Anne and Edward shared a common ancestor in John of Gaunt. Edward was descended from John's son, King Henry IV, by Gaunt's marriage to Blanche of Lancaster, while Anne was descended from Joan Beaufort, a daughter by Katherine Swynford. This meant that there was an impediment of consanguinity.

If Warwick's plan to overthrow King Edward was to work, he could not afford to wait until his daughter was married to Margaret's son. The Treaty of Amboise was agreed at the end of November sealing an alliance between Warwick, France and the House of Lancaster. Warwick had already promised Anne to Prince Edward to cement the deal, so the negotiations did not include the more usual financial agreements relating to Anne's marriage to the Lancastrian prince. If the earl's plan succeeded, Anne would have an extensive household, income and property rights as the wife of the Prince of Wales. It was perhaps for this reason that no jointure was settled upon Anne in the event of her outliving Edward in lieu of any dower rights.

Warwick, together with Clarence, Oxford and Jasper Tudor, would go ahead of the royal party to take back the throne. In the meantime, Anne was given into the care of Margaret of Anjou, and King Louis arranged for Matthew Fontenailles to travel to Lyons to seek the required dispensation. It should have been a formality, but the dispensation when it was granted described Anne as a damsel of Salisbury, which meant that it was invalid as Anne never resided in that diocese. A correctly worded dispensation was needed if the marriage was to go ahead. The difficulty was only resolved after Warwick sailed for England.

While the earl prepared for his invasion, Edward's sister Margaret and her husband the duke sent repeated warnings to England about the earl's plans. According to Commines the king preferred to hunt rather than to prepare to defend his kingdom. He was either very confident or complacent in the face of danger, even if Calais did remain closed to Warwick. Arrangements were drawn up for the seizure of Clarence's lands and for them to be placed in the hands of receivers, but they were not implemented at the time. By now Clarence had realised that it was unlikely Warwick would support his desire to become king. His resentment was fuelled by letters that he received from his family via an unnamed lady who visited Isabel. Philip de Commines reported a conversation that took place with Lord Wenlock in Calais: 'he told me it would be easy to reach a settlement because that day a lady passed through Calais, on her way to my lady of Clarence in France.'[7] De Commines' account goes on to explain that she was ostensibly carrying an offer from the king to Warwick, but that the real purpose of her visit was to win Clarence back to the king's side. Wenlock's failure to uncover the unknown woman's true intent meant that Isabel's husband received the correspondence. The king was supported in his attempts to persuade Clarence to resume his rightful place through the efforts of their sisters, in particular Margaret of Burgundy, and by Isabel's godmother – the Duchess of York. Whether or not Cecily had colluded with Warwick to bring about the marriage of Isabel to Clarence, she now set about healing the breach within her family. His own self-interest and the mediation offered by his sisters swayed Clarence's resolve, but he bided his time. It is not known what Isabel's view of the matter might have been.

Isabel said farewell to her husband and to her father as all of Warwick's womenfolk were to stay in France. The probable reason, aside from the need for a safe interval before their return to England, was that while Anne and Edward awaited a dispensation to marry and until Warwick fulfilled his side of the bargain, Anne was required to remain as surety for her father. The earl and Clarence, together with Oxford and Jasper Tudor, sailed from La Hogue in Normandy on 9 September. They landed in the west of England, probably at Dartmouth, on 13 September 1470. Tudor departed for Wales to raise troops. Oxford hastened to Essex where he began to recruit his own men with the intention of meeting Warwick and Clarence in London. The invaders were supported by Warwick's affinity which launched uprisings in Kent and Yorkshire.

A rising in Yorkshire was carefully planned to begin before the arrival of Warwick's fleet. Its purpose was to lure the king away from his capital. King Edward was at York when he heard the news of Warwick's landing. Despite the warning he received from Burgundy, he was unprepared for the fleet's arrival or the invasion that followed. It was impossible for him to reach London before his cousin and brother. He marched south to the Midlands where he expected to gather reinforcements led by Lord Montagu, but rather than remaining loyal to his king, Montagu now chose to support his own brother. The loss of the earldom of Northumberland still rankled.

It swiftly became clear that magnates loyal to King Henry VI were gathering in support of the invasion. Several towns refused to provide assistance to the beleaguered Yorkist monarch. Edward, recognising that he had been outmanoeuvred, fled to King's Lynn and sailed to the Low Countries with Lord Hastings and his brother Richard on 2 October, leaving the queen and their three daughters to take sanctuary in Westminster Abbey. Elizabeth's mother Jacquetta was also with them. Warwick's earlier accusations of witchcraft were sufficient reminders that a woman without powerful protectors was a woman at risk.

Warwick and Clarence entered London unopposed. On 3 October 1470 King Henry VI was released from the Tower and led through the streets by the hand before being restored to his throne. Ten days later the king was taken in procession to St Paul's for a ceremonial crown-wearing. The *Croyland Chronicle* described the Readeption of King Henry VI which formally began on 15 October and the manner in which official documentation was given: a double annotation in reference to the length of his reign – forty-eight years since he succeeded his father, but the first year since the throne was recovered from the Yorkists.[8]

A Lancastrian regime was quickly re-established, but Warwick was the puppet master controlling events at home. George Neville, Archbishop of York, became Lord Chancellor once more; Oxford was appointed Constable of England; and Clarence was reappointed Lieutenant of Ireland under the Lancastrian regime. Sir John Tiptoft was swiftly arrested and executed on the commands of Oxford whose father and brother had died on Tiptoft's orders. Warwick did nothing to save his brother-in-law. He remembered the impalements at Southampton. The Lancastrian restoration restored the fortunes of men like Jasper Tudor, the Lancastrian Earl of Pembroke, and it pardoned Warwick's brother Lord Montagu of his former loyalty to the Yorkist cause, but the redistribution of land, power and titles angered many others.

It seemed likely that Anne Neville would sit upon the throne, but it was only on 13 December 1470 that she and Prince Edward were finally married at Amboise. The marriage was uncanonical because it occurred during Advent, a season when weddings were prohibited by the medieval Church. The only alternative would have been to marry after Twelfth Night on 6 January, but no one, apart from perhaps Anne herself, wished to delay any longer than absolutely necessary. Isabel's marriage had been a family affair, but Anne's wedding was lacking in male guests. Instead, it was recorded that Countess Anne and Duchess Isabel were present, as was Margaret of Anjou. Historians speculate as to whether Anne's marriage to Edward of Lancaster was consummated. An alliance between the House of Lancaster and Warwick provided Margaret with the support she needed to attempt to retake the throne, but the earl was her enemy and an unconsummated union was more easily unmade than one where the couple shared a bed. The queen had many reasons for mistrusting Warwick and she may have concluded that the marriage need only be temporary until her ends were achieved. Conversely, Warwick would have known that a consummated marriage was less easily annulled and Anne was of an age where the marriage debt could be paid.

On 15 December Countess Anne, Duchess Isabel and Princess Anne accompanied Margaret of Anjou to Paris where King Louis provided them with a glittering reception. The royal party spent the rest of the winter in France before travelling to Dieppe in January, although it is unclear whether Isabel returned to England ahead of her mother and sister. Warwick sent Sir John Langstrother and Lord Wenlock, who had switched sides by that time, to fetch his family, Margaret of Anjou and Prince Edward. The party gathered at Harfleur on 24 March 1471.

King Edward IV spent the winter in the Low Countries where he sought the support of his brother-in-law Charles, Duke of Burgundy. Initially Charles was not sympathetic but with French attacks on Burgundian territories and England's declaration of war on Burgundy, he began to provide Edward with the resources he needed. It suited Charles the Bold to have an anti-French monarch on the throne in England. Edward gradually amassed men and money to return to England and overthrow the Lancastrian government. The *Croyland Chronicle* speculated that the Duchess of Burgundy sought the reconciliation of Clarence to his brother to help achieve her husband's goal.

In January 1471 Charles gave Edward sufficient funds to provide a fleet. The Yorkists arrived off the Norfolk coast on 12 March but were repelled by Oxford's men. The fleet continued northwards. On 14 March 1471 Edward disembarked at Ravenspur in Holderness on the Humber. He initially claimed, just as Henry of Bolingbroke did in 1399, that he was interested only in his father's title and estates. At York he told the mayor and aldermen, who refused to allow him inside the city wall with more than fifteen men, that he would never have claimed the crown if it were not for the 'exciting and stirring of the Earl of Warwick'.[9]

Warwick, who was at Warwick Castle, wrote to Sir Henry Vernon with a commission of array announcing that Edward had arrived with an army and that he himself would fall back to Coventry. He commanded his own followers to gather their men and meet with him there. As Edward marched south, bypassing Pontefract which was held by Montagu, the Yorkist army was swelled by the king's allies. Although Warwick's brother initially held off from attacking Edward, he took the precaution of shadowing the king's army with a much larger force of his own.

At Nottingham the king discovered that Newark was occupied by a large Lancastrian army commanded by Exeter and Oxford. By this time a steady stream of Yorkist supporters swelled Edward's own ranks. When the Yorkist army advanced upon Newark, the Lancastrians withdrew further south to rendezvous with Warwick as they had been instructed. Warwick closed Coventry's gates. It was a tactical mistake. In different circumstances Edward might have found himself penned into Nottingham by the armies of Warwick, Exeter, Oxford and Montagu; instead, it was Warwick who found himself in a difficult situation as the size of King Edward's army increased with each passing day.

If Clarence had not made his mind up before, he did so now. On 3 April the inconstant duke deserted his father-in-law and met with the king and their brother Richard between Burford and Banbury where they were reconciled. The combination of family pressure and a sense of self-preservation prevailed. The Yorkist need for Clarence's troops to tip the balance in Edward's favour ensured that Isabel and her husband were welcome back in England. The meeting was described by Margaret of Burgundy in a letter to her mother-in-law. Having attempted to negotiate on Edward's behalf with Isabel's father, who refused to agree terms for a surrender, Clarence marched with his brothers on London taking custody of King Henry VI on 11 April. The Lancastrian monarch was returned to the Tower along with the Archbishop of York. Edward went to Westminster where he was reunited with his wife and family, including his infant son Prince Edward who was born while the queen was in sanctuary.

Unaware of the speed with which events were unfolding, Countess Anne boarded a vessel at Honfleur. Her daughter, Anne, now married to Prince Edward, travelled with the royal household on a different boat. The weather was stormy and the seas rough, and the fleet turned back to harbour. It took a further two weeks to make a successful crossing. Margaret's fleet finally departed on 13 April. The queen's vessel containing Anne and her husband Prince Edward arrived at Weymouth in Dorset on Easter Sunday, 14 April 1471.

Their arrival coincided with the Earl of Warwick's defeat at Barnet by King Edward's army. The battle, fought early on a foggy morning, was closely fought. There were occasions when Warwick's army had victory in its grasp. Oxford's force, on the right wing of the Lancastrian line, routed the Yorkists commanded by Lord Hastings, chasing them into Barnet where they took the opportunity to loot the town as well as to hunt down their enemies. By the time Oxford regrouped his men and returned to the battlefield, the opposing lines had shifted on their axis by 90 degrees. The confusion of war and fog resulted in Montagu's men attacking Oxford's contingent, mistaking them for their enemies because of their livery badge which was a five-pointed star (or mullet), rather than a star with streams as it is often described.[10] In the confusion it was sufficiently similar to the king's own livery badge of the sun in splendour and it caused a disaster for Warwick.

Cries of treason led to chaos in the Lancastrian lines and a retreat. Lord Montagu was killed on the battlefield. Warwick died as he fled. Edward instructed that his forces should offer no quarter to his fleeing opponents and more than 1,000 men died. Exeter was left for dead on the battlefield until someone realised that he was still alive. His wounds were attended to and he was taken into sanctuary at Westminster. The Duke of Somerset fled to Wales where he joined with Jasper Tudor who was still recruiting troops. Oxford managed to escape to Scotland with his two brothers before sailing to France. He left his wife Margaret, who was Isabel and Anne's aunt, behind in England at Castle Hedingham. Oxford would not see his wife again until the fall of the House of York, and Margaret would be presented on occasion with letters from her husband asking for money and men that she could ill afford. Oxford was not attainted for treason; in all likelihood, it was because Warwick was not attainted so it followed that neither could his subordinates. Despite this, all his lands were forfeit to the Crown, and Margaret could not claim her jointure rights because her husband was still alive.

King Edward and his brothers went to St Paul's to give thanks for their triumph and to view the shattered remains of Warwick and his brother John Neville, Marquis of Montagu, who were stripped naked and placed on public display. Edward did not want any rumours that Warwick survived the battle. Two days later the bodies were released and sent for interment at Bisham Abbey alongside their parents.

Chapter 9

Lancastrian Princess

Anne Neville, now Princess of Wales and in the household of Margaret of Anjou, learned of her father's death at Cerne Abbey when Somerset arrived with the news on 15 April. The Countess of Warwick was informed of her loss at Southampton and abandoned all thought of being reunited with her younger daughter. Instead, she hastened to Beaulieu Abbey where she claimed sanctuary. She would remain with the Cistercians for the next two years.

Common law originally stipulated that anyone claiming sanctuary could remain for 40 days before facing trial or leaving the country for permanent exile via the nearest port, but by the fifteenth century, men and women often remained in the shelter of the Church indefinitely. This form of asylum was limited to those foundations that held sanctuary by right of a royal charter and was known as chartered sanctuary. Westminster Abbey, where Elizabeth Woodville sought refuge, was the principal foundation associated with chartered sanctuary. Ordinarily a felon or debtor entering sanctuary had to confess to the sins and crimes they committed. Countess Anne confessed her sins and swore to keep the peace within the precincts of the abbey and to obey all its regulations. Once she met those requirements, so long as she did not stray from the abbey's boundaries, she could not be arrested to be taken elsewhere against her will. The sanctuary administrator entered her name in Beaulieu's sanctuary register along with the reasons that she sought shelter. Unfortunately, the register no longer survives.

The Lancastrian queen wanted to turn back for safety, but the French ships that had carried her to England had already returned home. She was persuaded by her supporters to continue in the direction of Wales where Jasper Tudor awaited them with an army that grew by the day. She and Prince Edward took the decision to continue their campaign after Somerset and the Earl of Devon argued that Warwick's death made the chances of retaking the throne more favourable. This was because so many Lancastrian adherents were enemies of the earl and had refused to answer his call to arms. Somerset began a successful recruitment drive in the south-west. Margaret of Anjou and Anne stayed in Exeter for two weeks as men from Devon and Cornwall poured into the city.

Anne was still with her husband and mother-in-law when their army marched to Taunton, Glastonbury and Wells. The outcome of Barnet meant that Warwick had failed to fulfil his part of the marriage agreement, but there was nowhere else for her to go. Now Anne learned what an army might do when the Lancastrians sacked the Bishop's Palace at Wells. By 30 April she was at Bath. On 1 May Anne was with the Lancastrians when they fell back to Bristol, after learning that King Edward had amassed another army and had moved via Windsor and Abingdon to Cirencester on his way to intercept them. In Bristol the Lancastrians were grateful to receive 'money, men and artillery'.[1]

On the night of 2 May, the Lancastrians received further marching orders. They were to cross into Wales to meet with Jasper Tudor. Anne, having no alternative, went with them to Berkeley. She might have hoped for a respite, but the Yorkists was close behind them. At one o'clock in the morning the Lancastrians broke camp once more. They trudged through the night, intending to cross the Severn at Gloucester into Wales. Anne's distant kinsman, Sir Richard Beauchamp, denied the army access to the bridge forcing the Lancastrians north with the intention of fording the river. They travelled 44 miles before making camp at the hamlet of Gupshill, south of Tewkesbury, at about 4.00pm on 3 May 1471. Margaret and the ladies with her spent the night at Gobes Hall. Anne and the other Lancastrian noblewomen who accompanied the queen had covered a distance of more than 50 miles in less than forty-eight hours, as had the Yorkists who continued their pursuit.

Margaret, when told of the situation, was eager to cross into Wales as soon as possible, but Somerset persuaded her that they should stand and fight rather than risk being caught as they made the crossing in the swollen river. The next bridging point was at Upton-on-Severn. The Yorkists were almost upon them and the only real option was to make a stand. It was the closest that Anne had ever been to a battle and, given Warwick's recent death, the 14-year-old girl must had had a troubled night's sleep. The following day would either see her as the wife of the victorious heir to the Lancastrian throne or a fugitive once more.

The following morning Margaret of Anjou and the ladies she had in her company including Anne; Lady Katherine Vaux; Marie of Anjou, the dowager Countess of Devon;[2] and Margaret, the wife of Sir Hugh Courtenay of Boconnoc, parted from the army. Some writers believe that Margaret of Anjou was 'an agonised spectator'.[3] According to local legend she viewed the battle from the top of the abbey's tower. In reality she and her women were more likely to have been hustled away from immediate danger. There are different opinions as to where Anne might have been during the battle and what happened to the women in the royal party in its immediate aftermath. The *Historie of the Arrivall of King Edward IV in England*, usually abbreviated to *The Arrivall*, was written by a Yorkist eyewitness.[4] It suggested that Margaret went to 'a poor religious place'[5] after Prince Edward was arrayed for war and took his place leading the centre of the Lancastrian line. It is possible that her party travelled south-west for 4 miles to Deerhurst Priory, a monastic house associated with St Mary's Abbey in Tewkesbury. Here, she and the other women may have awaited the outcome of the battle and perhaps prayed in the Saxon church. The link with Tewkesbury Abbey is an important one because Abbot John Strensham, who Anne knew because of her familial links with the abbey, may have suggested the location. King Henry VI made the alien priory of St Denis a denizen in 1443 so that it avoided confiscation under the Act of Parliament of 1415. Four years later he seized the priory's possessions to help pay for his college at Eton and gave the priory to Tewkesbury Abbey. King Edward IV restored the priory to St Denis on the understanding that it would not pay any funds to its original mother house in France and that all the monks were English. When it proved impossible for Deerhurst to maintain a prior, four monks and a secular priest,[6] the Yorkist king regranted the priory to Tewkesbury.

An alternative destination considered more likely by some historians is Little Malvern Priory where Anne might have been housed with the queen in the prior's lodging. It has also been suggested that Evesham Abbey might have provided shelter.[7] A more intriguing possibility is that Margaret's party sought shelter at the moated manor of Birtsmorton Court to the north of Tewkesbury. Sir John Nanfan of Birtsmorton and Trethewell was once Henry VI's esquire of the body as well as a retainer of Anne's own Beauchamp grandfather. Sir John died in 1459 but his wife Jane still resided in the family home, as did their son Sir Richard

Nanfan whose Lancastrian loyalties would see him well rewarded in the reign of Henry VII. He was also an associate of Lord Wenlock who was part of the Lancastrian army at Tewkesbury – the crests of both men can be found at Sir John Norreys's home at Ockwells Manor at Bray in Berkshire.

The Battle of Tewkesbury was fought between two armies of roughly the same size on 4 May 1471. The *Arrivall* described the king's use of artillery on the Lancastrians as well as the shower of arrows that rained death on the field. The Lancastrians had been forced to abandon their own artillery in order to set the pace of their march, but they held the high ground surrounded by hedges and ditches giving them some advantage. Somerset, leading the right flank, attempted a frontal assault on the Yorkists, manoeuvring his men along a lane obscured by trees so that the king could not see their direct approach. Prince Edward, supported by Lord Wenlock at the centre of the line, made no move to support the duke's attack. The king was surprised by Somerset's appearance, but his men held their ground before pushing the Lancastrians back the way they came. Gloucester's vanguard joined the melee, as did the commander of the light cavalry sent by Edward to reconnoitre some woods that he feared might contain a Lancastrian ambush.

It was not long before the Lancastrians, commanded by Somerset, broke and fled, followed by the rest of their army. Lord Wenlock was killed on the battlefield, in some accounts with an axe wielded by the furious Somerset who believed that Warwick's lieutenant had betrayed them. If so, his actions caused the men under Wenlock's standard to flee. The Lancastrians were trapped by the Rivers Avon, Severn and Swilgate. There were two bridges and a ford which became congested and greasy with blood as the fleeing men were cut down. Other fugitives drowned as they attempted to escape their pursuers.

Many Lancastrians were caught on the narrow field still known as Bloody Meadow. According to *The London Chronicle*, Anne's 17-year-old husband was killed during the rout, reporting that 'there was the prince slain with many others'.[8] The *Warkworth Chronicle* added the detail that the prince was fleeing in the direction of the town when he was caught and that before he was slaughtered, he called out to his brother-in-law Clarence for mercy.[9] By 1473 continental accounts began to suggest that Edward was killed by the Yorkists in cold blood. Later accounts rendered by Tudor chroniclers describe the prince being 'crewelly murderyd'[10] after he was brought before King Edward, either by his attendants or by Gloucester. It would be suggested that Edward of Lancaster's murder occurred not to remove a threat to the Yorkist crown, but to clear the way for Anne's marriage to Richard of Gloucester.

Exhausted Lancastrians, including Somerset, sought sanctuary in the nearby abbey. They were followed by the victorious Yorkists who entered and began to kill them before, if the *Warkworth Chronicle* is to be believed, a monk bearing the sacrament in his hands confronted the king. The *Arrivall* suggested a general pardon was agreed. The men inside the abbey were safe, or so they believed. The *Warkworth Chronicle* describes a brief stalemate before the Yorkists dragged their enemies from the shelter of the abbey two days after the battle. Tewkesbury did not have the right to harbour men suspected of treason so the king was within his rights to act as he did.

Edward lost no time in having Somerset summarily condemned and executed along with twenty other prominent supporters of King Henry VI. *The Chronicle of Tewkesbury Abbey* confirms the Warkworth version of events and adds that the Yorkists sacked both the abbey and the town. As a result of the bloodshed and destruction, the abbey had to be cleaned and reconsecrated at the end of May having been unavailable for divine service in the month following the battle. Afterwards, according to the *Tewkesbury Chronicle*, the remains of Anne's young husband were quietly buried somewhere in the choir of the abbey. A modern brass, with a Latin inscription, commemorating Edward of Lancaster was placed in the choir in 1796. More than thirty important Lancastrians were buried in the abbey.

The news of the defeat was carried from the battlefield to the waiting women. One possibility is that Lord Thomas Stanley was delegated to tell the queen and his niece by marriage the terrible news. Stanley was married to Anne's aunt Eleanor Neville in 1454 and if not already widowed, he would soon be free to make a second marriage to Lady Margaret Beaufort. His political relationship with Warwick was a complicated one. Originally Lancastrian he came to terms with Edward in 1461 and served alongside his brother-in-law against Lancastrian forces in the north. When Warwick and Clarence had been forced to flee in March 1470, he refused to deliver assistance. But in the autumn of the same year he provided armed support to the earl when he arrived in England with an army at his back. Stanley, a political survivor best known for his aversion to committing his men to open battle, would soon make his peace with Edward IV.

Margaret of Anjou's only option now was to remain hidden, avoid capture and make her way to the safety of Wales before returning to France. *Fleetwood's Chronicle* maintained that Margaret and Anne remained hidden for three days after the battle. The king did not remain long in Tewkesbury departing in haste on 7 May when word arrived that the Bastard of Fauconberg had landed in Kent and was inciting rebellion in that county and in Essex. There was also trouble brewing in the Lancastrian north. The grieving women did not retain their freedom for long though. They were discovered and captured by Lord Stanley's younger brother William who fought on the Yorkist side.[11]

King Edward was at Worcester when a messenger arrived with the news that Margaret of Anjou had been captured. Sources stated that Margaret was a broken woman. The Tudor historian Polydore Vergil commented that she spent the rest of her life in mourning. Her beloved son was dead. The same sources do not say how Anne felt about her widowhood. Even if she did not love him, she had been with Margaret's court since the previous year and may have mourned the loss of both her husband and at least some of the Lancastrian nobility who accompanied the queen. She would almost certainly have been afraid of what the future held for her. Anne, the daughter of a politically astute family, must have realised that she needed to distance herself from her mother-in-law.

William Stanley arrived in Coventry on 11 May with his prisoners. Anne, weary and mourning the deaths of her father and husband, might have liked to take the opportunity to remind Gloucester of a shared childhood in Middleham if he was still with his brother's court. She needed a powerful ally if she was to retrieve anything from the situation in which she now found herself. Margaret, beside herself with grief at the death of her beloved son, screamed curses at Edward. The Earl of Northumberland arrived with further good news for the king. The northern rebellion had come to nothing once the news of the Battle of Tewkesbury arrived. In London, Earl Rivers, supported by the citizens of London, repulsed Fauconberg's son who abandoned the men he recruited to his cause before joining his fleet at Sandwich.

On 21 May 1471 King Edward IV and his lords arrived back in London in triumph. Richard of Gloucester led the procession that wound its way through the streets. Queen Margaret was paraded in a cage through the capital's streets behind the Yorkists before being taken to the Tower. That night, or soon after, King Henry VI died of 'pure displeasure and melancholy'.[12] The Milanese ambassador reported that King Edward IV had taken the necessary step to remove the last remaining impediment to his reign. It is likely that the Lancastrian king was murdered, especially as when his body was exhumed from its grave in St George's Chapel, Windsor, in 1910, his skull was found to be in several pieces. The skeleton was not subject to professional forensic examination and could have suffered damage during its original exhumation in 1484 from Chertsey Abbey for reburial in Windsor.

The direct line of the House of Lancaster ended with Henry's death. According to the agreement made by Warwick with Margaret, Isabel's husband was now the Lancastrian heir. In reality, the nearest blood claim was held by Lady Margaret Beaufort whose husband Sir Henry Stafford was grievously injured at Barnet. Margaret married for a fourth time to Lord Thomas Stanley before a year of widowhood was completed. The union offered her protection and the possibility of engineering a return from exile of her son Henry Tudor who was now in the care of his uncle Jasper.

Warwick's rise and fall from power coincided with a comet. *The Great Chronicle* recorded that 'This yeare after Christmas appeared a blazing star, and continued a week and more'.[13] He blazed an ambitious path but ruined Countess Anne's fortunes in the process. All the estates and castles that his forefathers gained through marriage lay at the feet of King Edward IV, who was about to begin his second reign with a male heir in the royal nursery. Margaret of Anjou spent the next four and a half years in captivity in the Tower and in Windsor and Wallingford. She was accompanied by Lady Katherine Vaux who lost her husband at Tewkesbury. In 1475 Margaret was ransomed by King Louis of France for 50,000 crowns, in return for which she was required to renounce the rights to her parents' estates. Katherine returned to France with her mistress who died in 1482.

It is unlikely that Anne, who was Clarence's sister-in-law as well as the king's cousin, was paraded through London or incarcerated with her mother-in-law. However, both she and her mother Countess Anne were the widows of men deemed to be traitors by the Yorkist regime. The wheel of fortune turned so that both women were brought low. By contrast, Isabel was the wife of the king's brother and welcome at court, despite Edward's earlier refusal to sanction her marriage. It is impossible to know what Isabel thought of Clarence who had been a firm friend to her father one day and his enemy the next. Clarence's feelings may also have been mixed. His dislike of the Woodville faction was not at an end. With the birth of Prince Edward on 2 November 1470, he was no longer his brother's heir presumptive.

For the time being, Isabel and George took up residence in Warwick's London home, L'Erber, on Dowgate Hill where George began to assert his claim to Warwick's estates which were forfeit to the Crown. Matters were complicated by the fact that Anne Beauchamp was *suo jure* Countess of Warwick. Her husband might have been dead, but the title was not vacant. The countess also held the vast Beauchamp and Despenser lands in her own right, as well as a third of the Neville estates which were her widow's right. Nonetheless her estates were confiscated as though she was not their legal owner and Clarence cast an acquisitive eye over the whole of the immense inheritance.

Countess Anne remained in sanctuary at Beaulieu Abbey claiming the mercy of both Church and king. Her decision may even have confirmed her guilt in the minds of the Yorkist government – what need had the countess of mercy if she was not guilty? She might have feared that once she was made Edward's prisoner, she would be obliged to take the veil and be shut behind convent walls which would effectively render her dead to the world. She might also have been afraid of the legal consequences of being Warwick's widow. She had travelled extensively with her husband and was privy to his plans for their daughters. Parliament might, with some justification, have passed an act of attainder against her, permitting Edward to confiscate her lands into Crown hands.[14]

Countess Anne was not the only member of Isabel and Anne's family to have to seek the refuge of sanctuary in the aftermath of Barnet. Margaret, Countess of Oxford, was forced into the sanctuary of St Martin-le-Grand by April 1472. King Edward confiscated all of the earl's estates, giving them to his own brother Gloucester, leaving Margaret nothing to live on other than the charity of those who were sympathetic to her predicament and 'the necessity of working with her needle'.[15] She could not claim a widow's legal rights since her husband was in exile, rather than dead. Oxford was captured in 1474 and spent the next 10 years as a captive in Hammes Castle in Calais. Margaret's difficulties continued. By 1477 Sir John Paston had cause to speculate about her plight. It was only in 1482 that she was granted a pension of £100 each year which was renewed by Gloucester when he became King Richard III.

Whatever personal affection King Edward had for Countess Anne was laid to one side so that she could be separated from the land and power which she represented. The countess wrote a series of letters petitioning for her own rightful inheritance together with its revenues:

> with her own hand, and not only making such labours, suits and means to the king's highness, smoothly also to the queen's good grace, to my lady the king's eldest daughter, to the lords the king's brethren, to my ladies the king's sisters, to my lady of Bedford, mother to the queen, and to other ladies noble of this realm.[16]

In addition, she was entitled to her full dower rights which were held to be separate from any of a man's estates that were confiscated by the Crown. She pleaded that the king 'weigh in your conscience her right and true title of her inheritance, as the earldom of Warwick and Spencer's lands to which she is rightfully born by lineal succession'.[17] No one moved to protest for the countess's rights – least of all Clarence. The king became increasingly exasperated by the countess's correspondence until he wrote to the abbot demanding that he keep Warwick's widow in more close confinement. There is no indication of how Isabel might have felt about the fact that her mother was effectively imprisoned at Beaulieu. The countess had not even a clerk to write the letters that she penned, not only to the king but to all the aristocratic women, including Jacquetta Woodville, who had at one time or another experienced the difficulties of attaining their rights in a world dominated by men.

Chapter 10

From Scullery Maid to Duchess

Anne was scarcely married before she was widowed. Rather than being the dowager Princess of Wales with all its associated rights, she was the penniless widow of a Lancastrian pretender and the daughter of a traitor. Her formidable father was no longer alive to provide his protection. Her uncle Lord Montagu was dead and the Archbishop of York faced an uncertain future, even though King Edward released him from the Tower at the beginning of June. Anne was entirely dependent upon the goodwill of her royal cousins who are likely to have kept her under strict observation in the months following Tewkesbury for fear that she might be pregnant with a new Lancastrian heir.

With Warwick dead it was now Clarence, legally her brother by marriage, who became Anne's guardian. It seems likely that the two sisters were reunited and that where Isabel went, Anne accompanied her. However, she was not free to leave Clarence's household even if she wished to do so. If Countess Anne was not permitted to retain her own lands as was Clarence's intention, it meant that his sister-in-law Anne was, theoretically at least, a co-heiress along with her elder sister. In the meantime, without jointure or dower rights, Anne lacked the agency to make her own decisions and while she remained unmarried, Clarence controlled Warwick's fortune in its entirety.

It is possible that Clarence tried to persuade Anne to enter a convent, especially once it became clear to him that his brother Richard wished to make the girl his bride. Gloucester would undoubtedly affirm her claim to her half of the estates. He was also one of the few men who would be able to provide a counter-balance to Clarence's assertion of power. It was alleged that after Richard expressed an interest in Anne that Clarence hid her from potential suitors. According to one story recorded by the *Croyland Chronicle*, the duke hid her at his Coldharbour house as a kitchen maid. In another she was disguised as a scullery maid in a cookhouse. Whether Isabel supported her husband's desire to control all

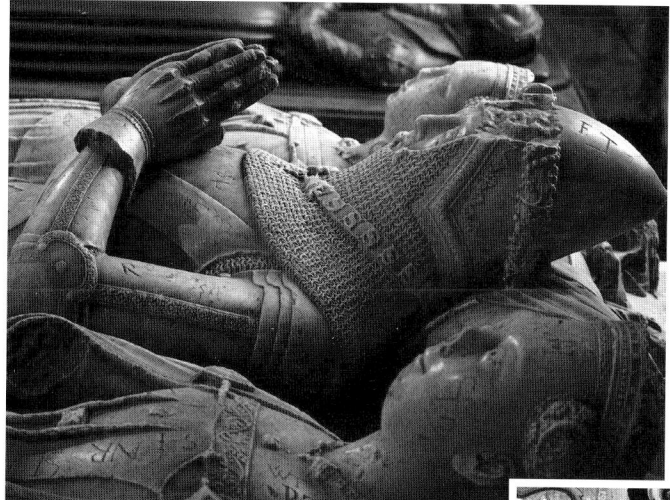

1. Alabaster effigy of Ralph Neville, 1st Earl of Westmorland (c.1364–1425) with his two wives, Margaret Stafford and Joan Beaufort, in St Mary's Church, Staindrop, County Durham. (© *Kyle Hewgill*)

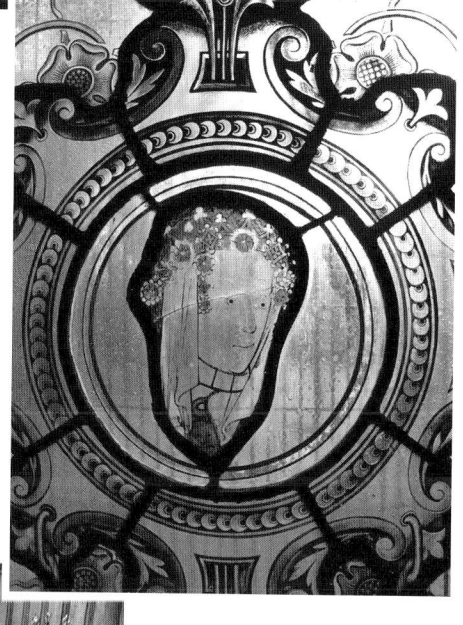

2. Stained glass image depicting Joan Beaufort, Countess of Westmorland, in St Andrews Church, Penrith, Cumbria. Originally thought to be of Cecily Neville. (© *Kyle Hewgill*)

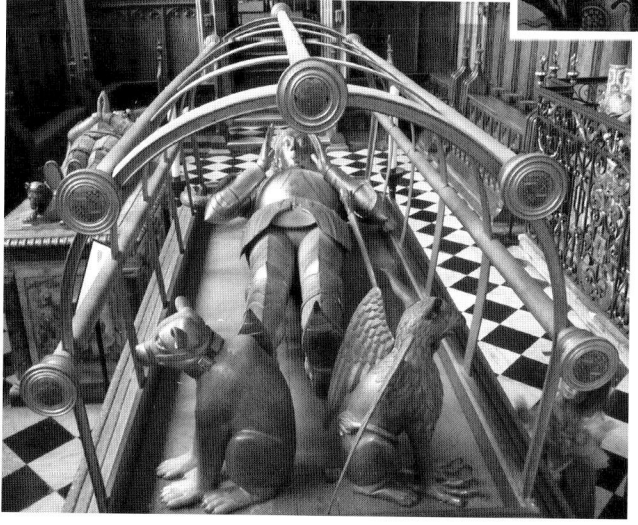

3. Gilded bronze effigy of Richard Beauchamp, 13th Earl of Warwick (1382–1439) in the Beauchamp Chapel of the Collegiate Church of St Mary, Warwick, Warwickshire. (© *Wikimedia Commons by Robin Stevenson*)

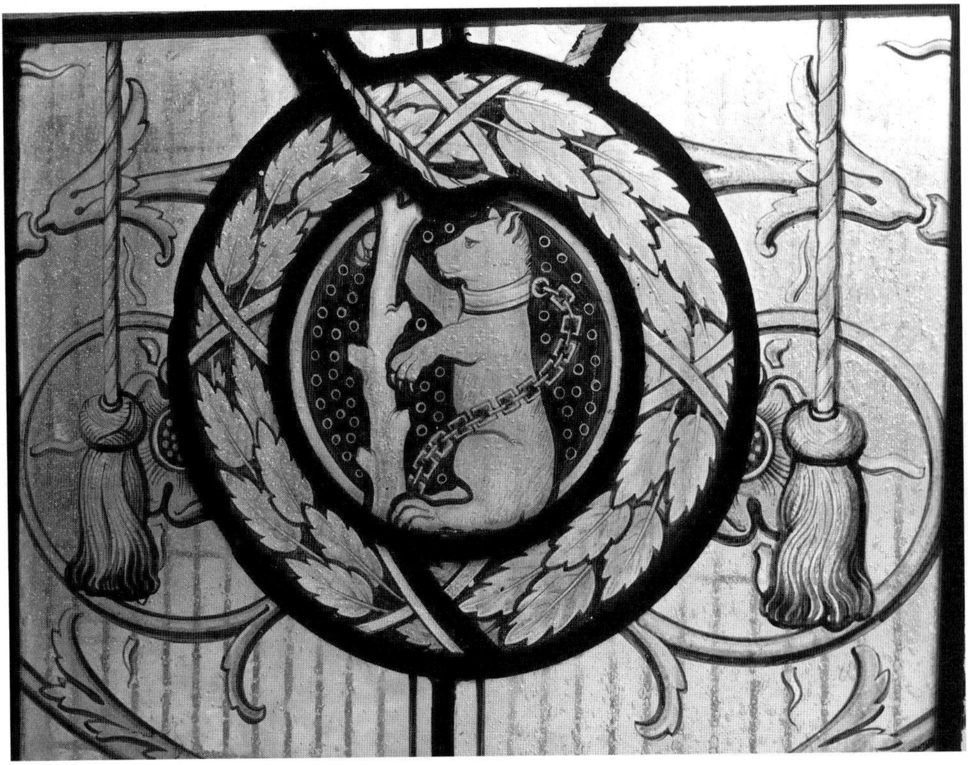

4. Bear and ragged staff in St Andrews Church, Penrith, Cumbria. (© *Kyle Hewgill*)

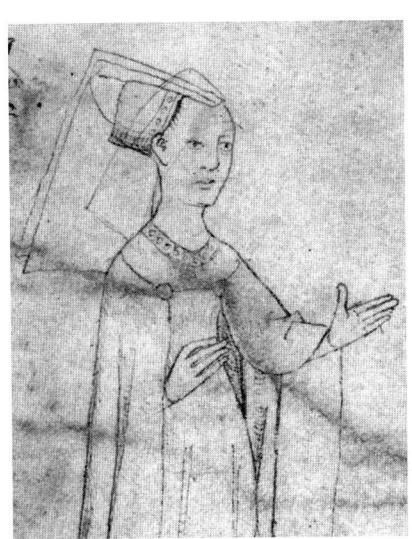

5. Anne Beauchamp, Countess of Warwick, from the Rous Roll. (© *FLHC FB4/Alamy*)

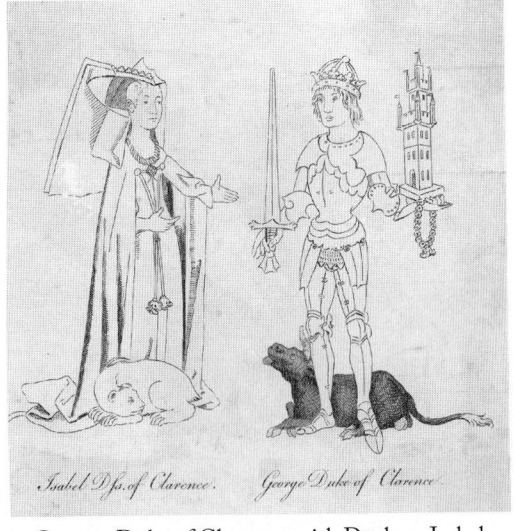

6. George, Duke of Clarence, with Duchess Isabel, the daughter of Richard Neville from the *Rous Roll*. (© *Chronicle/Alamy*)

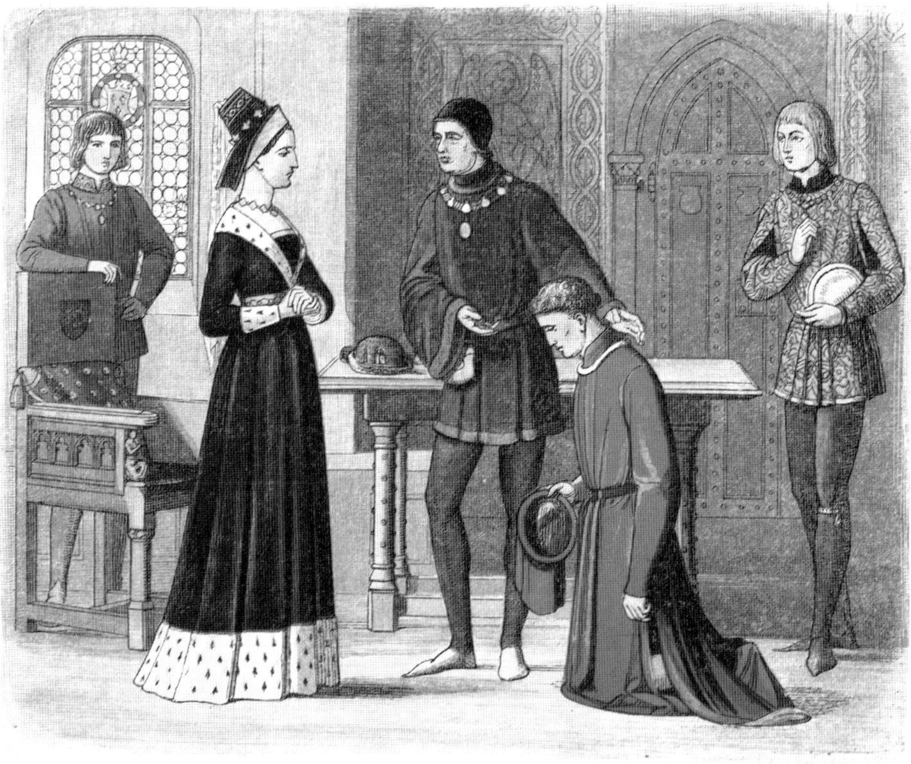

7. *The Earl of Warwick Submits to Queen Margaret* by James William Edmund Doyle (1864), from *A Chronicle of England BC 55 to AD 1485*. (© *Historica Graphica Collection/Heritage Images/Alamy*)

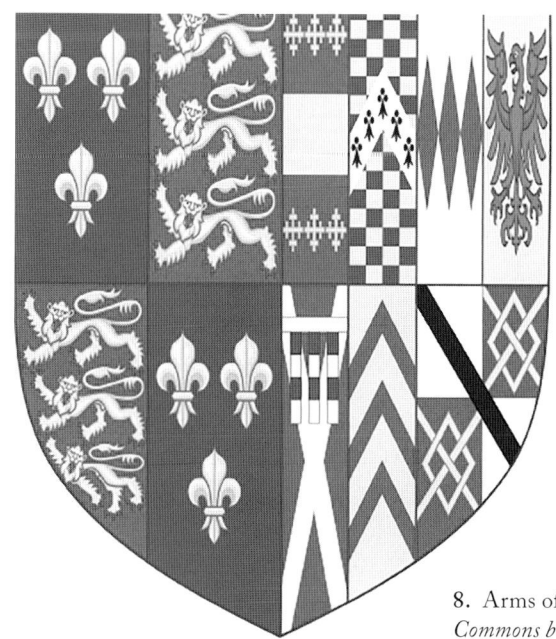

8. Arms of Anne Neville. (© *Wikimedia Commons by Sodacan (CC BY-SA 3.0)*)

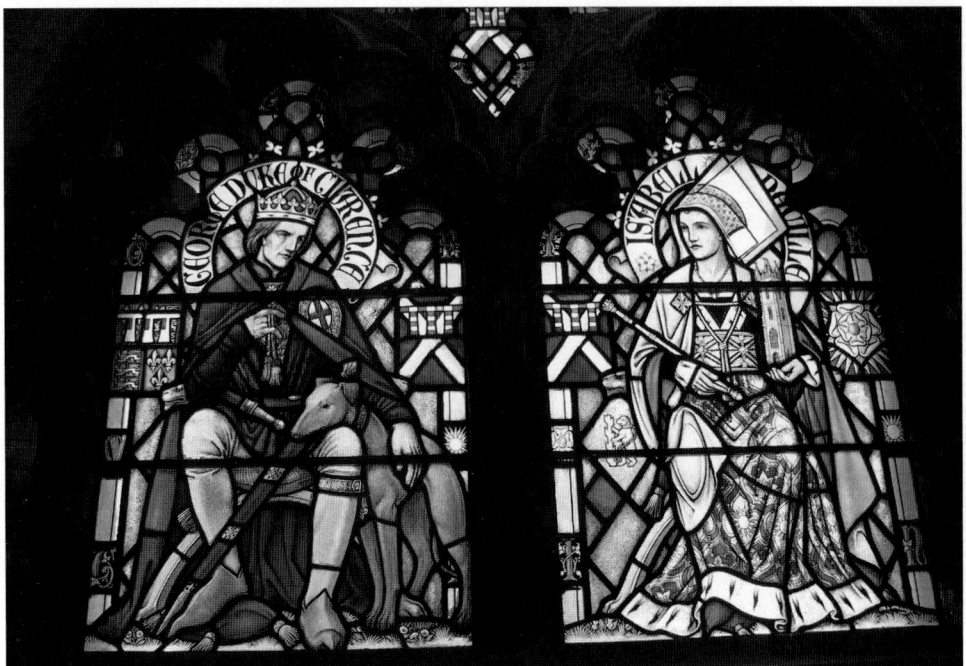

9. Stained glass image depicting George, Duke of Clarence, and Isabel Neville, Cardiff Castle. (© *Wikimedia Commons by Wolfgang Sauber* (*CC BY-SA 3.0*))

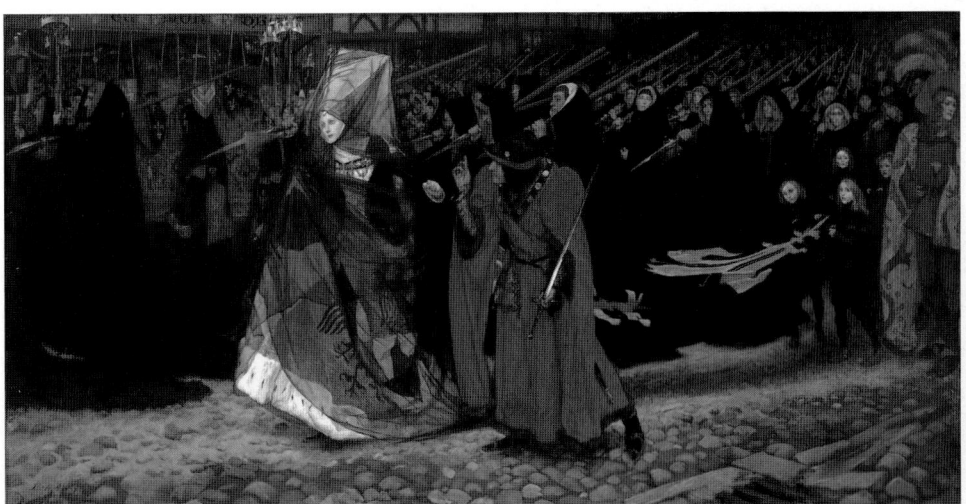

10. Richard, Duke of Gloucester and the Lady Anne by Edwin Austin Abbey (oil on canvas, 1896). Edwin Austin Abbey Memorial Collection. 1937.2224. (© *Yale University Art Gallery* (*Public domain*))

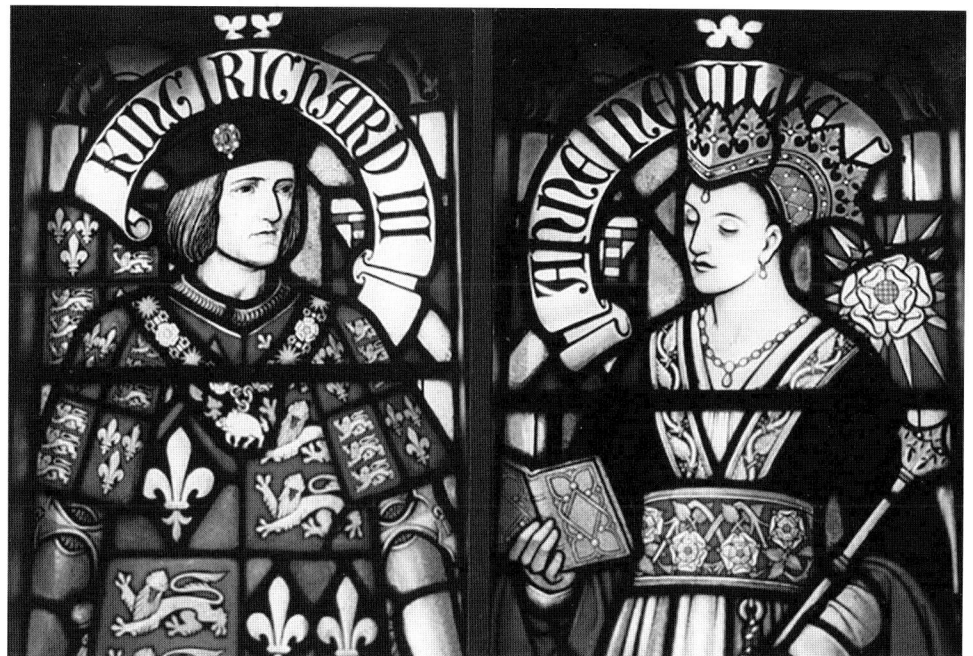

11. Stained glass image depicting King Richard III and Anne Neville, Cardiff Castle. (© *Wikimedia Commons by Verteran MP (CC BY-SA 3.0)*)

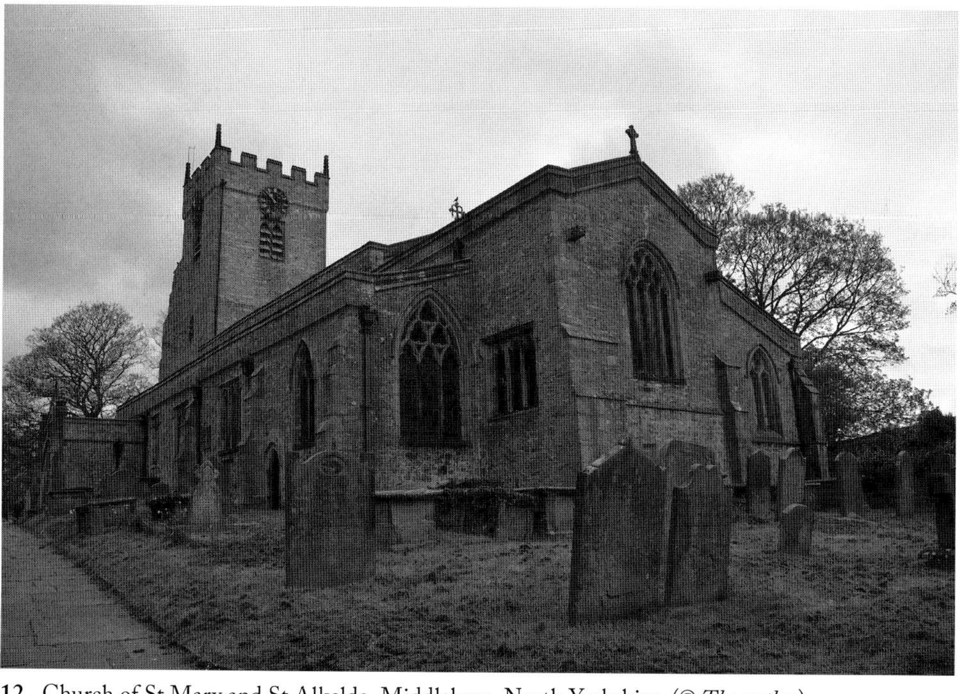

12. Church of St Mary and St Alkelda, Middleham, North Yorkshire. (© *The author*)

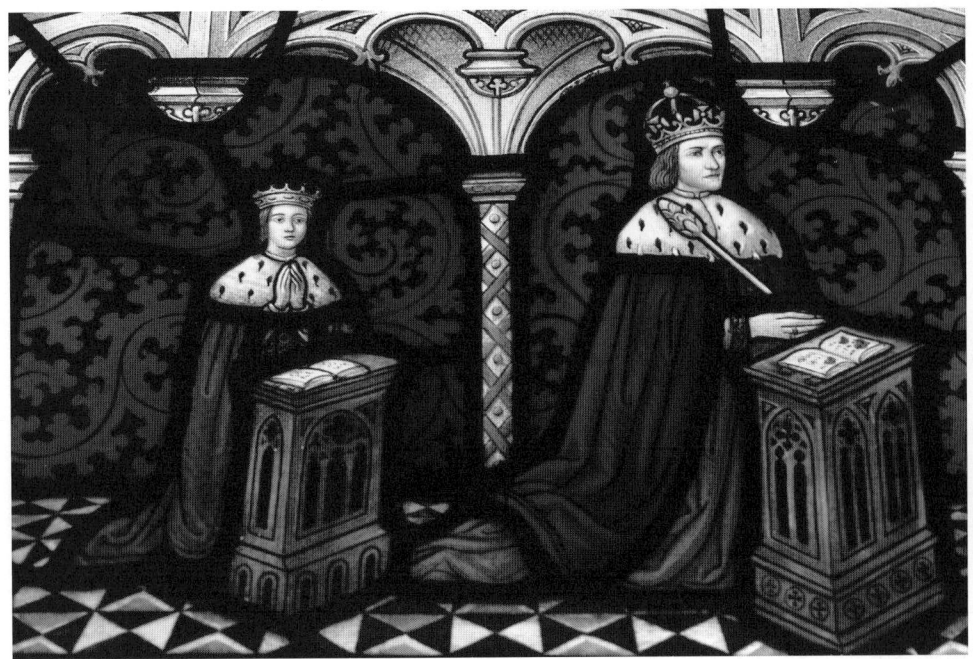

13. King Richard III and Edward of Middleham, Church of St Mary and St Alkelda, Middleham, North Yorkshire. (© *Kyle Hewgill*)

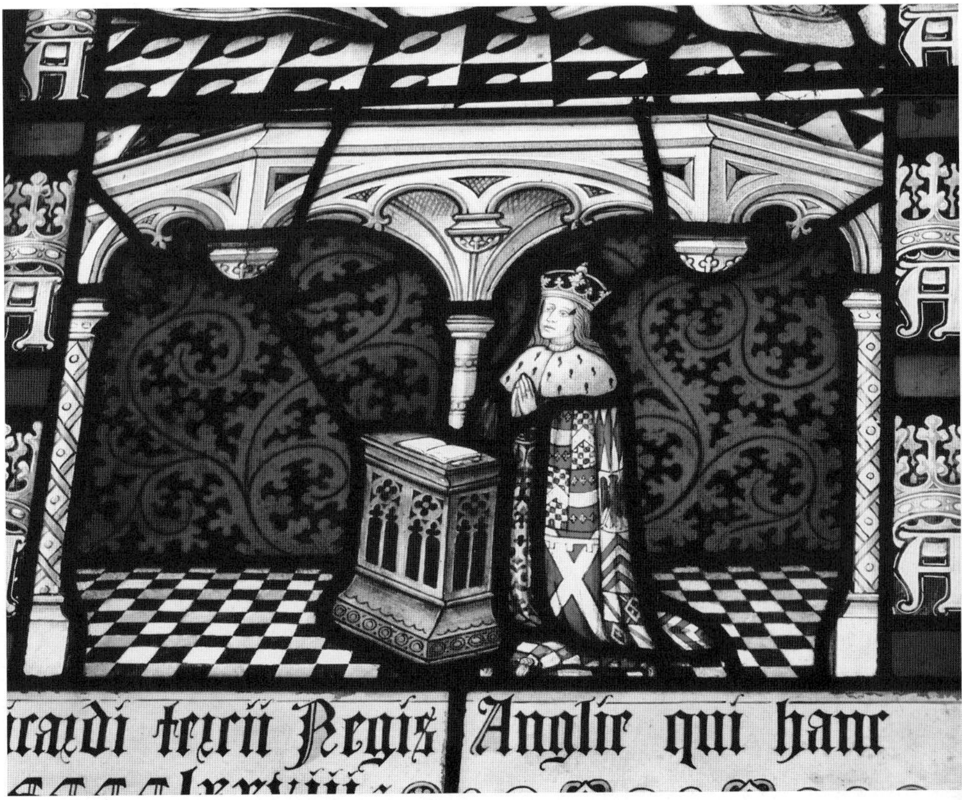

14. Queen Anne, Church of St Mary and St Alkelda, Middleham, North Yorkshire. (© *Kyle Hewgill*)

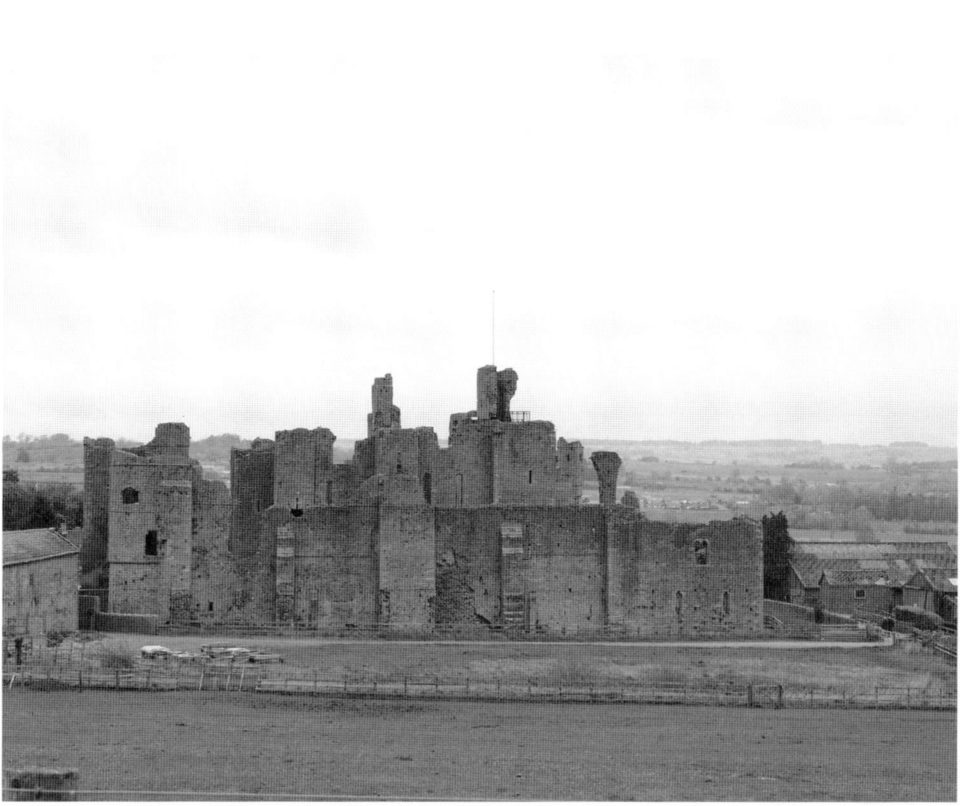

15. Middleham Castle, North Yorkshire. (© *Kyle Hewgill*)

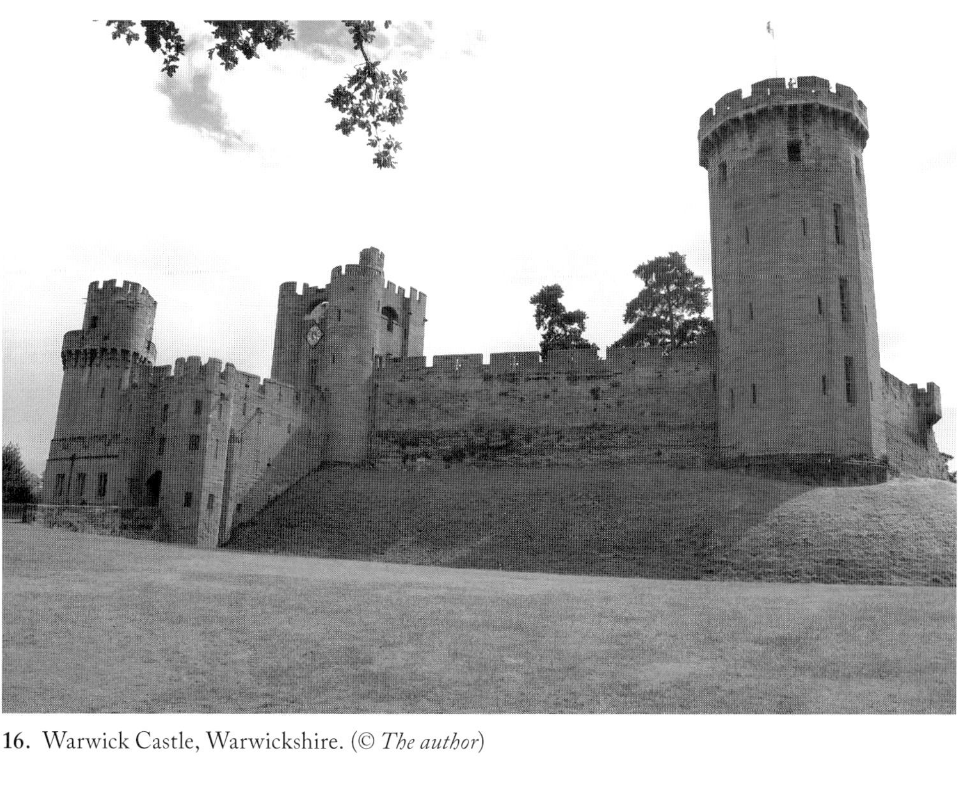

16. Warwick Castle, Warwickshire. (© *The author*)

17. Tewkesbury Abbey, Gloucestershire. (© *Kyle Hewgill*)

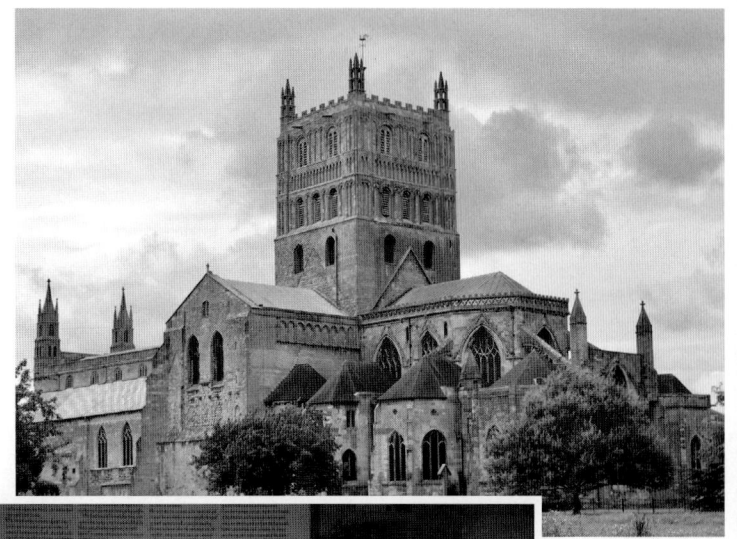

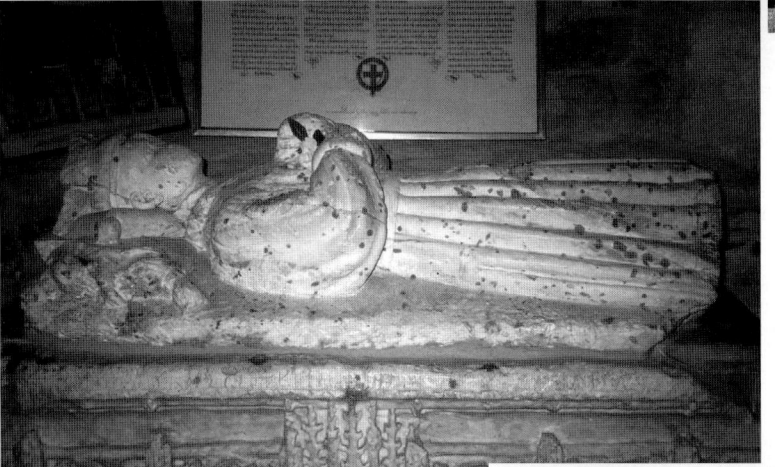

18. Effigy thought to be Edward of Middleham, Church of St Helen and the Holy Cross, Sheriff Hutton, York. (© *Janet Senior*)

19. Unknown woman, formerly known as Margaret Pole, Countess of Salisbury. (© *Art Collection 3/Alamy*)

of the Warwick inheritance is unknowable. The unity between the king and his brothers, which had been achieved in the spring of 1471, began to crumble once more.

The lands which Richard might have expected to accumulate as a reward for his loyalty in the aftermath of Edward's restoration did not materialise. The king recognised that attainder and its associated forfeiture of estate, which might have provided a basis for enriching Gloucester, was not a recipe for peace. But Edward needed someone he could trust to maintain order in the north of the country as well as to fill the void left by Warwick. In the summer of 1471, the king gave Gloucester control over Duchy of Lancaster estates in the north-west as well as parts of the Nevilles' northern stronghold including Middleham, Sheriff Hutton and Penrith in tail male. Amongst the estates were two-thirds of the Lordship of Richmond which were held by the Earl of Salisbury prior to their grant to Edmund Tudor in 1452 but which Tudor never possessed and which never left Neville hands. The Neville inheritance would in more normal circumstances have passed to Anne's uncle Lord Montagu, and subsequently to his son George, Duke of Bedford. Despite this it was logical that Gloucester sought to marry Anne as such a union might ensure a degree of loyalty from former Neville tenants.

Clarence remained unamenable to the proposition, whether his brother was married to Anne or not. The king had granted Clarence the honour of Richmond in 1462 despite the fact that Warwick retained possession of the majority of the lands. On 5 August 1472 Clarence was licensed to enter the remaining one-third of the estates associated with the earldom of Richmond, which had been held by Jacquetta, Duchess of Bedford – the mother of Edward's queen until her death in May that year. The historical conflict of ownership was compounded by the fact that Edward had granted the two-thirds of the property previously held by the Neville family to Gloucester the year before.[1] Clarence was unable to take possession despite his licence because Richard was already in occupation. The rancour between the brothers became more profound. The Croyland Chronicler was admiring of the way that Gloucester disputed his case and the depth of his legal knowledge. Even so, Clarence proved unyielding regarding the estates that rightfully belonged to Countess Anne and the Neville estates. Gloucester was forced to ask the king to intercede. It suited Edward to listen to the arguments that raged back and forth between his two younger brothers, although he had no intention of permitting Clarence the kind of influence that Gloucester would eventually come to wield in the north of England.

Gloucester identified Clarence's stratagem of hiding Anne and enabled her flight from his custody. The *Croyland Chronicle* told a story of Gloucester tracking Anne down to where Clarence hid her, having fulfilled the king's business in Kent against the Bastard of Fauconberg's rebels in the aftermath of the Battles of Barnet and Tewkesbury. Anne evaded her brother-in-law and his lackies between the end of December 1471 and February 1472. Under medieval law, in removing Anne from Clarence's control, Gloucester would have been open to the charge of *raptus* as it was against her guardian's wishes that Gloucester marry Anne. Abduction and rape are two different laws today, but in the fifteenth century they were punished by the same law, as was unsanctioned elopement. Anne may well have consented to her flight from Clarence's protection, but it would still have been considered abduction which in turn raised the possibility of Gloucester's excommunication and a prohibition on the couple's subsequent marriage.[2] To circumvent this possibility, Richard removed Anne from Clarence's household and placed her in sanctuary at the church of St Martin-le-Grand where she chose to remain while Gloucester began the process of obtaining permission to marry her and to acquire her share of the inheritance. She was dependent upon Gloucester but she was not part of his household. Clarence could threaten legal action against his brother, but Richard had very clearly not abducted Anne so long as she remained in sanctuary.

By the end of February 1472, Clarence agreed to the marriage in principle but John Paston wrote that the duke remained determined that even if his younger brother did marry Anne that he should have none of her inheritance. Even as the two brothers wrangled, it was not totally certain that either of them would benefit from marriage to Isabel or to Anne. Countess Anne refused to yield her rights and continued to argue her case from her sanctuary. Despite a lifetime at Warwick's side, she maintained that the earl's treason could not be ascribed to her. Countess Anne's obligations were to her husband. Under law they were one person from the time of their marriage – a wife was effectively under the protection of her spouse. It meant that she could not be guilty of treason against King Edward, any more than she could have been taken to trial for debt or breach of contract during Warwick's life. Both those liabilities would have lain with her husband. However, as the widowed *suo jure* Countess of Warwick, Anne did have a right to her own property as well as to her dower lands. Under those circumstances, neither of her daughters were eligible to inherit.

Most women, especially those as young as Anne Neville, remarried after the death of a husband. Marital alliances were an important part of medieval life, although it was as affluent widows with dower rights and jointures that they exercised most independence. Often viewed as little more than a cypher or shadow, there is an element of female agency in Anne's escape from Coldharbour and subsequent marriage to Gloucester. There was no social, familial or economic benefit for her to collude with Clarence's withholding of consent. Anne knew Richard from a shared childhood at Middleham and, according to *Waurin's Chronicle*, Gloucester was the husband that Warwick originally selected for his younger child. Setting the possibility of love aside, a marriage to the king's trusted younger brother would ensure she was rehabilitated within Yorkist society. She would once again have access to security and a lavish lifestyle rather than being regarded as the widow of one traitor and the daughter of another. Besides, there was only one man in the realm who might act as a counterweight to Clarence's determination that she remained unmarried and that was his younger brother whose loyalty to the king was unquestioned. It was also in King Edward's interest that Clarence, who had demonstrated the depths of his ambition, should not be permitted access to the whole of the Warwick inheritance lest he should aspire to be king once more. With Warwick's former wealth and tenantry at his fingertips, he might prove a destabilising influence on Edward's regime.

As the wrangling continued, Gloucester began the process of applying for a papal dispensation to marry Anne. In addition to the created consanguinity through their relationship as first cousins via their Neville ancestry, they were related by the Despenser line and through Anne's marriage to Edward of Lancaster who was Gloucester's kin. They were also related as brother and sister-in-law by reason of Clarence's marriage to Isabel. In medieval eyes this also created an impediment to marriage in the first degree because of the affinity that was created by their siblings' union.

A papal dispensation was granted on 22 April 1472 for the relationship created by Anne's marriage to Prince Edward, but it did not dispense with the impediment of being brother and sister in the eyes of the law, or any of the other prohibited relationships they shared.[3] The Church recognised that relatives of a couple did not become one another's blood relatives, but it would, for example, prevent a widower marrying his late wife's sister. The document held in the Papal Penitentiary left gaps that would have easily rendered the marriage invalid. Baptism also created a spiritual relationship between the baptised and their godparents which created a further impediment to marriage. Richard's mother Duchess Cecily was Isabel's godmother, but there is no record either of Richard's godparents or Anne's. Richard may have been named after his father, but it is also possible given the family connections that either Salisbury or Warwick was the duke's sponsor. Both Gloucester and Anne would have recognised the complexities of ecclesiastical law surrounding matrimony and the labyrinthine nature of aristocratic kinship networks. If their union was unwelcomed by the king, an annulment could not only be sought but granted on a technicality.

The wedding probably took place a short time after the dispensation was granted at an unknown location. The bride was 16 years old and the groom was 19. It has been suggested that the couple went to the manor of Stanford in the Vale which was part of Countess Anne's Despenser inheritance. It is claimed that the wedding took place in the church of St Deny's south porch which was built during the 1470s. The porch is decorated with the rose and fetterlock of York impaling the ragged staff of Warwick. Unfortunately, there is no written evidence to confirm the story. Stanford did become part of Anne's share of her mother's estates before it was granted to Queens' College Cambridge.

The king took the opportunity of Anne's marriage to his brother to consolidate Gloucester's northern landholdings. In 1472 a parliamentary act was passed exchanging Scarborough Castle and other Crown lands in Yorkshire for the Manor of Chesterfield which was originally part of Alice Montagu's inheritance. The king may have used the manor as a sweetener for Clarence, giving it to him by right of his duchess. In time it found its way into the hands of Isabel's daughter.[4]

The matter of Countess Anne's inheritance and the Warwick estates was becoming tiresome for King Edward. In addition to his brothers demanding a resolution, Countess Anne continued to correspond with him until he wrote to the abbot to prevent such freedoms. It is likely that members of his extended family broached her case with him as a result of her extended letter writing begging for justice. On this matter at least, his own queen might have had some sympathy with the countess. Elizabeth Woodville was said to despise and fear Clarence, whom she believed aspired to the throne.[5] It is also likely that the Bishop of Durham intervened on the countess's behalf. Barnard Castle was part of her inheritance, having been given to Guy of Warwick by King Edward I. Since 1470 the lordship lay in the hands of the bishops of Durham who expected a say in the matter. If her rights were voided, then Clarence would argue that the castle was more rightfully his and it was likely that Gloucester, when married to Anne, would counter-claim.

When Parliament was called in 1472, Countess Anne sent a petition to the Commons demanding her legal rights. If the petition was read it was not accepted. Instead, the document eventually made its way into the keeping of Gloucester.[6] The issue of Countess Anne's inheritance was debated by the Privy Council, Parliament and by the men and women in receipt of the countess's letters. It was to no avail. Parliament passed a resolution in July 1473 'that the countess of Warwick was no more to be considered, in the award of her inheritance, than if she were dead.'[7] Two further acts of Parliament in 1474 deprived Countess Anne and George Neville, 1st Duke of Bedford of what was rightfully theirs. Countess Anne's estate, illegally seized by the king, could be divided as though she was dead. All that remained was to settle the form that the division would take. In the end Gloucester received northern estates and some lands in Wales, while Clarence took the southern half of what belonged to the countess, including the lordship of Glamorgan.

The Neville estates were also provided with a legal solution: the king broke the entail. Gloucester and his male descendants would only be able to enjoy the Neville properties while the Duke of Bedford or one of his successors was alive. If the boy died without heirs, the Neville estates would revert to the Neville family. The king's support for his younger brother came at a price. Gloucester would resign his position as Great Chamberlain of England so that Clarence might assume the role when it was offered to him. Gloucester's brother also retained the fee farm, or fixed amount of annual rent, for Richmond.

Clarence was not satisfied with the king's resolution and remained bellicose. It has been suggested that he returned to the Yorkist side before Barnet because Edward promised him the whole of Warwick's former estates.[8] Now, Countess Anne and Warwick's inheritances were divided equally, but it meant that Clarence lost half of what he held before the king's judgement. At the same time, Clarence also lost estates in Staffordshire and Derbyshire, including his favourite manor of Tutbury which were returned to the Duchy of Lancaster. The king consolidated what was his and also ensured that Clarence did not become an overmighty subject. The Croyland Chronicler speculated whether or not the three brothers were as good friends as they had once been. John Paston writing on 2 April 1473 stated that:

> The world seemeth queasy, for all the persons about the king's person have sent for their armour, on account of the quarrel regarding the inheritance of Anne.[9]

Clarence's bile may also have been increased because Gloucester acquired East Anglian estates previously belonging to Warwick's brother-in-law John de Vere, 13th Earl of Oxford. Elizabeth Howard, the elderly dowager countess, was entitled to both dower and jointure rights. Legally Gloucester should have waited for her death before acquiring her share of the estates now granted to him. However, in order to prevent the dowager providing support to her son after Barnet, she was sent to Stratford Nunnery and from there into Gloucester's keeping. Feofees, or trustees, legally held Elizabeth's lands by grant, but it was the countess who continued to benefit from their use. By January 1473 the dowager signed the release that transferred her enfeoffed estates to Gloucester in return for an annuity of 500 marks and the payment of her debts. Oxford later alleged that his mother only parted with her property under duress. One of the countess's feoffees, Henry Robson, reported that the dowager was confined to a chamber and told that unless she agreed the transfer of her land, Gloucester would have her sent to Middleham. This might have seemed a welcome prospect to Countess Anne, immured in Beaulieu surrounded by guards sent by the king.

In the meantime, Anne, now Duchess of Gloucester, took up residence in the north of England at Middleham. Richard assumed the wardenry of the West March and took on the responsibility for administering the north of England. His marriage to Anne gave legitimacy to his role and assisted with the transition of the Neville affinity into Gloucester's own following. Even Sir John Conyers, who provided leadership for Robin of Redesdale's rebellion in 1469, became one of the duke's retainers. With the wealth of the north in his hands, Gloucester was the dominant force. In 1483 this was confirmed by the hereditary lordship of Cumberland and Westmorland, not to mention whichever parts of lowland Scotland he might be able to conquer. Anne remained in the shadows. There are no known household accounts belonging to the duchess or charters made in her own right.

Countess Anne emerged from sanctuary at the end of May 1473 and was escorted north to Middleham to join Anne's household. There were unfounded rumours that the king restored her to her inheritance and that she granted everything to Gloucester. More likely, thanks to the intervention of the Bishop of Durham, that Barnard Castle was now in the duke's hands contrary to Clarence's desires.[10] John Paston II wrote that the 'Countess of Warwick is now out of Beverley sanctuary, and Sir James Tyrell conveyth her northward, men say by the King's assent; whereto some men say that the Duke of Clarence is not agreed.'[11] He was in error about the location of the sanctuary, but the mood was uneasy. That autumn there were further rumours that the brothers were arming their tenants. Eventually the king was forced to threaten Clarence with an act of resumption to ensure that words did not escalate into warfare.

The countess's status remained opaque. Later, Rous claimed that she was held in custody by her son-in-law. There are records of a servant, William Catour, being sent to York to shop on her behalf.[12] If she was a captive, at least the countess's existence was more palatable than in the immediate aftermath of Barnet. The close-knit Neville affinity that lived near to Middleham ensured that Countess Anne and her daughter were not isolated. The gentry of Wensleydale and beyond served Gloucester, who proved to be a fair lord, as they once served Warwick. Anne perhaps saw more of her half-sister Margaret Huddleston and renewed their former acquaintance. It was at about this time that Gloucester arranged for Margaret's brother-in-law, William Huddleston, to marry Anne's cousin Isabel, one of Lord Montagu's daughters. It meant that the Huddlestons acquired the manor of Sawston. Gloucester further tightened the loyalty of the Neville affinity around himself by marrying another of Montagu's daughters, Elizabeth, to Thomas, Lord Scrope of Masham.

Chapter 11

The Duchess of Gloucester

From the time of their marriage until spring 1483, Anne and Richard resided mainly in the north where Gloucester succeeded to Warwick's power base. Anne's life took up where it had left off before her father's flight from England in 1470. Men like Sir Ralph Ashton, the High Sheriff of Yorkshire, served Gloucester as they had once served Anne's father and grandfather. Men who were part of the extended Neville kinship network transferred their allegiance to Gloucester. Sir John Conyers, married to one of Lord Fauconberg's daughters, played a prominent role in the Neville affinity from the 1450s onwards and is thought by many to have been Robin of Redesdale. But he was also amongst the men who came to terms with Anne's husband. Anne renewed her association with her half-sister Margaret Huddleston and her aunt Lady FitzHugh of Ravensworth Castle. After three years of uncertainty, Anne's life took up rhythms familiar since childhood amongst landscapes and faces she recognised, although her separation from Isabel was now permanent.

There were ripples of discord and reminders that Warwick all but destroyed the political pretensions of the Nevilles with his ambitions. Anne's uncle, George, the Archbishop of York, never managed to return to the king's good graces after the Readeption, even though Edward released him from the Tower. In 1471, George went to his newly built home at Moor Park, or The Moor as it was known, near Rickmansworth in Hertfordshire, where he became involved with a fresh plot against Edward. It is likely that he corresponded, if not actively plotted, with his brother-in-law Oxford who mounted an attack on Calais before attempting to land in Essex. He finally landed in Cornwall where he seized St Michael's Mount at the end of September 1473. The king, feigning ignorance of the archbishop's duplicity, invited the erstwhile bishop to Windsor to hunt. All affability, he suggested that George invited him to stay at The Moor. George believed that he was forgiven and hurried home to prepare for the royal visit. Instead, he was seized on 24 April 1472 and taken first to the Tower before being smuggled under cover of darkness to Hammes Castle in the Calais Pale where he was 'kept prisoner for many a day'.[1]

For a time Anne and Isabel may have believed that their uncle was dead. The king confiscated the archbishop's property and all his possessions. He even broke the archbishop's bejewelled mitre and used the gems for a crown. Gloucester interceded with the king for the archbishop's release. It was one of the few occasions when he and Clarence were in accord following the division of Countess Anne's estates. The archbishop was allowed to return to England at the end of 1475. He was made an abbot at Westminster on 6 November and sent to Blyth Priory in Northumberland where he died on 8 June 1476.

Between 1473 and 1476,[2] Anne provided her husband with an heir, born at Middleham and raised there, according to local belief, in the south-west tower or Prince's Tower which was part of the south range of Middle Castle. Like her mother and sister, she followed the usual practice of retiring to her chamber the month before she was due to give birth. The dates for Edward of Middleham's birth are based on supposition regarding Anne's marriage to Gloucester and on circumstantial evidence relating to Edward's likely age founded on financial accounts and later chronicles. Polydore Vergil, the Tudor chronicler, believed that the boy was 9 years old when he died. Anne's son was named Edward after the king who was likely to have been the infant's godfather. Anne may have become pregnant for a second time and given birth to a boy named George if an entry in the *Tewkesbury Chronicle* is correct. If this was the case Edward was born in 1473/74 and a short-lived second son followed in 1476.[3] Equally the Tewkesbury chronicler may have made an error in the name, although it raises the possibility of Gloucester seeking to mend the animosity that arose between himself and Clarence. Certainly, the records suggest that Edward was a young child still in the care of women rather than being schooled in a more masculine environment as might have been expected of an older boy at the time of his death.

By the time of her younger daughter's pregnancy, Countess Anne was living as part of Gloucester's extended household so she was able to care for Anne as her pregnancy progressed. It is plausible that the so-called Middleham Jewel, found by metal detectorists on the path between Middleham and Coverham Abbey, which dates from between 1470–1475 was worn as a protective amulet by either Countess Anne or her daughter. The lozenge-shape pendant depicts the Crucifixion, the nativity and the Lamb of God as well as fifteen tiny depictions of saints. An extract from the Mass, originally picked out in blue enamel, frames the Crucifixion scene. The front of the lozenge is set with a blue sapphire which was believed to enhance prayers, cure ulcers, headaches and stammers. Even more interestingly, the amulet contains a two-word charm, 'tetragrammaton' and 'ananizapta', against epilepsy. It is not totally clear what 'ananizapta' means but it appears to be associated with another name for God.[4] As with the sapphire, the word was regarded as having protective properties against epilepsy and plague. The pendant was somewhere between a prayer and a magical incantation. The back of the jewel slides open to reveal fragments of silk embroidered with gold. It is unknown whether these were the original contents or whether the opening was for a holy relic.

It has been speculated that the nativity scene was designed to protect its wearer from the dangers of childbirth. The *Agnes Dei* or Lamb of God was also connected with childbirth. Taken together, the iconography suggests that the jewel was owned by a high-ranking lady, in all likelihood a member of the Neville family, who would have been very unhappy to have lost such a significant item designed as it was to protect its wearer as well as to demonstrate the wearer's piety and wealth. Whoever commissioned the piece wanted to protect someone they loved. There is no evidence as to its owner, but its discovery at Middleham and the time frame for its creation point either to Countess Anne or to Anne Neville herself. The duchess tends to be portrayed as sickly, but there is little evidence of ill health prior to the winter months before her death, and there is no reference to the falling sickness as epilepsy was then known.

More recently a tiny gold Bible was uncovered near Sheriff Hutton, another Neville stronghold. It may have been part of a birthing girdle, on account of the engravings of St Margaret of Antioch and of St Leonard, both patron saints of childbirth. It is believed that the miniature Bible was made by the same goldsmith who crafted the Middleham Jewel.[5] It raises intriguing possibilities that Countess Anne, both her daughters and other female members of the Neville family wore this jewel, or ones like it, during their pregnancies and when they gave birth. John Tiptoft wrote a letter in

1452 to Henry Cranebroke about his deceased wife Cicely Neville whose first husband was Henry, Duke of Warwick. In it he made a reference to a protective 'Juel' owned by his wife which possessed 'holesum virtues' reinforcing the theory that she may have died in childbirth.[6] Gloucester's mother, Duchess Cecily, another member of the Neville family, was also known to own an *Agnus Dei* pendant decorated with the Trinity. In 1440 Joan Beaufort, Countess of Westmorland, bequeathed a Trinity jewel to her eldest son, the Earl of Salisbury. There is some speculation that the Middleham Jewel might originally have been Joan's, in which case several generations of women relied on its efficacy during childbirth and perhaps against illness as well – some with more success than others.[7]

Anne and her half-sister Margaret Huddleston shared the perils of pregnancy and worries of motherhood at a similar time to one another. Richard Huddleston, named after his father, was born in 1476 followed three years later by a sister named Margaret. The relationship between the two half-sisters was important because it enabled Gloucester to maintain the familial bonds and ties of dependency associated with regional affinities. Anne's nephew would one day be the Lord of Millom. However, it is likely that Anne looked with envy upon Margaret's second pregnancy. Anne does not appear to have become pregnant again, despite the fact that she and Gloucester continued to share a bed until her final illness in 1485. Like her own mother she would have prayed for more children, even though she had fulfilled her duty as a wife with the provision of an heir. It is possible that the tuberculosis which is thought likely to have killed her contributed to her lack of fertility. It has been suggested that Anne suffered from a symptomless disease called tuberculous endometritis which causes infertility.[8] It was a secondary disease with primary infection somewhere else in the body, most commonly the lungs. There is a possibility that Countess Anne's own fertility was similarly affected. Since Isabel Neville gave birth on four occasions, there is no suggestion that she might have suffered from tuberculous endometritis.

At Middleham the duke and duchess provided their son with a nursery close to the room where he was born. An inventory of 1538 identifies a nursery on the first floor above the bakehouse for warmth and close to Anne's privy chamber so that she could oversee her son's care. The court rolls reveal that the boy's wet nurse was a woman named Isabel Burgh, the wife of Henry Burgh, one of Gloucester's favourites who must have recently given birth to a child of her own. Isabel is also likely to have been a relation of Alice Burgh who is thought to be the mother of Gloucester's illegitimate son, John of Gloucester or Pontefract. Although the identity of John's mother is uncertain it is known that Alice, described as Richard's 'beloved gentlewoman'[9] was rewarded with an annuity of £20 on 1 March 1474 at Pontefract for 'certain special causes and considerations'.[10] The Burghs, possibly from the Burgh family of Knaresburgh,[11] appear to have been part of the gentry circle at Middleham tied by kinship and affinity in the service of Anne's father and, apparently, even more closely to Gloucester himself who fathered John when he was about 18 years old.[12] The date of the grant suggests a later date for the birth. Richard may already have been married to Anne when he demonstrated his own fertility. After Edward was weaned, Isabel returned home to her own family.

Anne Idley, the Mistress of the Nursery, remained with Edward's other attendants. She was appointed to oversee Edward's household under Anne's direction. She was the widow of Peter Idley who wrote a book of moral instruction for the education of boys. Idley died in 1473 leaving his widow and family by his first wife. Peter's son agreed to pay Anne an annuity of 5 marks a year if she moved out of her home at Drayton Manor following a dispute over Idley's estates.[13] Anne took the post supervising the nursery at Middleham, but, in 1478, Gloucester wrote to the Oxfordshire justices of the peace asking them to find out why William Idley and his sister Elizabeth had not paid the agreed annuity to their stepmother. Jane Collins or Colyns was also part of the household that formed around Edward. She was paid £5 for a year's service in the summer of 1483 and a further 48s 9d for items purchased by her for the prince. In October the same year she was awarded an annuity of 10 marks for life. Agnes Cooper may also have been part of Edward's household which was dominated by women even in the last year of his life. In addition to caring for his physical needs, the women were also involved in teaching him manners, correct behaviour and religious instruction. Like his mother before him, he was expected to know the Lord's Prayer, the Apostle's Creed and the Ave Maria.

It was not an entirely female household. The abstracts of Richard III's Second Register[14] were started in May 1483 but presented by Geoffrey Franke, the Receiver of Middleham, in October that year, by which time

Richard was king. The document reveals six male servants are listed together as part of the costs associated with Edward's household. Two of them, Pacok and Metcalf, ran by the side of the boy's carriage, but they were paid extra for this service. The household also included a fool called Martyn who was paid 12d.

Clearly Anne and her son enjoyed entertainment. Martyn's was not the only diversion on offer at Middleham. Mummers' plays took place in the great hall of Middleham Castle during the Christmas season. Often the chosen story was the tale of St George and the dragon. The players may have been local to Wensleydale, or they may have been travelling professional actors. There was singing, dancing and acrobatics. It is also likely that the duke and duchess travelled to York to see the mystery plays performed by the city guilds. It was not a lonely or unhappy existence. Edward owned a pack of dogs and his father provided a man to look after them. There were rabbit warrens on the Middleham estates as well as enclosed parks where Duchess Anne and her son might ride and hunt. One or two of the dogs might have been more akin to pets. The Duc de Berry's *Tres Riches Heures* illustrates the popularity of dogs amongst the aristocracy from small lapdogs to hounds more used to chasing and retrieving game. In the medieval world, pets demonstrated their owner's wealth. By the end of the fourteenth century Chaucer depicted the prioress of the *Canterbury Tales* feeding her lapdog roast meat. There is no record of Countess Anne or either of her daughters owning a pet of any kind, but small dogs can be found in the book illustrations, literature and art of the period. Nor were they the only pets that wealthy owners chose to lavish their affections upon; monkeys, caged birds, squirrels and even ferrets had their place.[15]

Anne, reading Peter Idley's book of manners, must have approved the importance of learning self-control and meekness. They were the same values which she learned at Countess Anne's knee. Idley also emphasised the importance of friendships. It is possible that Edward was not alone in his nursery, despite Anne's failure to produce more heirs for Richard. As well as children who were part of the extended Neville family, the duke was father to two illegitimate children. Katherine was older than Anne's son, but it is unclear whether Richard's illegitimate son John was born before Richard's marriage to Anne or after. It is also uncertain whether Katherine and John shared the same mother or not. It has been speculated that Katherine's mother may have been Katherine Haute who was in receipt of an annuity from the duke. She was part of the extended Woodville family which raises some intriguing questions about the nature of Richard's relationship with the faction.[16]

Wives were expected to remain chaste and to accept their husband's illegitimate offspring who were reliant for their place in society on their legitimate relations and therefore likely to be more loyal. Anne is known to have enjoyed a close relationship with her illegitimate sister Margaret. Their shared great-grandmother was Joan Beaufort, the legitimated daughter of John of Gaunt and his 'scandalous duchess' Katherine Swynford. Anne's grandmother Alice Montagu was her father's only legitimate heir, but Alice's illegitimate brother John was recognised in the 4th Earl of Salisbury's will and followed his father into a military career serving in France during the 1430s and 1440s.[17] He did not achieve the notoriety of Anne's kinsman Thomas, the so-called Bastard of Fauconberg who served Warwick with great loyalty during the duchess's childhood gaining infamy in *The Great Chronicle of London*, the *Yorkist Arrival* and *Croyland Chronicle*.

During 1475–76 Gloucester was absent from Yorkshire on his brother's short-lived French military campaign. He was home within three months to spend the winter with his family. The duke's absence on official business was not unusual. He was the Warden of the West Marches and, from 1482, the Lieutenant of the North ruling the region on behalf of his brother. Anne was expected to oversee the management of their estates in his absence and conducted business matters as her husband required. Gloucester can be found listed in the House Books of the City of York dating to the 1470s. But there is no record of Anne being petitioned by its civic officers in the way that Countess Anne was given gifts when Warwick was alive, suggesting that the authorities regarded the Duchess of Gloucester as being without influence. Anne's lack of presence in the written record has given rise to speculation about the extent to which she was in partnership with her husband or lost within his shadow. Nor is there any documentary evidence that the Duchess of Gloucester had her own funds. It appears that Anne's independence was very limited indeed. It is easy then to paint Richard as manipulative and controlling. Archaeological evidence provides an alternate possibility. It comes in the form of a copper alloy plaque which may have originally been attached to the lid of a casket. It has 'the entwined initials R and A and a French motto, *A Vo Plaisir* (for your pleasure)'.[18] Love was not part of the world of medieval marriage and is difficult to evidence but it could simply be that the duke loved his wife and wanted to take care of her after the traumas she faced when she was barely out of childhood. There is insufficient evidence to paint Anne as Gloucester's victim, any more than there is enough material to write about a love affair that grew from a shared childhood.

On Sunday 21 July 1476, Gloucester was at Pontefract as the bodies of his father, Richard of York, and brother Edmund were exhumed from their graves at the priory of St John. The coffins were placed on a hearse and a requiem Mass conducted the following morning. The duke accompanied the bodies south to Fotheringhay as chief mourner. The cortège, with the royal standard flying at its head along with York's falcon and fetterlock, was an impressive sight. As well as nobles, officers and heralds, there were 400 men on foot carrying lit torches.[19] Richard arrived with the cortège at Fotheringhay on 29 July. Anne, who might have been pregnant depending on her son's date of birth, was probably already there along with the rest of the king's family. It may have been the last time she saw Isabel, who was also pregnant at the time, assuming that Clarence set aside his difference with his brothers for the occasion.

That winter Anne travelled with Gloucester to London. She took the opportunity to shop for new clothing and furs as well as silk cloth. Richard's account notes the purchases for 'the most dear consort of the lord'[20] which was a conventional description for a marriage partner. There was no restriction on what Anne might wear or even eat because she was the wife of a royal duke. She could wear sable, cloth of gold and purple fabrics which were restricted to the royal family from 1463 onwards.[21] Sumptuary laws also allowed her, if she wished, to wear shoes with long toes or pikes of more than two inches.[22] By the end of December though, Anne and her mother were plunged into mourning when news reached them that Isabel was dead.

It is likely that Anne travelled to court whenever Gloucester was required by his brother to be present, but Mancini reported that Gloucester preferred to live mainly in the north so Anne spent more time with her son Edward than Countess Anne spent with either of her daughters during their early years. The countess, no longer occupied by housewifery or the political intrigues of her husband, was also present in Edward of Middleham's life. Like so much else about the family's domestic arrangements, we cannot know about the intricacies of the relationship between the boy and his grandmother. Nor is there any evidence that Anne or her family travelled to any of the estates that once belonged to her mother, although Gloucester visited a number of them to conduct his or the king's business.

At Barnard Castle, once Countess Anne's property, Gloucester added an oriel window to the great chamber to allow light to flood in and open up a view across the River Tees. It helped turn the formidable stronghold into a more comfortable residence where Anne might sit and sew, read or talk with her ladies. A carving of Gloucester's boar emblem was carved into the ceiling above the window. He also ordered the building of the three-storey garderobe turret on the side of the adjoining Mortham Tower which was raised at the same time to create three new storeys.[23] The duke also gave orders for the reroofing of the great hall next to the tower in order to improve its proportions. Circumstantial evidence suggests that the Round Tower was modified at this time.[24] Other building works undertaken by Gloucester included the residential range at Penrith Castle. Clearly Gloucester liked modern amenities and wished to be comfortable. The duchess and her mother may have lived in the north of England, but it does not mean that they dwelled in cold fortresses – their surroundings were nothing if not luxurious. They were also far from the intrigues at court, but Anne would soon find herself plunged back into the political maelstrom.

Chapter 12

The Duchess of Clarence

Fortune, it seemed, favoured Isabel Neville in May 1471 because of the decisions made by her husband prior to the Battle of Barnet. She was back in her rightful place in society, 'an excellent princess'[1] rather than a fugitive. This was in contrast to Anne, who was reliant on George's goodwill, or their mother, who was little more than a prisoner at Beaulieu. Isabel dressed once more in clean chemises of fine linen or silk. Her skirt, tight-fitting bodice and houppelande or over-gown with its sweeping floor-length sleeves and folded back collar were made from the richest and most costly of fabrics, trimmed with fur or embroidered with gold thread and jewels. She was welcome with her husband at court.

Clarence's household cost more than £4,000 a year in wages and expenses. Isabel's ladies included a baroness and five gentlewomen. She was served by a chamberer, five female servants, a chamberlain, an almoner, a chaplain and a clerk to care for her jewellery and plate. When Isabel sat down to her meals, there was a server, a cupbearer and a kitchen full of staff to fulfil her dietary requirements. Servants cared for her birds of prey and horses. The duchess's retinue were paid quarterly and it was 'appointed that all ladies, gentlemen, and chamberers, attending upon the said Duchess, take such fees, rewards and clothing, as shall please the Duchess'.[2]

Her duty was to undertake the housewifery of her home and estates and to provide her husband with heirs. She was assisted in the former by Clarence's ordinances drawn up in 1468, some six months before his marriage.[3] It is worth noting that many of the people who served Clarence received neither payment nor livery, giving service in return for food and lodging. Little wonder that the duke was concerned about theft and ordered that his household should be carefully supervised. There was a regular weekly stocktake in order to control expenditure and prevent pilfering. Servants were entitled to fees or perquisites, to give perks their full name, but only at the duke and duchess's convenience.

The couple was conventionally pious, hearing mattins, Mass and evensong. Isabel's mother-in-law, who lived mainly at Berkhamstead, arose each morning at 7 to hear mattins. The daily routine that mirrored the canonical hours was a familiar one to Isabel and to any noblewoman who owned a book of hours. It was part of the rhythm of everyday life. Decorum was an essential element in a pious and well-ordered household. Clarence wanted only servants who were 'wurshipful, honeste, virtuouse conversation, absteyninge themselves from suspected places'.[4] Like many other households, gambling was forbidden to servants except during the twelve days of Christmas. The ordinances by which the duke and duchess ran their household were similar in many respects to those maintained by Duchess Cecily and, in all likelihood, by Countess Anne in happier times. Noblewomen aimed to present the world with a well-regulated household. The need for economy and piety was sharpened by King Edward's own household ordinances compiled in the *Liber Niger* of 1471 which created a set of complex rituals emphasising the king's royalty. The efficiency of the royal system was to be shared by both Clarence and Gloucester and, as a consequence, by Isabel and Anne.

Isabel became pregnant at the end of 1472 while her mother remained in sanctuary and her sister sought to marry Gloucester against Clarence's wishes. It meant that the duchess was without the close female family support that she might otherwise have expected. She may have turned to Clarence's mother who was also Isabel's godmother. Duchess Cecily gave birth to twelve children during her marriage, of whom five died soon after birth or while they were still infants. At court Elizabeth Woodville had given her husband another daughter named Margaret on 10 April 1472 and was pregnant again that Christmas. Edward's second son, Richard, would be born in August 1473. The queen would give birth to ten babies in 14 years. However, it is unlikely that Elizabeth and Isabel shared confidences. The queen disliked Edward's brother who resented the Woodvilles in his turn.

Medieval medicine devised diets to rebalance the humours of pregnant women experiencing morning sickness or strange cravings. Advice of the period included avoiding excessively sweet or savoury food. A diet that included poultry, bread and fragrant wine was recommended. Raisins, quinces and pomegranates may also have been purchased if Isabel was told about their perceived benefits.

Duchess Cecily may have recommended a woman to take the place of Countess Anne, or Clarence could have sought a respectable widow with knowledge of childbirth from amongst his own following. Although there is no named midwife who tended Isabel during her second and subsequent pregnancies, it is plausible that one of her ladies, Ankarette Twynyho née Hawkeston, the widow of William Twynyho[5] of Keyford near Frome, met the criteria. The woman's sons were amongst Clarence's loyal supporters. The Twynyhos were also known to Duchess Cecily. The previous year, on 8 November 1472, Ankarette's brother-in-law John Twynyho, a wealthy wool merchant and lawyer who served in various offices in Gloucestershire, was granted a licence by the duchess for the foundation of a chantry in Lechlade Church, Gloucestershire.[6] There is also some circumstantial geographical evidence for Ankarette's presence in the birthing chamber. The Twynyho residence near Frome was only 8 miles from Farleigh Hungerford, near Bath, where Isabel went into labour. As a respectable widow with a reputation for supporting women in childbirth and with ties to Clarence's family, Ankarette was an ideal midwife for Isabel who had experienced the trauma of stillbirth during her family's flight from England in 1470.

Farleigh Castle had been gifted to Gloucester by the king in 1462. Clarence is not known to have held the castle or resided there, although his presence in the wider area is recorded during the previous year. For instance, he was at Salisbury Cathedral on 5 February 1472 for Vespers.[7] It is not known whether Gloucester ever stayed in the castle, but it seems that Clarence most likely did, even though the relationship between the two brothers was strained. Either Isabel went into labour before her time or an accommodation was reached by the two brothers on some matters at least.

Women were encouraged to accept the pains and perils of childbirth because the Church regarded the pain of childbirth as women's atonement for Eve's original sin. Isabel was carefully tended during her pregnancy and the onset of labour, unlike the dangerous birth that she endured in 1470. A month before she gave birth, Isabel withdrew to a specially prepared birthing chamber where the doors and windows were closed and covered by heavy tapestries. Cold was something to be avoided, but it was usual to keep one small window open to permit some ventilation.

The darkened room was filled with soft furnishings, warmth and the scent of soothing herbs.

Isabel was attended by her ladies, her friends and those of her family who were welcome, as well as by midwives. Whoever acted as Isabel's principal midwife would have been a respectable woman of mature years who had children of her own. Midwifery was learned from experience and whoever cared for Isabel had a reputation for keeping both mother and child safe during the birthing, or being able to deal efficiently with any difficulties that might have arisen.

Clarence, his duchess, her mother-in-law or even Countess Anne from the safety of Beaulieu may have arranged to borrow a holy relic. These relics were often girdles. Isabel's cousin Elizabeth of York is known to have paid a monk for providing her with the Virgin Mary's girdle prior to the birth of her seventh child by King Henry VII. If a relic was not available, Isabel's women may have provided amulets containing powerful words that were tied to the labouring duchess.[8] When Isabel's labour began, all belts and ties holding her clothing in place were unlaced.[9] Even the ribbons in her hair were removed. The loosening was symbolic of easing the woman of her burden. As she laboured, her ladies provided her with herbal drinks, massaged her stomach, thighs and genitals with oils of lilies and roses, camomile or spikenard which were said to lessen the pain. One fifteenth-century manuscript advised hyssop steeped in hot water or wine. Some midwives made their patients sneeze by giving them irritants to sniff in the belief that sneezing would help matters progress. Isabel's chamber is likely to have been equipped with a birthing stool, a chair cut in a half-moon shape so that the woman could sit while the midwife knelt in front of her or sat on a lower stool to monitor progress. Another one of Isabel's ladies would have supported the duchess from behind.

The baby, named Margaret, arrived on 14 August 1473. She was washed and cleaned before being swaddled and handed over to a wet nurse while Isabel delivered the afterbirth. Clarence provided a household of nursery staff to care for Margaret – some of them may even have cared for Isabel and Anne during their childhoods. A woman was appointed to oversee Margaret's staff which also included menial servants. As well as a wet nurse she would have been equipped with a rocker whose job it was to sit and keep the cradle in which Margaret lay gently moving back and forth while singing soothing songs. Rockers were usually young girls.

Safely delivered, Isabel spent the next month in the birthing chamber. Mortality rates due to childbed fever were high during this period, as were the risks of a newborn child dying. The confinement allowed Isabel to rest and regain her strength. Her ladies cooked for her and celebrated the birth of a healthy child. Theologians believed that the very act of giving birth made the woman impure. They made a connection between giving birth and the sinfulness of conception. Isabel would not have been permitted to attend Margaret's baptism as she would not have been allowed into a church; instead, she remained in her chamber being fed fortifying foods such as broth, eggs and bread.[10] Tended by her ladies she may also have been visited by female family members and friends who would have come to rejoice with her the birth of a healthy child and Isabel's survival. At the end of 40 days Isabel was cleansed by a ritual known as churching. A priest met her at the entrance of the castle's chapel dedicated to St Leonard, sprinkled her with holy water and gave the duchess a blessing. She made an offering and received Mass. She may have paused to look at the wall painting depicting St George and the dragon and considered the symbolism of Christian faith overcoming the Devil and all his works. Perhaps she recalled the story of her ancestor Guy of Warwick slaying the dragon, or the sugar subtlety shaped like a dragon served when her uncle became Archbishop of York in 1465. Without benefit of written memory, it is impossible to know Isabel's thoughts. It is not even certain what she gave as an offering following the Mass. Many women gave gifts of candles by way of thanksgiving for a safe delivery. It is probable that the family celebrated a safe delivery by giving alms.[11]

Eighteen months later on 25 February 1475, Isabel provided George with a son named Edward who was born at Warwick Castle, Isabel and Clarence's principal residence since 1471. The boy was named Edward after his royal uncle who was also his godfather. The king gifted the child with the title Earl of Warwick. The boy's second godfather was John Strensham, Abbot of Tewkesbury. For the time being Margaret and Edward shared their nursery but it is likely that the birth of a son meant that the staff was expanded. During his infancy and early childhood, the nursery would normally remain a largely female domain overseen by a governess and directed by Isabel.

The king crossed the Channel on 4 July 1475 along with both his brothers to make war on the French. Unlike Countess Anne or Duchess Cecily, there was no need for Isabel or her sister to prepare for a protracted stay in a garrison town. Edward's brother-in-law Charles, Duke of Burgundy, failed to provide the support he promised to the English army and also refused to allow Edward to take his troops through towns controlled by Burgundy. The Duke of Brittany proved similarly uncooperative. By 12 August the king opened negotiations with King Louis XI which concluded with the Treaty of Picquigny signed at the end of the month. Louis paid Edward 75,000 crowns to go home; agreed an annual pension of 50,000 crowns; and ransomed Margaret of Anjou for a further 50,000 crowns. The treaty was concluded with the agreement that Edward's daughter Elizabeth of York would marry the French Dauphin. Clarence was present when the two kings met to sign the treaty on a specially constructed bridge, as was Edward's friend Lord Hastings. The duke was also one of the four arbitrators to whom the terms of the treaty referred. Fortune was smiling upon the duke: he had a beautiful wife; two healthy children; and he was finally taking his place at the centre of international politics.

Isabel became pregnant again early in 1476. In June news arrived that her uncle the Archbishop of York was dead. He was buried in the York Minster, but there is no record of a tomb for the disgraced bishop. In July the duchess is thought to have been at Fotheringhay along with the rest of the royal family for the reinterment of Richard of York and his son Edmund, Earl of Rutland, who had lain at the Priory of St John in Pontefract since Edward won his victory at Towton in 1461. Warwick's heraldic ceremonial for the reinterment of his own father and brother at Bisham, as well as the reburial of Isabel's grandfather, the 13th Earl of Warwick, in his mausoleum at St Mary's Church, Warwick on 27 December 1475 provided models for the costly reburial.

Gloucester filled the role of chief mourner for his father and brother. He watched as the bones were lifted from their graves at Pontefract on 21 July 1476. Each casket was the subject of religious ritual before being covered with a pall and carried into the choir of a nearby church. Vigil was kept wherever the caskets stood overnight before continuing their journey south. Each night new candles lit the darkness around the funeral hearses; each morning the coffins were blessed before continuing their journey down the Great North Road towards Fotheringhay.

The duke accompanied his father and brother's cortège with a retinue of mourners clad in expensive black garments – Thomas, Lord Stanley; Ralph, Lord Greystoke; and Humphrey, Lord Dacre, amongst others.[12] Men reaping in the fields stopped to doff their caps. Gentry and aristocrats who owed their allegiance to the House of York came to show their respects to the man who was never king. At Fotheringhay on 29 July, York's sons stood together along with other male scions of their family as well as those of Elizabeth Woodville. Their wives, daughters and sisters awaited them inside the church. The reburial rite was a lengthy one including psalms and antiphons.[13]

The notable absence from the record of the occasion was the duke's widow, Duchess Cecily. It is not a certainty that Clarence and his duchess attended the reinterment. It has been speculated that the dowager and her middle son preferred not to be in the vicinity of Elizabeth Woodville,[14] but if Cecily's absence was commented upon by the chroniclers, surely Clarence's would have been noted as further evidence of the division between the brothers. On 30 July Masses were said and King Edward made a gift at the altar on his father's behalf before being offered his father's arms. The solemn service was followed by a feast held at Fotheringhay Castle.

Summer passed. For reasons that are not known, Isabel was not at Warwick Castle when she went into labour with her fourth child. On 6 October, she was in the new infirmary at Tewkesbury Abbey. Most medieval women gave birth in their own homes and there is no indication as to why she was in the abbey hospital. Hospitals were not usually associated with women of Isabel's status or with childbirth. They were places for the poor, the elderly and those who were physically ill with no one else who might care for them. At least the abbot was able to offer Isabel use of a new chamber attached to the infirmary. It may have been that the child was premature or that Isabel was unwell. A hospital was the last resort. History does not record if Isabel had a long or difficult labour but on 6 October, she gave Clarence a second son who they named Richard. The day after his birth the infant was baptised in the abbey. Isabel did not travel to Warwick for another month. There is no record indicating who helped at her birth or who cared for her new son. She recovered sufficiently to return to Warwick by 12 November.

Isabel died on 22 December 1476. The *Croyland Chronicle* blamed childbed fever. Childbed fever or puerperal sepsis is caused by infection introduced during childbirth. It suggests a lack of hygiene either in the surroundings which Isabel found herself or on the part of her attendants. If Isabel did succumb to childbed fever, the infection made itself felt with the onset of shivering fits and a high fever a few days after she gave birth. As her pulse rate quickened and her belly distended, the pain would have been agonising. Usually, an infection of this kind caused death within days rather than permitting a new mother to recover sufficiently to make the journey from Tewkesbury to Warwick. The time lapse would suggest that if there was an infection, it was introduced later.

Death in childbirth was not unusual. It has been estimated that one in forty women died in childbirth during the Tudor and Stuart period.[15] Complications arising from childbirth included infection, haemorrhage and sepsis as well as obstetric complications such as a retained placenta or a ruptured uterus. Difficulties such as a breech birth, which are regarded as minor in the modern age, could also be fatal to mother, child or both during the medieval period. Frequent pregnancies increased the risk associated with childbirth. Although infection was a major cause of mortality amongst new mothers, Isabel might also have died from other causes. One possibility is that Isabel had tuberculosis.

Isabel's infant son died at the beginning of January 1477. Richard, like his mother, might have been infected due to a lack of hygiene or could have suffered injury during birth. Equally, if he was exposed to the bacteria that causes tuberculosis, he could have become infected in his mother's arms. If that was the case, the infant would have developed a fever, become lethargic and struggled to breathe. Whatever the truth, Clarence, struggling with fortune's fickleness, came to believe that Isabel and their child were both poisoned.

Yuletide preparations stalled as the household plunged into mourning and preparations were made for Isabel's burial. The duchess left no will so Clarence made a decision concerning his wife's final resting place which could, of course, be based on a conversation that took place during the weeks preceding Isabel's death but for which no evidence remains. She would not lie in St Mary's near her Beauchamp grandfather or even at Bisham alongside Warwick, Salisbury and Alice Montagu. The duchess would be interred near her Despenser ancestors and her uncle Henry Beauchamp, 1st Duke of Warwick.

A sad cortège returned Isabel's embalmed body to Tewkesbury Abbey on 4 January 1477. Abbot John Strensham received the hearse carrying her body in the abbey choir. Together with the bishops of Worcester and Landaffe, the duke's own chaplains and in the presence of the monastic community, Isabel's funeral office was performed. That night the duke held a vigil over the coffin and on the following morning, which was the Feast of Epiphany, three Masses were celebrated for Isabel's soul – the first at the altar of St Mary, the second for the Trinity and the third for Isabel's eternal rest. The hearse and coffin remained in the choir for the next thirty-five days until a new vault was built behind the high altar.

Medieval Christians believed in the Last Judgement which would take place at the end of time when Christ would resurrect the dead. They also believed that each individual soul was judged immediately after death and sent to a spiritual destination to await the day of judgement. It would only be when body and soul were finally reunited that Christians would find their way to their final eternal home, be it Heaven or Hell. There was an intermediate state called Purgatory where souls went to expiate their sins before being admitted to Heaven. Salvation or reduced time spent in Purgatory could be achieved through good works and through the intercession of saints. Masses for the dead were an essential part of the translation from an earthly body to eternal salvation. Clarence may have believed he had time to endow a chantry chapel and to make arrangements for Masses to be said for the souls of both Isabel and himself. He might even have considered how his endowment could have a charitable purpose which would make the prayers and Masses even more efficacious. The duchess was finally interred on 8 February 1477. Burial in the abbey church gave Isabel's soul immediate spiritual benefit. The closer a body was placed to the high altar and the Body of Christ, the better. The building of the crypt left room also for a splendid chapel and effigy in due course. Clarence may have considered the chantry chapel and two-storey tomb built in 1430 by Isabel's grandmother for her first husband Richard Beauchamp, 1st Earl of Worcester, as a model for his own future intentions.

Although George was distressed by Isabel's death and sought to blame an outside agency both for her demise and that of their son, it took very little time for the first marriage proposal to arrive in the hands of the grieving widower. Margaret of York, Clarence's sister, suggested her own stepdaughter as a possible bride. Mary, the daughter of Charles the Bold of Burgundy, had been mentioned as a possible wife for him before he came under the influence of the Earl of Warwick. Since her father's death on 5 January 1477 at the Battle of Nancy, Mary was not only a very wealthy heiress but the titular head of state. She was also betrothed to Archduke Maximilian of Hapsburg. Edward IV declined the proposal on his brother's behalf. The proposed union would have alienated the Hapsburgs and dragged England into conflict with King Louis XI who was eager to secure Burgundy for France.

A short while afterwards it was suggested that Clarence marry one of James III of Scotland's sisters. King Edward declined that offer as well. The rejections gave Clarence further grounds for discontent against his elder sibling. The reconciliation achieved in 1471 became strained once more and in all likelihood, the grieving duke began plotting against his brother soon after Isabel's death.

Although Clarence considered taking another wife, he did not forget Isabel nor his duty to support prayers and Masses for her soul. He arranged for Isabel, their two surviving children and himself to be admitted to the Guild of the Holy Cross at Stratford-upon-Avon. The original purpose of the guild was for the its chaplains to pray for the souls of dead members of the fraternity. However, the guild was also involved in arbitration between members, giving charity and providing free education. Like many other organisations there was a direct connection between the guild and the town's commerce. It was a way of maintaining social and business contacts as well as having an association with the region's gentry and magnates. When Clarence enrolled his family, he paid an entry fee or fine as it was described in the records of the guild of 5 marks.[16] Isabel's formal posthumous admission to benefit of prayers was not an unusual one.

Fortune was not yet done with Isabel. Clarence's reaction to his wife's death would have catastrophic consequences for him. There would be no bronze or alabaster effigy to commemorate Isabel with her feet resting on a chained bear, proclaiming her identity to the world; no chantry chapel echoing with the murmur of repeated prayers speeding her and Clarence's souls heavenwards; and nothing for future generations to construct a physical identity for Isabel Neville, Duchess of Clarence.

Chapter 13

Witchcraft, Murder and Treason

Crazed by grief, Clarence accused Isabel's gentlewoman Ankarette Twynyho of murder by poison and witchcraft. She helped care for the duchess during her final weeks and may have acted as Isabel's midwife on more than one occasion, although there is no certainty. There is no existing record of her being at Tewkesbury in October. Documentary evidence suggests the opposite. The duke stated that on 10 October 1476, four days after Isabel gave birth, Ankarette was at Warwick. Most records indicate that Isabel travelled home to Warwick the following month.

Either the fault lies with the record, the duke made a mistake, or it was a deliberate piece of misinformation to ensure that any trial took place in Warwick rather than in Tewkesbury, even though Clarence was lord of both the manor and borough for Tewkesbury. It would perhaps have been more difficult for him to influence proceedings.[1] The duke also came to believe that his infant son was poisoned by another servant named John Thursby. He became so convinced that his family were being murdered, he was accused of attempting to send his heir, Edward, out of the country to Ireland in a bid to keep him safe.

It was three months before Clarence made his accusation and moved against Ankarette. It has been conjectured that the duke was required to go to Ireland[2] soon after Isabel's interment. History can only speculate about the duke's state of mind. It did not help that at least one member of the Twynyho family, who Clarence regarded as long-standing members of his affinity, was now employed by the Woodville family. John Twynyho, Ankarette's brother-in-law, was employed by the queen's son Thomas Grey, Marquis of Dorset.

On 12 April 1477, Clarence sent twenty-six armed servants to Keyford near Frome where Ankarette was living following the disbandment of Isabel's household. Richard Hyde and Roger Strugge arrived early in the afternoon, kidnapped the terrified woman and took her to Bath. From there they travelled to Cirencester on 13 April and on the evening of

Monday 14 April, the armed guard arrived with their prisoner at Warwick Castle. Clarence's men were shadowed throughout their journey by Ankarette's daughter Edith and son-in-law, Thomas Delalynde. After a journey of more than 70 miles in three days, Ankarette was cast into a cell, having had all her jewellery and money stolen, while Clarence's men ordered her family to leave Warwick. Edith and Thomas retreated 6 miles to Stratford-upon-Avon where they could only await the outcome of Ankarette's ordeal.

The following morning, Ankarette was tried for the murder of Isabel at the Guildhall in Warwick. It was said that she gave the duchess poisoned ale 'falsely, traitorously and feloniously'.[3] The account went on to accuse Ankarette of administering the poison from 10 October until Sunday 22 December, causing Isabel to sicken and to die. John Thursby, who was from Warwick and already in Clarence's custody, was accused of the murder of Richard. The justices sitting on the bench, including John Hugford of Emscote who would become the Constable of Warwick Castle the following year, had no choice for fear of Clarence's anger other than to condemn both prisoners to death. Ankarette and John were executed that afternoon, having been drawn through Warwick to the gallows at Myton. The time from trial to execution was three hours.

A third man, who did not appear at the Guildhall, escaped Clarence's vengeance. The duke believed that while Ankarette and Hugford administered the poison, Sir Roger Tocotes of Bromham masterminded the plot. He was an influential member of the Wiltshire gentry, not to mention part of the extended Beauchamp family. The knight served the Kingmaker and was in France with the earl in 1470, but defected with Clarence back to King Edward IV before the Battle of Barnet. Prior to Isabel's death Tocotes was one of the duke's advisors and was with him during Edward's French campaign. It has been suggested that the man counted as Clarence's friend.[4] However, like the Twynyho family, Tocotes' loyalty was not reserved for George alone. In the aftermath of Isabel's death Tocotes served King Edward IV[5]. The duke would also accuse the king of wanting his death. Clarence grew increasingly afraid of being poisoned in the same way that he believed Isabel was murdered. Either the duke mistook the symptoms of Isabel's illness for something sinister, suffered a mental health crisis, or there was some truth in his accusations. Without further evidence it is impossible to draw any conclusions.

The whole sorry affair was compounded when John Stacy, an astronomer from Oxford, was accused at about the same time of trying to murder Richard, Lord Beauchamp, by means of a lead image created at the behest of Beauchamp's adulterous wife. The *Croyland Chronicle* reported attempted murder through witchcraft, but did not include in its account the information that Stacy admitted during his interrogation about predicting the deaths of King Edward and his eldest son by use of astrological charts, which amounted to assassination by divination. He implicated Thomas Black, an Oxford clerk, and a second man, Thomas Burdett, who was a member of Clarence's own household, but it was not until 1477 that the case was brought to court. It was not the first time in the fifteenth century that a monarch's death had been encompassed by witchcraft, or that a member of the royal family was ruined by the accusation. In 1441 Eleanor Cobham, wife of Humphrey, Duke of Gloucester, was arrested and charged with treason following the interrogation of three of her servants. Her astrologer, Roger Bolingbroke, was hanged at Tyburn because he cast the horoscope that ascertained Humphrey of Gloucester's chances of ascending to the throne as King Henry VI's heir presumptive. Bolingbroke was also alleged to have melted a wax image of the king to hasten his end. Humphrey was forced to retire from political life and was himself arrested on a charge of treason, but died before the case could be tried.

If allegations of involvement with the dark arts were not enough, Clarence's servant Burdett was also accused of writing treasonable verses aimed at dethroning King Edward.[6] The publication of Burdett's writing prompted King Edward to appoint a commission of oyer and terminer to investigate the case more thoroughly. The enquiry was presided over by the Marquess of Dorset as well as other members of the Woodville family.[7] A week later all three men were found guilty of constructing a star chart to predict the death of both the king and Prince Edward. The punishment for attempting to kill the monarch through sorcery was death. Burdett was hanged, drawn and quartered on 20 May 1477, still protesting his innocence.

Clarence's fragile self-control snapped. It may have appeared to him as though Burdett's death was yet another example of intrusion by the Woodville faction into his life. Or it may have appeared to be direct retaliation for the manner in which he flouted the legal system to ensure

Ankarette's judicial murder. By coincidence, on the same day as Burdett went to the gallows, the Twynyho case was transferred to Westminster for judicial review. With Isabel gone there was no one to advise the duke, to guide or even to counsel restraint. Instead, the shadow of Isabel and her infant son seemed to serve only to inflame Clarence. He burst into a council meeting at Westminster to read Burdett's statement of innocence made at the foot of the gallows in full. It may have been that Burdett prepared his speech beforehand and it was a copy of this document that found its way into Clarence's hands.

The king was absent from the meeting but when he learned of Clarence's outburst, he refused to act on the provocation that his brother offered. Instead, three weeks later after due consideration, he demanded that Clarence appear at court to explain his behaviour. The meeting between the two brothers was uncomfortable. The king was facing yet another Lancastrian insurgency at the time of the duke's most recent outburst. A man purporting to be the Earl of Oxford was trying to raise support for a rebellion in East Anglia. It did not matter that Oxford remained incarcerated in Calais or that the pretender was swiftly apprehended. Now Edward was forced to address his brother's anger about Burdett's execution, even though the man may well have published verses challenging Edward's right to rule and promoting the claims of Clarence to the throne.

And then there was Ankarette's case. Even though the matter was never formally addressed, Clarence had taken the right to interfere with the legal process upon himself. It was a crime known as accroachment, a word that had much in common with usurpation. The duke assumed a power for which he had no right or authority. Worst of all, it came to the king's ears that Clarence was feeding rumours that Elizabeth Woodville was not Edward's legal wife, that Edward was himself a bastard and that he used sorcery to corrupt his subjects. The stench of treachery was in the air and Edward, known for his easy good humour, finally lost patience. It must have seemed that Clarence was once again in the thick of the troubles that beset him. Edward had always forgiven his ambitious younger brother, but now he publicly upbraided Clarence. The *Croyland Chronicle* added that George was arrested for matters known only to the king when he was taken to the Tower in the autumn of 1477.

It was an opportunity that the Woodville faction could not afford to ignore. George's ambition for the crown was well known. Parliament was called and an attainder bill was introduced against the duke in January 1478, including his part in the Readeption of King Henry VI in 1470. Gloucester, fearing that the Woodvilles were behind George's arrest, became concerned that he might also be at risk. Only Sir Thomas More's account of the episode sought to implicate Richard in his brother's fall. Mancini, who was in England from 1482, placed the blame squarely on the shoulders of Elizabeth Woodville. He claimed that she feared for the future of her own children while Clarence lived. Whatever the truth of the matter, *Hall's Chronicle*, published in 1548, commented on the confusion and conjecture surrounding Clarence's trial. King Edward personally read the charges against the duke including his illicit marriage to Isabel at Calais; his support for Warwick; the Lancastrian parliamentary statute of 1470 which made George's claim to the throne; and his attempted marriage to Mary of Burgundy within weeks of Isabel's death. Clarence's proven intrigues, plots and treachery had always been forgiven in the past.

There was nothing more tangible in the accusations made against Clarence on this occasion, or at least none that the king or his councillors were prepared to discuss in public. Amongst the charges was one that stated he 'cause (ed) a strange Child to be bought to his Castle at Warwick, and there to have be put and kept in likeness to his Son and Heir'.[8] It was said that the duke asked the Abbot of Tewkesbury, John Strensham, and two other men, John Tapton and Roger Harewell, to find a child who looked like 2-year-old Edward. Clarence intended that his son be taken to Ireland or Flanders. One of Clarence's servants, John Taylor, was sent to fetch Edward from Warwick, but failed to make the exchange when the men charged with supplying the substitute toddler refused to hand the boy over. Taylor was later forgiven by the king for his part in Clarence's attempted deception, perhaps because his loyalty was to Isabel's son. He went on to become forester and bailiff of Clarence's Worcestershire lands and, in 1485, Gloucester, by then King Richard III, made him keeper of the king's park at Morelwood in Gloucestershire.[9]

Another clue as to the exact depth of Clarence's treachery lay in a report from the Milanese ambassador to France dated 6 July 1473. In it he recorded that the Earl of Oxford persuaded King Louis XI to support him financially by presenting 'twenty-four original seals of knights and one duke, who have promised and pledged their troth to make war on King Edward.'[10] Louis came to believe that the seal was a forgery, but Clarence is a convincing argument for the identity of the duke plotting against the king.[11] When George was given an opportunity to defend himself, he showed no remorse for any of his actions. The duke's choice of advocate for himself and for his executed man Burdett was inflammatory. Dr John Goddard, a Franciscan friar, was known for his anti-Yorkist views. In September 1470, at the time of the Readeption, he preached outside St Paul's Cathedral advocating the rights of King Henry VI to the throne and denouncing Edward. Unsurprisingly no one else wished to speak on George's behalf.

In February the Duke of Buckingham, Edward's newly appointed High Steward, pronounced George's guilt. The king may have believed that Clarence was plotting once again and wanted his brother's wings clipped, but he could not bring himself to read the death sentence, even though he signed the indictment. George remained in the Tower for another eleven days before being executed on 18 February 1478 without having asked for pardon or mercy. The *Croyland Chronicle* reported in 1486 that Clarence was drowned in a butt of malmsey wine rather than the more usual beheading, although the contemporary *London Chronicle* made no mention of the manner of his execution. Mancini described a 'jar of sweet wine'[12] in 1483. Commines, writing ten years after the Milanese ambassador, also reported death by drowning. In later times a picture of an unknown Tudor lady is often described as a portrait of Isabel's daughter Margaret, Countess of Salisbury, because of a bracelet bearing a barrel charm worn by the sitter said to be in remembrance of Clarence. The story of his execution also gave rise to the idea that Clarence was a dissolute alcoholic, but as with many good yarns there is no documentary evidence of Isabel's husband being intemperate.

Edward, having paid his brother's debts, arranged for Clarence's embalmed body to be transported to Tewkesbury Abbey to lie in the stone-lined vault behind the high altar with Isabel. Mourners accompanied the body on its final journey and prayers were said for the soul of the duke,[13] but any plans for a chantry and alabaster tomb stalled despite the fact that both Polydore Vergil and Sir Thomas More believed that the king regretted George's death.

The duke's attainder meant that Isabel's young son Edward would not inherit a dukedom. Half Countess Anne's estates now lay in the hands of the Crown, not because of the attainder against Clarence but because Edward, who turned 3 years of age the week after his father's execution, was a royal ward. He was permitted to inherit by right of his mother who was deemed by Parliament to be one of Countess Anne's co-heiresses. Had the Crown granted the estates to Clarence rather than allowing him to claim them by right of his wife, they would all have reverted to the king. Instead, Edward gained use of his nephew's estates until the boy achieved his majority as well as controlling the right to arrange the boy's marriage. The new earl and his elder sister Margaret left Warwick Castle and travelled to London on the king's orders where Warwick was housed in the Tower – it was after all a royal residence as well as a prison. The governor of the Tower was Thomas Grey, Marquis of Dorset, the king's stepson. In 1480 the king sold Edward's wardship for £2000 to Dorset.[14] The marquis' wife gave him a daughter named Dorothy in the same year. The probable intention was that the young earl, and his half of Countess Anne's fortune, should marry into the Grey family. The king also granted Dorset possession of some of Warwick's estates in Gloucestershire, Hampshire and Wiltshire. It is likely that Isabel's son was sent to one of Dorset's estates so that he might be raised and educated amongst his new family. Isabel's daughter Margaret remained in the financial care of the king who provided her with clothing and servants. It is probable that she remained in the royal household with her cousins.[15]

Shakespeare, drawing on Sir Thomas More's account, painted Anne's husband Gloucester as responsible for Clarence's downfall and death in order to put himself closer in line of succession to the throne. Isabel Neville's husband would be remembered as 'false, fleeting perjured Clarence'.[16] Of Isabel there was no mention at all. Nor was she even permitted to rest in peace. Clarence and Isabel's coffins were disturbed during the eighteenth century when alderman Samuel Hawling, his wife and son were interred in their vault only to be evicted from it in 1829, the supposed bones of the duke and duchess gathered from where they were scattered and placed in a repurposed stone coffin. Four hundred years after Isabel's death, the vault was fitted with an iron gate and a brass plate engraved with two suns in splendour reading:

> Dominus Georgius Plantagenet dux Clarencius et Domina Isabelle Neville, uxor ejus qui obierunt haec 12 Decemberis, A.D. 1476, ille 18 Feb., 1477.
> Macte veni sicut sol in slendore, Mox subito mersus in cruore

Translated, the inscription reads 'Lord George Plantagenet, Duke of Clarence, and Lady Isabelle Neville, his wife, who died, she on Dec. 12, 1476, he on Feb. 18, 1477. I came in my might like a sun in splendour, Soon suddenly bathed in my own blood'.

Successful aristocratic women married well and bore large numbers of children for their husbands. If they were long lived, like Katherine Neville, Duchess of Norfolk, they became rich through successive marriages. Isabel, the eldest daughter of a mighty magnate and the wife of a prince, is marginalised by the historical narrative, largely airbrushed from cultural retellings and is even sidelined on her memorial simply as the wife of a son of York, although the bear and ragged staff of Warwick can be found on the Victorian floor tiles in Tewkesbury Abbey. Isabel's daughter Margaret remembered rather better the weight of ancestry handed to her by her mother. Her coat of arms bore her father's royal arms, but the rest of the quarterings reflect her Beauchamp, Montagu and Neville ancestry. Even more poignantly, Margaret named her only daughter Ursula – meaning 'little bear'.

Chapter 14

The Lord Protector's Wife

King Edward IV became ill at the beginning of April 1483. Dominic Mancini, an Italian cleric and chronicler, recorded that the king caught a cold during a fishing expedition at the end of March. Philip de Commines suggested that Edward succumbed to an apoplectic fit having grown very fat from his excesses. The Tudor chronicler Edward Hall speculated that it was tertian fever or malaria that caused the king's death. Realising that his end was imminent, Edward appointed Gloucester as protector of his 12-year-old son. Anne's husband was always loyal to his brother and was known to be an able soldier and administrator.

Edward IV's death on 9 April 1483 brought to a head a deadly rivalry that was to have seismic consequences for the Plantagenet dynasty. The Woodville faction were reluctant to share power with their rival who was far away in the north. More judicious councillors were already concerned about the extent to which the king's often unpopular Woodville relations surrounded him. Anthony Woodville, 2nd Earl Rivers, was at Ludlow as the Governor of the Prince of Wales' household. The king's grieving widow objected to Gloucester's appointment as protector fearing that he would have too much power. She sent a message with instructions that Anthony should bring the new king to London to be crowned as soon as possible. King Edward V could, in theory, become a legal adult, even though someone would need to govern on his behalf behind the scenes.

Events appeared to be overtaking Gloucester who might reasonably have expected from the precedent of the past to run the country as King Henry VI's uncles had done during his minority, or indeed as John of Gaunt had ruled on behalf of his young nephew King Richard II. Lord Hastings, Edward IV's chamberlain and Anne's uncle by marriage, wrote advising Gloucester to reach London as soon as he was able. The *Croyland Chronicle* asserts that Hastings was concerned that he himself might fall victim to the Woodvilles. Another messenger was sent by the Duke of

Buckingham, Anne and Richard's kinsman, informing Gloucester of Edward's death. Buckingham clearly expected trouble.

As soon as he learned of his brother's demise, Gloucester went to York where the city's officials gave an oath of loyalty to King Edward V. He left the city on 23 April, having written to Anthony Woodville, Earl Rivers, the king's uncle, asking to meet him and the king on their way to London so that they could enter the capital together. The coronation was due to take place in less than a fortnight, but Anne did not travel with her husband as he hastened south with a force of men loyal to him. It is impossible to know what Richard planned or how much Anne knew of it in advance.

On 24 April Edward V, with his Woodville entourage, left Ludlow. It had taken ten days since the messenger arrived from London to prepare for the journey. By 29 April Anne's husband was at Northampton with Buckingham when he received news that his 12-year-old nephew, King Edward V, was at nearby Stony Stratford with his uncle and his half-brother Sir Richard Grey, who had been in London but had left the capital to meet the new king. He may have been carrying a message from Elizabeth Woodville urging them to make haste.

Rivers left the king at the Rose and Crown Inn and went back to Northampton to explain that there was not enough accommodation for all of them. By all accounts he enjoyed a cordial evening with Gloucester and Buckingham. He awoke the following morning to discover that he was a captive. Gloucester arrested Grey and Edward V's chamberlain, Thomas Vaughan, before taking custody of the king. Rivers was sent to Sheriff Hutton while the other two men were sent to Middleham and Pontefract. The remainder of Edward V's retinue, which had accompanied him from Ludlow, were dismissed. Gloucester informed his shocked nephew that his Woodville relations and his attendants were conspiring against him. He then continued to London, having sent letters to the council proclaiming that he had saved the king from his enemies.

Polydore Vergil believed that Richard planned to usurp the throne before he began his journey from York, but more recent historians have speculated that it was Buckingham who persuaded the duke to turn on Edward V's protectors on 30 April. Buckingham had his own grudge against the Woodville family. He was married to Elizabeth Woodville's sister Katherine and resented the humble origins of his bride. He might also have begrudged the fact that if he had married one of the Kingmaker's daughters, it would have been him who inherited half of Countess Anne's fortune. He also had his own claim to the throne.[1]

When Elizabeth Woodville learned the events of Stony Stratford, she escaped on 30 April, under cover of darkness, into sanctuary at Westminster for a second time with her younger son Richard, Duke of York, and her daughters as well as her eldest son from her first marriage, Thomas Grey, Marquis of Dorset.

On 4 May, the day he was supposed to be crowned, King Edward V arrived in London flanked by Gloucester and Buckingham. Four carts containing weapons, all bearing the Woodville insignia and originating from Ludlow, preceded the royal procession. This was to be the proof that the Woodville faction had intended to deprive Gloucester of his role as protector, if not his life. Mancini wrote that the charge was a false one, but did believe that the Woodvilles planned a coup. The weapons were intended for a campaign against the Scots. Whatever the truth of the matter, Gloucester's arrest of Rivers meant that there could be no turning back from the course upon which he was now set. Earl Rivers was of much the same opinion. He made his will and prepared himself to die. By mid-May the young king was moved from the Bishop of London's palace where he was initially lodged to the Tower of London. By then a new date, 22 June, was set for the coronation.

On the same day that Gloucester entered London with his nephew and ordered the capital's inhabitants to swear loyalty to the new king, Anne's young cousin, George Neville, the son of Lord Montagu, died. In 1475 Parliament divided the Neville inheritance between Isabel and Anne on the proviso that the estate was only to remain in Gloucester's hands so long as George Neville or his heirs survived. Anne's husband knew that his northern estates and hegemony would only pass to his own son so long as George was unable to claim what was rightfully his. It was also essential according to the terms of the Act of Parliament ratifying Gloucester's possession of Warwick's northern estates that George produced heirs of his own. In 1480 the boy's wardship was granted to Richard and he became part of the duke's household. In time a marriage into a family loyal to Gloucester would have been arranged that ensured George was without the funds or power to pursue his rightful claim to the Neville inheritance. Now, with George's death, Gloucester was effectively only a life tenant and would not be able to pass the northern estates that once belonged to Warwick to his son. It would be Richard, Lord Latimer, who benefited from the Neville inheritance while George's sisters became the co-heiresses for the estates of their late mother, Isabel Ingoldsthorpe. Gloucester needed to look to mend the fortunes of his family.

Anne, mourning the loss of her cousin as well as Edward IV, arrived in London on 5 June 1483 assuming that she would be attending the coronation of King Edward V on 22 June. By then Gloucester had given a solemn oath of loyalty recognising the succession of his nephew. He even wrote to Elizabeth Woodville, still in sanctuary, confirming his loyalty. Anne concluded her journey at Crosby Place, Bishopgate, a short distance from the parish church of St Helen's[2] rather than at L'Erber or her mother-in-law's London residence at Baynard's Castle. It is unclear whether Gloucester owned or rented Crosby Place, but as it never became a Crown property after Richard's fall it seems more likely to have been rented. The house was large and modern, having been completed by Sir John Ashby in 1470.

Five days later, following a council meeting, Gloucester summoned help from York claiming that Elizabeth Woodville was plotting to murder him. The letter arrived on 15 June carried by Sir Richard Ratcliffe. Any troops that the city sent were required at Pontefract by 18 June.[3] Fired up by the duke's words, men set about gathering their troops and arming for war. Rivers was moved from Sheriff Hutton to Pontefract where he was executed on 25 June before an army led by the Earl of Northumberland began its journey south.

By then events had taken a dramatic turn in London during a council meeting held on 13 June in The Tower. It began, according to More's account, with Gloucester expressing a desire for a dish of strawberries from Cardinal Morton's garden at Holborn. A messenger was dispatched to fetch some. The meeting was interrupted and Gloucester left the room. When he returned, he was both angry and agitated. Richard explained that he believed there was a conspiracy against him. He claimed that he was unable to breathe and that his body was withering from the effects of witchcraft performed by Elizabeth Woodville. He held out his arm as proof. Forensic evidence obtained in 2013 reveals that there was no foreshortening of his arm, but the scoliosis that was twisting his spine, causing one shoulder to be higher than the other, could have resulted from muscle spasms, or the problem could have been caused by something completely unrelated.

Six members of the council were immediately arrested. Shortly afterwards Lord Hastings was dragged from the meeting and executed on Tower Green, having been found guilty of treason by Gloucester. Richard was within his rights as Constable of England to have Hastings executed without further trial, but it was also very convenient. In all probability, Hastings was conspiring with the Woodville faction. King Edward IV's former mistress Jane Shore was carrying messages for her new lover to Elizabeth Woodville in sanctuary in Westminster. In all likelihood, Hastings was loyal to King Edward V and had proved unyielding in his determination to see the young king crowned. He may have been sounded out by William Catesby, a lawyer in his own service but recruited by Gloucester. Sir Thomas More would later describe Catesby as lacking in faith.[4] When the proclamation announcing Hastings' execution was read out, it reminded the populace that Hastings enticed the king into debauchery.

Gloucester also saw to it that Jane Shore was charged with conspiracy and tried in the ecclesiastical court for adultery. She was made to do public penance, dressed in just her shift, before being imprisoned in the Fleet. It was a reminder both of the duke's own morality and his brother's flagrant history of womanising. Mancini and Commines both wrote of the court's immorality because the king gave himself, 'wholly to pleasures and took no delight in anything but ladies'.[5]

Three days later Edward V's younger brother Richard of York emerged from sanctuary into the care of his uncle. By then Westminster Abbey was surrounded by troops. At about the same time as the Duke of York joined his elder brother, Anne's nephew the 8-year-old Edward, Earl of Warwick, formerly Dorset's ward, was taken to Crosby House and given into the care of the duchess.[6] At the same time as Anne's own son remained in Middleham, it was an opportunity for her to get to know her nephew.

With his royal nephews under his control and Hastings dead, the way was clear for Gloucester to take the throne for himself. The coronation was delayed once more. Anne's husband is either portrayed as an ambitious child killer or a virtuous prince who took the only course available to him once he understood that Edward was bigamously married to Elizabeth

Woodville. Commines related that Robert Stillington, the Bishop of Bath and Wells, who was briefly imprisoned in the Tower after Clarence's trial in 1478, revealed that he had performed a marriage ceremony between Lady Eleanor Butler and Edward:

> The bishop discovered to the Duke of Gloucester that his brother king Edward had been formerly in love with a beautiful young lady and had promised her marriage upon condition that he might lie with her; the lady consented, and, as the bishop affirmed, he married them when nobody was present but they two and himself. His fortune depending on the court, he did not discover it, and persuaded the lady likewise to conceal it, which she did, and the matter remained a secret.[7]

It has been suggested that the reason for his arrest was because Clarence had some knowledge of Edward's first marriage. The exact nature of the king's relationship with Lady Eleanor Butler remains open to speculation, but on Sunday 22 June, the date of the postponed coronation, Dr Ralph Shaa, the half-brother of London's mayor, preached a sermon at the cross outside St Paul's. It was entitled 'Bastard Slips Shall Not Take Root'. He declared that King Edward V and all his siblings were illegitimate. The *Croyland Chronicle* reported that the illegitimacy of Edward IV's family stemmed from the fact that when the king married Elizabeth Woodville in 1464, he was already precontracted in marriage to Lady Eleanor Butler. The promise of marriage followed by intercourse constituted a legal wedding. No ecclesiastical court made any pronouncement on the union of Edward to Elizabeth Woodville or the subsequent birth of their children, but no one had forgotten the scandal of Elizabeth's own clandestine marriage and its subsequent revelation.

Shaa also resurrected the slurs against Duchess Cecily made at the end of the 1460s by Anne's father. The cleric proclaimed that Edward IV was himself illegitimate. The king – tall, blond and handsome in his youth – did not look like his father, the Duke of York. Mancini wrote that Richard had 'corrupted preachers of the divine word' to achieve his own ends.[8] The man who was known for his lifelong loyalty to his brother and whose personal motto was *loyalté me lie* (loyalty binds me) was either driven by an impossible situation to claim the crown, or had been overcome by the same ambition that brought Anne's own father down. The purge of Gloucester's enemies continued. Thomas Grey, Marquis of Dorset, who was Warwick's legal guardian, fled. In Yorkshire, under the direction of Richard Ratcliff, Earl Rivers, Richard Grey and Thomas Vaughan went to their deaths.

On 26 June Buckingham petitioned Richard to take the crown on behalf of the realm's lords and commoners because Edward IV's marriage to Elizabeth Woodville was unsafe. Gloucester gave his assent to the proposal, then went to Westminster Hall and sat upon the king's marble bench in exactly the same way that his elder brother claimed the throne in 1461. Like Edward before him, he stated that the king's principal duty was to administer law. No one wanted a return to the battles that had intermittently punctuated the last thirty years or so.

Anne's son, Edward of Middleham, described by Vergil as being about 9 years of age, became the Duke of Cornwall, but he remained at Middleham that summer as events unfolded in London. He was growing fast. He was provided with a new gown of green cloth that summer and Dirick the shoe maker was paid 13s 1d for a pair of shoes. Amongst the other expenses as events unfolded in London were the costs of choosing a king of West Witton for the rush-bearing celebrations and 5s for the purchase of a feather 'for my lord prince'.[9] He made journeys to nearby Jervaulx Abbey and to Coverham Priory. Jane Colyns gave Edward coin for the offerings he made at their shrines and also at Fountains Abbey, near Ripon. Her expenses were reimbursed from the boy's household accounts. At the end of the summer Edward's expenses were absorbed into Richard's own accounts. By that time the boy had turned from the son of a duke without the prospect of inheriting his forefather's northern lordship into the heir to the throne – which perhaps accounts for the purchase of a magnificent feather for his hat.

Chapter 15

Queen Anne

The coronation had been cancelled three times since the beginning of May, but now, with Buckingham appointed to oversee the details of the first joint coronation since Isabella of France was crowned alongside Edward II in 1308, preparations became frenetic. On 27 June 1483 Peter Courteys, the Keeper of the Great Wardrobe, was called upon to create an indenture specifying the robes and accessories that he and his department would need to supply for the forthcoming coronation. Orders were given that everything had to be ready by 3 July. There were only six days and nights for all the furriers and cloth merchants in London to provide their wares and for an army of tailors, seamstresses and skinners to cut and stitch everything that was required. Luxury fabrics from Italy, including cloth of gold, had been arriving since April, but Edward IV's son was a child without a wife and now robes and liveries were required for Anne and all her ladies. Henry Ive, the queen's tailor marshalled his staff to cut and sew the exquisite materials sent to him by the Great Wardrobe.

Meanwhile, a silkwoman called Alice Claver started to make buttons and tassels from gold thread. Extremely thin strips of beaten gold were wound around a core of silk or linen thread before being worked. Claver was a widow who traded in her own right for more than 30 years having completed a lengthy apprenticeship. She is known to have supplied goods to Edward IV, Richard III and Henry VII. On this occasion it was her responsibility to provide silk ribbon, laces, fringing, tassels and buttons to the Great Wardrobe.[1]

On 4 July 1483, Anne moved with her husband from their lodgings to the Tower's royal apartments by barge. It was traditional for kings to go to their coronations in Westminster Abbey from here. They would have been escorted by the mayor, his aldermen and the city companies. When Anne sat down to her meal that night, only fish was served as it was a Friday. The men serving her and Richard were the squires who would shortly be made Knights of the Bath, amongst them was her illegitimate half-sister's husband Richard Huddleston. Anne had no official part to play in the ceremonies that evening so she was able to retire to her chamber. Did Anne think of Elizabeth Woodville still in sanctuary, or of her two sons suddenly rendered illegitimate? The last recorded sighting of 12-year-old Edward and his 9-year-old brother Richard was made in *The Great Chronicle* on 16 June 1483. A week after the coronation on 13 July, Edward's attendants were dismissed. By the end of the summer, rumours began to circulate that the two boys were dead. Or perhaps Anne remembered her former mother-in-law Margaret of Anjou ransomed in 1475? Maybe she even thought of King Henry VI whose doom was sealed by the death of Edward of Lancaster at the Battle of Tewkesbury. Warwick's surviving daughter understood all too well fate's vagaries and must have recognised that queens of England were no more secure than daughters of ambitious earls, unless the king could control the realm. There was no room for sentiment or doubt in the unsparing realities of fifteenth-century politics.

Anne's ladies awoke her early on 5 July and attired her for the day. She wore a fine lawn smock next to her skin under a kirtle, surcoat and mantle. Later that morning, after hearing Mass and dining with the newly made knights, Anne retired once more to her chamber to prepare for the procession to Westminster where Richard would hold a vigil the night before he was crowned. Anne's own vigil robes symbolised her purity. Her kirtle was made from white damask cloth of gold and trimmed with miniver. The ladies-in-waiting would have laced it closed and then helped her into the heavy mantle made from the same materials as the kirtle. Its train was made from more than 27 yards of shimmering white damask cloth of gold bordered with ermine. Her long reddish-gold hair was brushed until it shone and a jewelled circlet was placed upon her brow. More usually Anne would have worn her hair drawn tightly back from the forehead beneath a butterfly headdress of a richly-embroidered cap described as similar to an 'inverted flower pot', with a folded and pinned wired veil arranged in a five-shape at the front of the cap, stretched out at the back to resemble butterfly wings.[2] Today, however, Anne wore her waist-length hair as a bride going to her wedding symbolising her virtue and humility.

As Anne prepared, the men and women taking part in the coronation procession were marshalled into order outside her windows. Anne and her husband were to be escorted by retinues that included the contingent summoned by Richard from York on 10 June.[3] The gentlemen of the north were originally from the Neville affinity, but Gloucester had won them over with his sense of justice. Now Anne's extended family, including the FitzHughs and Sir John Conyers, escorted the duke and his wife to their coronation. Amongst the throng that day were Scropes, Harringtons, Middletons and Ashtons whom Anne had known since childhood. The king's cavalcade left first, accompanied by the sound of trumpets followed by the clatter of heralds, sergeants and yeomen all wearing the king's white boar device. Anne may have looked at her husband in his purple velvet riding gown sewn with over 3,000 ermine tails and gilt spurs[4] as he set off; she may have thought of her father who went to such lengths to ensure that one of his daughters should be married to a future king of England. It seemed likely at that moment that his grandson would one day sit upon the throne.

Anne's procession was headed by her gentlemen ushers, William Joseph and John Vavasour, dressed in crimson doublets.[5] She was 'carried on an open litter between palfreys trapped in white damask'[6] rather than riding on a palfrey which was led behind her. She travelled beneath a canopy made from white damask and white cloth of gold, decorated with ribbon and gold fringe.[7] It tinkled as it moved, thanks to the bells that decorated its staves. Anne's retinue trooped behind her down Cheapside with its brightly-coloured banners, choirs of children and conduits spouting wine. The displays of pageantry, like so much else, had been in preparation for the coronation of Richard's nephew Edward V.

Chariots conveyed twelve of the most important of Anne's ladies. All of the ladies in the procession wore blue velvet gowns presented to them as part of their coronation gifts and liveries. Amongst them was Anne's own illegitimate half-sister Margaret Huddleston who received a gift from the king as an indication of her special favour.[8] Anne's ladies all knew first-hand the consequences of the Wars of the Roses. Many of them had played their own part in the conflict. Anne's great-aunt, Elizabeth Talbot, the Duchess of Norfolk, was the sister of Lady Eleanor Butler who had been named King Edward IV's legal wife, making the subsequent union with Elizabeth Woodville bigamous. Katherine Neville, another Duchess of

Norfolk, who was also Anne and Richard's aunt, had been married to Elizabeth Woodville's brother John despite their age difference. He had been executed on the orders of Anne's father in 1469 after the Battle of Edgecote. The four times married duchess survived all her children, but this was the last time that she would be seen in public. Richard's sister Elizabeth, the Duchess of Suffolk, was also there. Her father-in-law William de la Pole, blamed for the loss of English territory in France and financial mismanagement, had been murdered on his way to exile in 1450 after the Commons impeached him. King Henry VI had tried to save his favourite but to no avail. The ship carrying him to Calais was intercepted and Suffolk was executed. His body, with his head on a pole next to it, was left on the beach at Dover.

Lady Margaret Beaufort, the mother of Henry Tudor, was also present. Her first husband, Edmund Tudor, Earl of Richmond, was King Henry VI's half-brother. She had served Margaret of Anjou as part of the royal household. Her second husband, Sir Henry Stafford, was a relation of Anne's. He had switched his loyalties from the House of Lancaster to the House of York after the Battle of Towton in 1461, and served King Edward IV at Barnet where he was seriously injured. He died on 4 October 1471. The countess married Thomas Stanley the following year. Stanley had once been married to Anne's aunt Eleanor Neville, but he distanced himself from Warwick when it became expedient to do so. Stanley's transition from King Edward's household to Richard's was not entirely smooth according to Sir Thomas More's account. On the morning of Hastings' arrest and execution, Stanley was injured by an axe-wielding man-at-arms and was only saved from serious injury by falling under the table. Polydore Vergil noted that Stanley was apprehended with the bishops of York and Ely who were also at the fateful council meeting. He was released soon afterwards and the whole matter was smoothed over.

Anne's ladies-in-waiting, riding palfreys, followed after the carriages. There were women in the retinue that Anne knew from Middleham as well as her half-sister. Viscount Lovell's wife Anne was there. Lady Elizabeth Scrope of Masham, another of Anne's cousins, was also resplendent in blue velvet, as was Lady Mountjoy. The coronation was a family affair in other respects. Another cousin, Lord Maltravers, the heir of the Earl of Arundel, was present in Richard's procession. His mother Joan Neville was Anne's aunt. Nor was this Maltravers' first coronation; he had attended Edward IV's crowning in 1461 and, like his aunt Katherine Neville, had been required by Edward to marry into the Woodville family. His wife was Margaret Woodville, but there is no mention of Lady Maltravers amongst Anne's ladies. Joyce Percy, the wife of Sir Robert Percy of Scotton, was also in attendance. It seemed that Anne was surrounded by women to whom she was either related or had known for most of her life.

Anne was presented with a void, or light refreshment, of wine and spices at the end of her journey before supper in the great chamber of Westminster. Last minute preparations for the following day's coronation continued behind the scenes. The following morning, Anne was dressed in a clean smock before being helped into a surcoat and crimson velvet anointing robes. All her ladies were clad in their own red gowns and mantles. Shortly before 8.00 am, Anne's chamberlain led her into Westminster Hall where Richard and his retinue were already gathered. Both she and Gloucester were barefoot. Today Richard would be reborn, through his anointing with holy oils, as King Richard III, while Anne arrived as a duchess and departed the abbey as his queen consort. Bishop Stillington was at Richard's side as he approached the altar where the crown awaited. Lady Margaret Beaufort was given the honour of carrying Anne's train. No one could have guessed the hopes and fears that passed through either woman's mind as they made their solemn progress. Margaret, who had met with Richard before the coronation, was hopeful that her son Henry might soon be permitted to return from exile.

The king was anointed first as Anne looked on. The Bishops of Norwich and Exeter led her in her turn to the altar where she prostrated herself on cushions. When she arose, the circlet was removed from her head by one of her ladies who also unlaced the front of her gown. Her forehead and breast were anointed with holy oil amidst prayer before one of her ladies relaced the queen's gown. Francis Lovell, a familiar face from her childhood, now appointed to the post of Lord Chamberlain, purchased Anne a ring of sapphires and pearls at Richard's command before the coronation.[9] This was now blessed and placed on her right hand, and the circlet was replaced by a crown. She was then given a sceptre in her right hand and a rod in her left which depicted the dove of peace.

Anne was led to a raised dais where she curtseyed to her husband before taking her place on a throne positioned slightly lower than Richard's. A Mass followed, before the couple were led to a room near St Edward's shrine where they breakfasted and changed their robes – Anne wore a robe of purple velvet – before returning to their thrones. The crowning ceremony concluded when they processed to Westminster Hall before withdrawing to their chambers. At four o'clock in the afternoon Queen Anne re-joined her husband beneath the Cloth of State in Westminster Hall for another feast that lasted late into the night. Every cook and scullion in Westminster had been busy since before the sun rose and now roast crane and cygnets arrived, followed by peacocks dressed in their plumage, venison and fish. Anne was served by Lady Margaret Beaufort and the Duchess of Norfolk. The week ahead included more feasting, pageantry and a tournament.

Queen Anne was Richard's wife long before he became king. Although she was the daughter of a traitor and the widow of a Lancastrian prince in a Yorkist regime, she brought political advantage to Gloucester in the north on their marriage. Her position as Duchess of Gloucester was a secure one in a familiar environment while King Edward IV was alive. As queen she had already fulfilled her main responsibility in providing the king with a legitimate heir, if not a spare. It was also her duty to use her wifely influence as an intercessor for mercy from the monarch on behalf of his people. More recently, Elizabeth Woodville and Margaret of Anjou were both actors upon the political stage promoting their own interests. Anne's mother-in-law Duchess Cecily used the title King's Mother and played her own role in the country's affairs, both on the public stage and behind the scenes because of the relationship she had with her sons. Closeness to the throne brought influence which in turn gave consorts and royal mothers power. Anne's influence over Richard before he became king remains unknown because of the lack of written evidence.

Chapter 16

A Royal Progress

Anne's son, who remained quietly in Wensleydale with his household, received an unexpected gift from the City of York in the weeks after his parents' coronation. On 12 July 1483 the House Books for the city record that Edward was to be gifted with 'two barrels of wine, six herons, two dozen rabbits'[1] and the finest quality white bread. The mayor and aldermen delivered the gift themselves. Edward, the son of a duke and his representative in the north, knew that good manners were required from him even if the gift was not designed to appeal to a small boy.

Anne and Richard spent the week following their coronation at Greenwich. Edward, now a prince, became the Lord Lieutenant of Ireland. It was a role held by the boy's uncle and grandfather, and it was synonymous with the heir to the throne. For Richard, as newly crowned king, it was important that his subjects bore witness to his newly enhanced status. He began this process by going on a progress, beginning with a journey through the Thames Valley. The royal couple arrived at Windsor on 19 July 1483 before continuing to Reading.

The king would journey to Minster Lovell, Gloucester and Tewkesbury before travelling to Warwick at the beginning of August. Sir Thomas More speculated that before the king met with Anne, he gave Sir James Tyrell the order to murder his two nephews in the Tower.[2] While he was at Tewkesbury the king visited Isabel and Clarence's tomb and gave the abbot £310 as well as clearing Clarence's debts. It is probable that he also gave orders for a large flat blue stone to be installed, as described in *The Gentleman's Magazine* of 1826, which also detailed the marks left by the brass which once inlaid it. It has been suggested that there was also funerary brass, but both are long since vanished.[3]

By 8 August the king was at Warwick where he was met by Anne who arrived with the Spanish ambassador as well as her nephew Edward, Earl of Warwick. While they were at Warwick, John Rous presented his history of the Beauchamp family to Anne. This version contained an image of Anne in her coronation robes, her husband and her son who the queen had not seen since the end of May. The court remained in the castle for a week before travelling to Coventry, Leicester and then Nottingham where Edward of Middleham was created Prince of Wales on 24 August. John Kendal, the king's secretary, wrote a letter while they were in Nottingham which was sent to York ahead of the royal couple. In it he hinted that if the city put on a good welcome, the king would consider reducing the city's fee farm, or fixed rent, for 'there come many southern lords and men of worship with them'.[4] The royal couple, along with their lords and ladies, continued to Pontefract where they were joined by their son Edward who left Middleham on 19 August. From Pontefract, where Anne's grandfather was executed in 1460, the royal family travelled to York on 29 August where they were welcomed at Micklegate Bar by the mayor and aldermen in all their finery. The king sent Sir James Tyrell, who was now Richard's Master of Horse and Master of the King's Henchmen, back to London on a mission to collect apparel from the Wardrobe for Edward of Middleham's investiture as Prince of Wales which was to take place the following week. Polydore Vergil concluded that Tyrell's instructions were a cover to kill Edward V and Richard, Duke of York.[5]

In York, Anne and Richard's three-week visit was well underway amidst entertainment and splendour. On 7 September, the Trinity Guild, of which Anne and Richard were both members, performed in a creed play, probably in twelve scenes, paid for by York's officials, employing the wagons used by the annual Corpus Christi miracle plays.[6] The king's retinue made its way through streets hung with tapestries and banners, crowded with men and women wearing the king's white boar livery badge to the Minster. Richard, Anne and Edward were met at the west door by the dean and the clergy, and were anointed with holy water. Prayers for the king were followed by a *Te Deum*.[7]

The following day Anne put on her crown and processed though York's streets once more. It was the feast of the Nativity of the Blessed Virgin Mary. She and her family attended Mass in the Minster.[8] Edward was formally invested as Prince of Wales and Earl of Chester at the archbishop's palace, just as Anne's first husband was styled from infancy onwards and as Richard's nephew, Edward, had also been named. The first died at the end of a bloody battle while the second disappeared behind the walls of the Tower. As the queen led her son by the hand through the streets to the Minster afterwards, in a display that the *Croyland Chronicle* described as a second coronation,[9] she might have pondered upon the tricks played on princes by the wheel of fate. Or she might have basked in the loyalty shown by the north to her husband and son.

At the same time that Edward was invested, his cousin the Earl of Warwick and half-brother, Gloucester's illegitimate son, John of Gloucester, were both knighted alongside Edward.[10] Richard presented the Minster with twelve silver gilt figures of the apostles. He also gave decorated copes and a large cross standing on six steps decorated with the two thieves who were crucified alongside Christ, figures of angels and jewels.[11] It was an act of eye-catching piety, though whether it expiated the crime of a double nepoticide is another matter entirely. In the summer of 1483 Richard and Anne were nothing if not regal. The north had a monarch and consort of whom they could be proud.

It has been hypothesised that Anne's niece Margaret accompanied the royal party north, and that Isabel's children remained there as wards of their uncle King Richard III when the king and queen returned to London.[12] Had the royal line of succession been strictly followed, Isabel and Clarence's son should have been king rather than Richard. But as the Earl of Warwick was a child, he lacked supporters who might have pressed his own claims to the throne. Nonetheless it was perhaps expedient to keep him from the eyes of Londoners. The following week the king reduced the city's fee farm so he must have been pleased with the spectacle offered by the townspeople of York.[13]

It was during this visit to the city that Richard decided to found a chantry in York where one hundred priests would pray for his soul and the souls of his family. It is possible that he was considering York Minster as a family mausoleum. The relationship with York was one that he intended to nurture. On 21 September Anne and her son, Edward, went to Middleham Castle. It is unclear why Anne did not travel with Richard throughout the earlier part of his progress although the reason could have been suggestive of underlying ill health. As queen she was expected to take a leading role at court and in the spectacle of royalty. She fulfilled that role in York, in the heart of the Neville north, but she was notable by her absence elsewhere.

The king and his household departed for Pontefract. Richard had demonstrated himself to be a popular leader in the north of England, but his capital was in the south and his popularity there was waning rapidly. London seethed with rumours and whispers of sedition. The Yorkists were now divided between those men who supported Richard and those who upheld the rights of King Edward V. After rumours of the young king and his brother's death became more prevalent, many men gave their loyalty to the only potential heir to the throne not in Richard's custody – Henry Tudor.

The king continued to Lincoln and it was here that the celebrations surrounding his coronation came to an abrupt end. Buckingham, who had given his support to Richard and who had received significant rewards, transferred his allegiance from Richard to Henry Tudor either at the end of August or the beginning of September 1483. It is possible that Buckingham, a descendant of King Edward III, had his own ambitions for the throne. He may have felt that the king was not sufficiently grateful for Buckingham's own role as kingmaker, or there might have been another reason entirely. The truth will never be known. Although the rebellion bears his name, the uprising involved both Lancastrians and Yorkists including members of Edward IV's former household. Lady Margaret Beaufort, who had so recently played a role at Anne's coronation was part of the conspiracy, as was Elizabeth Woodville. Between them the two women helped to bring together the various groups who questioned Richard's right to rule.

Richard may have developed a powerful affinity in the north of the country during the previous decade, but he did not have the loyalty of the Midlands or the south. A series of risings was planned for 19 October 1483 across the south-east and south-west of the country, but in Kent the uprising started early on 10 October. The lack of co-ordination would have dramatic consequences for Buckingham who marched an army out of Wales in the company of Cardinal Morton, having refused Richard's request that he explain himself. Fortunately for the king, it proved impossible for the duke to meet up with rebels from the west led by the Bishop of Exeter – the same man who escorted Anne to the altar for her coronation – because of the torrential rain that caused the Severn and the Wye to flood. Henry Tudor and his uncle Jasper, troubled by storms at sea, failed to land their troops in time and turned back to Brittany.

Buckingham hid from the king's wrath, but was betrayed and executed in Salisbury on 2 November. All that was left was for Richard's forces to mop up the rebels.

Richard's claim to the throne was based on his legitimacy and his own morality which he contrasted with the immorality of his late brother. He used the same arguments to persuade people to accept his rule during Buckingham's rebellion. At Leicester, in October, before he marched against the rebels, he issued a 'proclamation for the reform of morals' against the rebel ringleaders. The Woodvilles and their ilk were 'horrible adulterers and bawds'.[14] He reminded the world that the Marquis of Dorset was a man of insatiable sexual appetite. Dorset fled from sanctuary via the West Country to Henry Tudor in Brittany.

By contrast to the corruption at the heart of Edward's court, Richard portrayed himself as a respectable man. The king's response to the rebellion was authoritative, but he chose to replace men of doubtful allegiance or who had gone to their deaths in the rebellion with men from the north who he knew he could trust. An influx of strangers from the north caused further resentment and suspicion in the south. Once it was safe to do so, Anne, a virtuous and quiet wife, returned to her husband's side leaving their son at Middleham. With her came a household of ladies from the north, including her half-sister, Margaret.

Chapter 17

An Enigma – Piety and Patronage

Anne's separation from her husband during Buckingham's rebellion meant that she could not fulfil a medieval queen's duty in its aftermath to plead for mercy for any of the rebels. There was an expectation that a consort would intercede for mercy with the monarch on behalf of their subjects as well as for the needs of their immediate family. Anne, largely undocumented, was not one of the fifteenth century's more colourful queens. Margaret of Anjou was actively involved in the politics and warfare of the period, while Elizabeth Woodville demonstrated the indirect power that a consort could wield through her influence. Queens were also required to be conventionally beautiful as well as personally virtuous and pious. Religious patronage was a demonstration of the latter. It might be achieved by pilgrimage, the giving of gifts, endowments, the granting of advowsons and, on a more personal level, even by the embroidery of vestments and altar clothes.

A poem dating from the fourteenth and fifteenth centuries entitled *How the good wiff taught hir daughter* depicts a mother teaching her daughter about a wife's duty to go to church and worship God. The poem suggests that conventional piety was a prerequisite to making a good marriage. The woman's role, it appears from the poem, was not only to care for her own religious wellbeing but for that of her family and wider household.[1] During the fifteenth century, women from aristocratic and gentry families were actively involved in the foundation of chantries and in projects that repaired, extended or beautified church buildings. In many cases it is the only remaining historical footprint to their identity.[2] As a queen, Anne's duty extended from the religious wellbeing of her family to the realm as a whole, but she remained in the shadow of her husband's public piety both as duchess and queen. She did not have the 'soveraynetee'[3] of a widow. She was more like Patient Griselda – charming, compliant and obedient to her husband's wishes. Even the chantry founded by Middleham's chaplain John Cartmel at York Minster to pray for Anne's grandparents, the Earl and Countess of Salisbury, was completed under Richard's aegis.[4]

Just as Countess Anne encouraged Richard Neville to assume guardianship of her Beauchamp heritage, Gloucester inherited traditions of patronising the churches that Anne's Neville forefathers once maintained. As Peter Idley wrote in the instructions for his son, 'thy wife thou love in perfect wise, in thought and deed, as heartily as though can.'[5] This suggests that Anne and Richard's marriage was perhaps a partnership. Even though her husband was the senior partner, the couple was bound together by loyalty and duty whether Richard was a duke or a king.

Anne joined the fraternity of the Corpus Christi in York in 1477 or thereabouts, when she was Gloucester's duchess. It was one of the most important guilds in the north of England. Whoever took note of her enrolment failed to pay attention. Rather than Anne, she is identified as Elizabeth. Francis Lovel and his wife, who was Anne's cousin, were already members. It is possible that the duchess joined because of the guild's intercessory role in her soul's salvation through her charitable offerings, but her motive, or Richard's, was just as likely to have been social or political.

She was also a member of the Sisterhood of Durham Cathedral Priory. It cannot be a total surprise that she felt an affiliation to Durham. Several of her ancestors were buried there, but as with York, Richard was also associated closely with Durham so the piety was a shared demonstration of both faith and patronage. In 1474 the monks of St Cuthbert's in Durham consulted with Gloucester on a legal matter. During April the monks entertained the duke and admitted him to the priory confraternity. In 1476 Anne was also admitted to the organisation. Anne is present, but her voice is indistinct. It was not unusual. Although many women became guild members, it was often because men took the course of becoming joint members with their wives. More often than not, the women who joined in their own right were widows.[6]

Patronage of chantries and churches was designed to ensure perpetual prayers for the donor, their closest family and anyone else identified in the licence or founding charter. Anne and her husband believed in the doctrine of Purgatory that stated souls went to a place somewhere between Heaven and Hell in order to be cleansed of their sins before journeying to their final destination. Prayers speeded the process. In 1483, a month after Buckingham's execution, King Richard issued a licence to James Charlton for a chantry dedicated to St James at St Mary's Church, Ricall some 8 miles south of York on the way to Selby. The chaplains were to say prayers for Richard, Anne and their son Edward during their lives and for their souls after death. The king also included prayers for his parents in the agreement.[7] Further licences for chantries were granted to William Chamberlain.[8] Anne is mentioned as a beneficiary of each chantry's prayers, but it is Richard who is the active patron. Like much else about Anne, there is no existing written evidence of her decision-making to give her a distinct voice in the creation of the chantries with which she and her husband were associated.

Richard's piety and status was publicly displayed at Middleham and Barnard Castle in the collegiate churches commissioned there prior to his accession to the throne. Work began with royal licence for them being granted by King Edward IV on 21 February 1477, shortly after Clarence's execution and the marriage of Richard, Duke of York to Ann Mowbray.[9] The foundations are usually associated with Gloucester but would he not have consulted with his duchess? The ordinance for the Collegiate Church of St Mary and St Alkelda at Middleham references Anne only in the context of requiem Masses. However, the collegiate church at Middleham not only signalled virtue, but also pointed to Anne's lineage and Gloucester's self-adopted stance as a northerner.

Anne is absent from the written record in the context of active church and chantry building. Instead, inferences must be drawn. Each of the stalls that was to be created in the quire of the college at Middleham was identified with either the Virgin Mary or a saint. It is within the choice of saints that a distant echo of Anne's voice may perhaps be heard. St George received mention, as did St Katherine, the patron saint of maidens whose saint day marked the arrival of Advent.[10] This popular saint was known to have a large female following so Katherine's inclusion as one of Middleham's saints might have been at the behest of Anne. Katherine was one of the Fourteen Holy Helpers of the medieval world who were especially venerated because it was believed that their intercession was particularly effective. Equally Katherine's invocation as an intervention against sudden death might have been sufficient grounds for inclusion, or even because of her association with Rouen where Duchess Cecily spent time.

Another possible, though tenuous, correlation to Anne can be established in the chair dedicated to St Barbara, another virgin and holy helper, who refused an offer of marriage arranged by her father. Barbara was eventually beheaded by her parent who was struck by lightning on his way home. She was often invoked against lightning strikes and fires, but Barbara was also the patron saint of artillerymen. Anne's father was known for his innovative use of artillery. He was certainly wealthy enough to furnish his artillerymen with the best equipment available. St Winifred is even more likely to have been chosen by Anne and her mother. Countess Anne's father Richard Beauchamp left money for a golden statue of himself to be dedicated at, amongst other places, St Winifred's shrine in Shrewsbury where her relics were housed.[11] Isabel Despenser, Anne's grandmother, left velvet cloth to the shrine in her will. As King Richard III, Anne's husband gave a gift to the chantry priests at Shrewsbury in 1484. The Beauchamp family associations with St Winifred hint that Richard listened to Anne's preferences on this occasion.

Richard provided further funds for the improvement of St Mary's Church at Barnard Castle. It was enlarged with a new porch and a two-storey vestry, roof, windows and new chancel arch. A corbel on one side of the arch was made in a likeness of Richard while the other may have been Anne, although some sources states that it is King Edward IV! The collegiate church would have supported a dean, twelve priests and sixteen choristers to say Masses for the souls of Richard and his family. The chantry, which was destined to become a royal peculiar, was never completed because of the brevity of Richard's reign. Although it is impossible to overlook Richard's achievements as a religious and architectural patron, it becomes impossible to give Anne further voice either as duchess or queen. By the summer of 1484 Richard, now the king, planned an additional college of priests in the north, this one in York itself. He intended that more than one hundred priests should say daily Masses and prayers for himself and his family. There were already more than one hundred perpetual chantries in York, second only to London, so it is likely that Richard was seeking to create a location where he, Anne and their descendants might be buried. The nunnery at Wilberfoss also received his support in return for prayers for himself,

Anne and Edward. Having made a start with his plans, the king began to issue decrees and make grants that would turn his college into a reality. Vergil, having described King Richard III's many alleged murders in great detail, including King Henry VI and Edward IV's sons, did not see the foundation as the work of a pious man rather the desperate actions of one whose hands were red with blood:

> ...to geave the hew and cowntenance of a good man, wherby he might be accowntyd more righteous, more mylde, better affectyd to the commonaltie, and more lyberall especially toward the powr; and so first might meryte pardon for his offences at Gods hand.[12]

Of Anne there was no mention, but St William's College, York, was founded by Anne's uncle George Neville, Bishop of Exeter, later Archbishop of York. Warwick provided much of the funding for the twenty-three chantry priests it housed in 1461. The land which Warwick donated was held inalienably by the college. Once again Anne's husband was fulfilling his obligations as the successor to the Neville lords of the North suggesting both loyalty and a degree of partnership.

As queen there was a precedent for Anne, in her own right, to patronise university colleges for the improvement of learning and the betterment of the clergy to provide for the spiritual welfare of their flocks, as well as providing patronage to family institutions. King Henry VI founded King's College Cambridge. Queen's College came under the patronage of his queen, its first charter being granted in 1446 to Andrew Doket, an advisor of the king; the second was issued in 1448 re-founding the college on a better site and recognising that no English queen had previously founded a college in Cambridge. One of the witnesses to the second charter was Anne's grandfather, the Earl of Salisbury, as was his brother-in-law, the Duke of York. The foundation stone to the college was laid by the queen's chamberlain, Sir John Wenlock, who would play such an important part in the lives of Isabel and Anne because of his changed allegiance from Lancaster to the Earl of Warwick in the aftermath of the First Battle of St Albans. Once the Yorkists were on the throne, the patronage of Queens' College transferred to King Edward IV's queen, Elizabeth Woodville, in part due to Doket's petitioning. With the death of Edward and the ascension to the throne of King Richard III, it was inevitable that Anne would become the next patron of the college.

It was the king and not the queen, following the pattern of their lives as duke and duchess, who issued a licence on 25 March 1484 stating that the college existed because of Anne's patronage. Further gifts of land, originating from Anne's inheritance, were also made in the queen's name. Amongst the gifts was the advowson of St Denys Church, Stanford in the Vale, where Anne and Richard may have been married in 1472. This grant was revoked after the Battle of Bosworth, the advowson returned to Countess Anne who immediately conveyed her rights to Henry VII.[13] The patronage of Queen's College would continue in the hands of the royal family, but it was Lady Margaret Beaufort, Henry Tudor's mother, who became involved with both Queens' College and Jesus College rather than Elizabeth of York who, like Anne, stayed out of the limelight. Although Anne's successor did sometimes take a stand on the public stage, her husband was careful to ensure there were no reminders that she had a better right to rule than him.

Without sources such as letters and diaries to give a more intimate insight into her mind, there is little indication of how Anne's beliefs may have evolved as fortune's wheel revolved. Book ownership, particularly by the women of the Neville family, offers a small window to personal belief and piety.[14] Anne Neville's great-grandmother Joan Beaufort, Countess of Westmorland owned a considerable library of devotional texts including a book of hours. Joan's affinity for books is known to have been shared by Anne's aunts, the duchesses Buckingham and York who left books to their family in their wills. The Beauchamp family also patronised the arts. Anne's grandmother, Isabel Despenser, the wife of the 13th earl, was the patron of Lydgate's *Fifteen Joys*. Unfortunately, although large numbers of beautifully illustrated books survive from the medieval period, only one can be traced specifically to Anne. It does not mean that she did not own any, simply that there are no bequests of books made to or by her, and evidence of ownership within the books themselves is lacking. It is highly likely that she owned a book of hours, for instance. They were especially popular texts designed for private prayer. Different prayers, psalms and hymns might be added according to the requirements of the person commissioning the volume. At the time of their marriage Gloucester is not thought to have owned his famous book of hours.[15]

It was certainly acquired after he became king because he amended the calendar for 2 October to note his birthday and he referenced himself as *Ricardus Rex* – King Richard. It has been suggested that Richard's Hours are sufficiently similar to those of Anne's uncle, Henry Beauchamp, for the book to have been a gift from either Anne herself or even Countess Anne, suggesting a better familial relationship than the one often painted by posterity.[16]

The only book Anne is known to have owned for a certainty is *The Booke of Gostlye Grace* by the mystic Mechtild (St Mathilda) of Hackborn.[17] Her name 'Anne Warrewyk' together with her husband's is written in the flyleaf,[18] lending itself to the idea that the couple shared their piety. In the north of England, it was often read by members of the Guild of Corpus Christi in York. More likely though was that Mechtild was recommended by Anne's mother-in-law Duchess Cecily, who is regarded as the devotional text's 'most prominent owner and reader'.[19] The text considers that everything comes from God and that an individual must find spiritual truth in a personal relationship with Christ grounded in oneness of the spirit. The shared devotional text, like much else about Anne and her husband, indicates a combined approach. However, because Richard is known to have owned many other texts and to have commissioned manuscripts once he became king, Anne is once again placed at a disadvantage within the historical record. It is impossible to know the extent to which Anne engaged with religious or secular books, let alone whether she discussed their content with her mother, sister or husband.

Either Anne or her mother commissioned John Rous to create the armorial roll-chronicle in English about the deeds of the Beauchamp earls presented to her in 1483 at Warwick on her way to York. In all probability it was so that her son Edward could learn about his ancestors. One image in the roll shows Anne in her coronation robes, Richard in the centre and Edward on the right – a miniature version of his father. A copy of the *De re militari* by Vegetius translated into English[20] is also thought to have been made for Edward because of the griffin of Salisbury depicted on its opening page, together with a decorated initial containing the royal coat of arms supported by Richard's emblem of the boar. The text also contains a decorated initial letter showing the arms of Anne Neville. She might have been a silent partner in her marriage, but Warwick's youngest daughter emerges as a model medieval wife – mild, pious and beautiful.

Chapter 18

Sudden Grief

Anne's son remained in the north throughout the summer and winter of 1483–84. His household was paid and his education continued. It is possible that his visits to Jervaulx and Coverham in the summer of 1483 were in preparation for his first communion. The purchase of a primer and psalter support this view.[1] There is no evidence that Edward joined the Christmas festivities at court that year. It might have been expected because the visible presence of an heir would have reinforced Richard's position. Either the boy was too young to attend, was in poor health or the king wanted to keep him out of London for another reason. At least in Middleham he was safe.

Anne was at Nottingham celebrating Easter on 20 April 1484 when news arrived that her son had died after a short illness. The *Croyland Chronicle* recorded that the king and queen were 'in a state almost bordering on madness, by reason of their sudden grief'.[2] Rous described the boy's parents as being stricken. Edward was their only child and they seem to have been unprepared for his death, suggesting that even if he was, as is sometimes intimated, a sickly child, that his illness was not regarded as life-threatening. *The Croyland Chronicle* described a 'short illness'.[3] Historians today speculate that the boy died from tuberculosis which was exceptionally contagious.

The king and queen left Nottingham almost immediately and returned to Middleham. No exact record remains as to exactly where Edward is buried. Locations from York Minster, Middleham, Jervaulx Abbey and Sheriff Hutton have been suggested. Records for the king's whereabouts suggest that he went to Middleham for two days at the beginning of May; Anne was with him so he may have attended his son's funeral. However, royal protocol dictated against monarchs attending the funerals of their children. There is a damaged alabaster effigy of a young boy in the north-east corner of the church of St Helen and the Holy Cross at Sheriff Hutton. His face is largely eroded, but on his head rests what appears to be a coronet. If Edward was buried in Sheriff Hutton, his remains are more likely to rest in the southern side of the church where other members of the Neville family are buried. Together with the coronet, the location and armorial bearings that can still be found in the church, the balance of probability suggests that this is the last resting place of Anne's only known child. Other research suggests that while the boy on the tomb is likely to be a Neville, the effigy dates from the first half of the fifteenth century rather than the second half. If Richard intended York to become the family mausoleum, it is likely that no effigy would have been commissioned. Instead, when the time was right the remains of Edward would have been reinterred inside a magnificent chantry chapel.

Richard faced a new vulnerability to add to his grief. Like King Henry VI before him, he was a king without an heir. To their contemporaries Edward's death could have been seen as a punishment from God or an indicator of Richard's unworthiness to rule. It was essential for the stability of the realm that Anne provided her husband with another son as soon as possible. But Anne became increasingly fragile. Like Edward she may have been suffering from the 'white plague', as tuberculosis was often called. Her health and vitality gradually wasted away as the disease took its inevitable course. Later Polydore Vergil would write that the king began to complain about his consort. But in the months immediately following their son's death, there was no rumour of the king seeking to set Anne aside.

All that remained from Anne's immediate family were Countess Anne and Isabel's children. Margaret and her brother Edward were well treated and may have stayed at Sandal Castle near Wakefield[4] which was where the king's permanent household was located rather than at Sheriff Hutton or even Middleham, even though Middleham was described as the 'Windsor of the North' because of its magnificence. On 8 June 1484 the king, who was at Pontefract, ordered fabrics including velvet, satin and cloth of gold for new clothes for Anne's nephew and niece as well as his own illegitimate daughter Katherine Plantagenet. The order included materials for Katherine's betrothed, William Herbert, Earl of Huntingdon, who carried the sceptre at Anne's coronation. It is probable that the clothes were intended for Katherine and William's forthcoming wedding.[5] The information about the clothing was only retained because of a lawsuit against Richard III's former solicitor, Thomas Lynom, heard during 1500, pertaining to payment for the cost of fabrics owed to Peter Courteys, the Keeper of the Great Wardrobe during Richard's reign. It is a reminder that just because there is a complete absence of Anne's own accounts from the historic record, it does not mean to say that they never existed. As queen, Anne had her own household and did not always travel with the king; if she commissioned the Rous Roll, the funds must have been available to her.

During the spring of 1484 Elizabeth Woodville emerged from sanctuary having reached an agreement with Richard and released her daughters into his care on the understanding that he would arrange suitable marriages for them. Cecily Plantagenet may have become part of Queen Anne's household with her elder sister Elizabeth, or it might have been arranged for her to join the household at Sandal. It was also settled that Cecily should marry Ralph Scrope of Upsall. The Scropes were part of the Neville affinity who transferred their allegiance to Richard while he was Duke of Gloucester. The marriage took place but Cecily later sought an annulment, claiming that she and her husband were related within prohibited degrees because both were descended from Joan Beaufort, the second wife of Ralph Neville, 1st Earl of Westmorland. As the illegitimate daughter of a king, the match was an appropriate one as well as a reward for Scope's loyalty to Richard. Later when the *Titulus Regulus* was reversed, the union was not suitable for the legitimate sister of Henry Tudor's queen.

On 21 August 1484 Richard made his sister Elizabeth's son, John de la Pole, Lieutenant of Ireland. It was a post traditionally held by the heir to the throne. The king also created the Council of the North and named Lincoln its president. It is likely to have been a strategy to ensure Richard's continued dominance of the region.[6] It was essential for the stability of the realm that the king should not appear weak. Already there were rumours that Henry Tudor was preparing an invasion fleet. Anne's uncle by marriage, John de Vere, 13th Earl of Oxford, had been imprisoned in Hammes Castle in the Calais Pale since 1474, but his presence on the other side of the Channel bothered Richard who ordered the earl's removal to England on 28 October.[7] It was too late. Oxford escaped in the company of the man ordered to keep him secure before making his way to join Henry Tudor. 'Giddy Fortune's furious fickle wheel'[8] was turning against Anne and her husband.

Chapter 19

Christmas 1484

During the Christmas season of 1484, rumours arose that Richard was contemplating setting Anne aside and making a marriage to his own niece Elizabeth of York, the eldest daughter of King Edward IV and Elizabeth Woodville. The *Croyland Chronicle* stated that the gossip arose from a trick played by Anne on Richard involving the two women changing their clothes. The monastic chronicler describes a mischievous scene that flouted court conventions and criticised the dancing and gaiety of the court that year. It sounds as though Anne and her husband were putting a brave public face on their private grief. It does not suggest a woman in fear of her husband. Perhaps the queen wished to put Elizabeth at her ease? Anne knew what it was like to be an outsider in an alien household from her time in Margaret of Anjou's company. It has been suggested that the familiarity with which Anne treated Elizabeth was that of a sister for a younger sibling.[1]

Polydore Vergil, no friend of the Yorkists, claimed that Richard blamed Anne for her failure to conceive, and that the relationship between husband and wife was stretched to the extent that the king planned her death. The *Croyland Chronicle* did not take this view, but did state that Richard sought to divorce his wife so that he might remarry. It also hinted of other matters that the chronicler rather coyly chose not to write about because they were distasteful. The unpleasant rumour that everyone knew was that Elizabeth of York was pregnant by her uncle. What is unknown is whether Richard ever considered marrying Elizabeth or the lengths to which Elizabeth, the eldest daughter of Edward IV, was prepared to go to regain her father's throne. Leviticus, from which the laws of consanguinity and prohibited degrees of relationship evolved, states that a man cannot marry his aunt. It does not say he cannot marry his niece, even though he would have been related to both in the same degree.[2] The Spanish branch of the Hapsburgs made three such marriages in the years after 1550.

It was true that Elizabeth was a decade younger than Anne, who was 28 years old, and that she was described by the Venetian Ambassador as 'very handsome'.[3] Tudor chroniclers were anxious to blacken the name of the last Plantagenet king in order to justify King Henry VII's claim to the throne, in exactly the same way that Richard sought to blacken Edward's reputation in 1483, and Warwick arranged for Henry VI to be depicted at the heart of a rotten court in 1461. Reports of the Christmas season of 1484 turned Anne into another one of her husband's alleged victims and Elizabeth into a fair maiden in need of rescue. It was a short step from whispers of an annulment to assassination. The evidence for Richard's dastardly plan was a purported conversation between an unnaturally garrulous monarch and the godly Thomas Rotherham, Archbishop of York, that 'the queen should not long lyve.'[4] Whether the king was likely to share his desire to murder his wife with a leading churchman or was expressing a genuine concern because Anne's illness was terminal is a matter of interpretation.

On 6 January 1485, the last day of the Yuletide festivities filled the court with the sounds of laughter and revelry. The sound rang hollow for the king, aware that his wife was more fragile than ever, that he had no legitimate heir and that Henry Tudor was planning to launch an invasion that summer. There was no need to kill Anne – it was obvious that she was fading away. What the chroniclers did not know was that in recognising his queen did not have long to live, Richard arranged for an envoy to depart for Rome in order to facilitate arrangements for a marriage between himself and Joanna of Aviz. Anne's husband planned that there would be an Anglo-Portuguese alliance which should be further cemented with a marriage for Elizabeth with Joanna's cousin, Manuel of Beja. Like Clarence before him, Richard understood the necessity of making an advantageous second marriage as soon as possible after the death of his first wife.

It has been suggested that Anne suffered from tuberculosis, a common airborne disease, which may have killed her son Edward as well as her sister Isabel. Today it is associated with poverty, but in the medieval period it was endemic. Besides destroying her lungs, consumption, or phthisis as the disease was known, would have gradually eroded most of Anne's internal systems. She may have suffered from the progressive wasting disease throughout most of her short time on the throne, although there is no specific evidence of her health failing any earlier. The fact that she did not accompany Richard on the entirety of the 1483 progress may be an indicator of her lack of strength. It is also possible that her health may have declined as a direct result of losing her only child. Intense grief could have weakened her immune system, resulting in latent *Mycobacterium tuberculosis* becoming active. She may even have succumbed to a viral infection. There is no record of Anne's health as an infant or child, although it is often suggested that she may always have been delicate. It would offer an alternative explanation for her absence from the written record. Richard may have taken responsibility for her household expenses and other duties associated with aristocratic women, not to deny his wife agency but to spare her – but without evidence it remains hypothesis.

After Twelfth Night 1485 Anne withdrew from public gaze. Her symptoms developed rapidly. It may have been a few weeks or Anne may have been ill before Christmas and disguised the extent of her fatigue and other symptoms. If she had a cough, it would have become more unpleasant. She may have already been spitting bloody phlegm which must have been alarming for both her and for her ladies-in-waiting. As all her internal systems were consumed by the disease and her appetite failed, flesh melted from her bones. The king made it known that the queen's doctors advised him to stay away from his wife's bed. She suffered from fevers, which would have been treated as an ailment in its own right rather than as a symptom as well as breathlessness and weight loss.

Anne experienced a range of treatments from the inevitable bloodletting to purgatives. Medieval doctors believed that fevers were the result of an excess of hot humour: blood. If Anne was haemorrhaging, it might not have been seen as a bad sign by the people caring for her. The humours within her body were trying to rebalance themselves. Her care might have included trying to balance the overproduction of phlegm, which was considered cold and watery by medieval doctors. She is also likely to have been treated with lungwort based on the doctrine of signatures and the work of Pliny, which identified the spotted leaves of the plant as being similar to diseased lungs. Hildegard of Bingen, writing in the twelfth century, advised an infusion of lungwort in wine for lung complaints. Anne would have been provided with other cures to balance the excess phlegm. But as her illness escalated, all that the queen's doctors could do was provide her with opiates to ease her pain.

It was said later that Anne was sick with grief. The rumour, according to Vergil, emanated from the king as a way of transferring suspicion for Anne's forthcoming demise from himself. Her husband's detractors presented her as being perceptive and brave:

> Whan the queen herd of such terrible rumors dispersyd already of her own death, supposing that hir days wer at an end, she went unto her husband very pensyffe and sadde, and with many teares demandyd of him what cause there was why he should determine hyr death.[5]

Shakespeare made use of the same account to write the scenes in which Richard III arranged for the murder of his long-suffering consort, having seduced her when she was Prince Edward's grieving widow. Unlike Isabel, Anne would not be totally consigned to the shadows. Instead, Anne's death became a vehicle by which Tudor propagandists, historians and playwrights emphasised her husband's villainy. John Rous, who was committed to the Earls of Warwick and owed his loyalty to Countess Anne and her daughter, wrote favourably of Richard during his lifetime but changed his tone towards the former king after Henry's accession. In the English version, Rous describes Richard as an 'especiall good lord'[6] but in the Latin version of the same text, sentences praising the former monarch are removed and his image is replaced with Anne's first husband, Edward of Westminster. The *Historia Regum Angliae* accused Anne's widower of murdering the queen by poison and imprisoning Countess Anne.[7] Anne's status as a Lancastrian princess was rehabilitated for the benefit of the countess, who sought to retrieve what was rightfully hers now that the Plantagenet sons of York were no more. The Lancastrians, in whose cause Warwick died, were back on the throne.

Tudor chroniclers missed an important fact. If the king did wish to be rid of a barren wife, he did not need to resort to poison. The couple were related within the prohibited degrees of consanguinity. Without the correct papal dispensation, the marriage was invalid. The original dispensation granted in 1472, when Anne was in sanctuary, failed to cover all the necessary relationships between the pair. The correct application for an annulment could have left Richard free to remarry as other men and women had done throughout the medieval period.

Anne died at Westminster on 16 March 1485 during an eclipse of the sun which was undoubtedly a bad omen for her widower. Men and women watching the moon pass in front of the sun knew that there was political upheaval ahead. The pair had been married for more than a decade, and when Richard addressed the Mayor of London and aldermen in the great hall of the Hospital of St John on 30 March, he sought to address the rumours of an intended union with Elizabeth of York. He added that he was 'nor willing nor glad, of the death of his queen but as sort and in heart as heavy as a man might be.'[8] Richard had known Anne since they were both children. He had fought with his brother Clarence for the right to marry her, and to all intents and purposes they had lived in harmony at Middleham until the death of King Edward. With the death of the queen, her household was disbanded. The king sent Elizabeth of York north to join her younger sisters and cousins.

In 1619, safely on the other side of the Tudor dynasty's rule, George Buck wrote a history of Anne's husband and recorded the content of a letter purporting to be from Elizabeth to John Howard, Duke of Norfolk, declaring her desire to marry Richard. As the letter has since been lost, there is no way of verifying Buck's view that Elizabeth was willing to marry her own uncle.

Anne was buried in Westminster Abbey on 25 March 1485, the Feast of the Annunciation, with all the honours due to a queen. The funeral was organised by the Lord Chamberlain, Francis Lovell, another of Anne's childhood companions at Middlcham. It was followed by interment on the south side of the high altar in a privileged position designed to speed her soul through Purgatory to Heaven. No memorial was commissioned to mark her last resting place. It has been hypothesised that Richard intended to move Anne's body to York Minster, but he had not yet established the perpetual chantry he proposed at York. Most medieval aristocrats wrote their wills safeguarding their possessions for their families long before their deaths. They also arranged for their passage through Purgatory to Heaven with equal care. Chantries were often created during their founder's lifetime. Something as important as eternal afterlife could not be left to chance. Chantry priests prayed for the souls of their founders and their families during their lives as well as after their deaths. Many chantry chapels became the final resting place for their benefactors. Richard began the process but he did not live long enough to complete it or to commission an appropriate tomb for his queen. Without the written evidence of a foundation charter or a will, history cannot be sure where Richard intended his family to be buried, especially as he and Anne founded collegiate churches in Middleham and Barnard Castle as well as a number of smaller chantries. The chantry at York Minster, if established, would have been the largest new foundation in the country, but fortune's wheel turned against Richard, and Anne's passing would remain unmarked. There would be no alabaster effigy of Warwick's younger daughter with her feet resting on a muzzled bear, and no royal mausoleum for King Richard III. It was only in 1960 that an enamelled brass plate was placed as near to Anne's grave site as was possible.

It is impossible to know how grief-stricken Richard was by Anne's death. *The Hours of Richard III*, the king's personal prayer book, was originally created in 1420, but it has the additional pages of Richard's own text including a prayer that has since become known as 'King Richard's prayer'. However, it was used in its basic form by many others during the period. It lists Richard's afflictions and amongst them is *dolor* or grief, which is unlike the standard text that usually references 'affliction' or 'tribulation'.[9] Having lost his wife and only legitimate heir, the king had much to mourn.

Less than a week after Anne's burial, Richard III issued a denial that he ever intended to marry his niece. He made his statement in front of the merchants and aldermen of the City of London in the great hall of the Hospital of St John. Richard began to openly negotiate for the hand of Joanna of Portugal, which would have linked the lines of York and Lancaster. The king was planning on ruling for many years and he believed he had time to raise another family. The negotiators discussed the possibility of Elizabeth marrying King John II's second cousin, Manuel, Duke of Beja. If such a marriage had taken place, Elizabeth's claim to the throne would have been more effectively neutralised than it had by the *Titulus Regius*, which was repealed by Henry VII; he also issued the instruction that all copies of the document making his wife illegitimate were to be destroyed.

For the majority of medieval women, independence came during widowhood when they exercised more rights and can, as a consequence, be located more frequently in the historical written record. Anne's brief life and shorter reign left her in shadows that darkened around her with the passage of time because there was no contemporary funerary monument to serve as a visible reminder of her life.

Chapter 20

Afterwards

By April 1485 it was apparent that there would be another round in the conflict between the Houses of York and Lancaster. In May, Anne's widower went to visit his mother, Cecily Neville. It was the last time the duchess saw her son. There is no known evidence that Cecily's relationship with Richard was ever anything but amiable. Like Elizabeth of York, Elizabeth Woodville and Lady Margaret Beaufort, the duchess could only await the outcome of the Battle of Bosworth which was fought on 22 August 1485. The Earl of Oxford, having escaped his prison at Hammes, led Henry Tudor's army into battle. A third force led by Lord Thomas Stanley, Lady Margaret Beaufort's husband, took no part in the action as its commander preferred to see who would hold the winning hand before committing his men.

Fortune finally turned against Richard when the Duke of Norfolk was killed and the king led a charge of his bodyguard, a small group of men, against Henry Tudor whose standard bearer, Henry Brandon, was killed. Richard was within striking distance of the man who sought to replace him on the throne when Stanley, witnessing the king's vulnerability, sent a force crashing down upon Richard and tipped the balance of the battle in the favour of his stepson Henry Tudor. Meanwhile, Henry Percy, who was in command of Richard's rear guard, either failed to realise that the king needed his assistance or chose to withhold his forces at a vital moment. When Richard's horse was killed beneath him, he fought on foot, refusing the offer of a horse to carry him to safety. He died on the battlefield like Anne's father and his own. Richard's broken body was stripped and brought to Leicester where it was exhibited naked for two days before being buried. In York the mayor's sergeant of mace recorded:

> King Richard, late mercifully reigning over us, was through great treason... piteously slain and murdered, to the great heaviness of this city.[1]

Men who fought for Richard III were imprisoned, executed, sought sanctuary or became fugitives. The majority submitted to Henry Tudor and swore an oath of allegiance to the Tudors. Percy was briefly imprisoned, but later restored to his earldom. Yorkshire took its revenge for the death of Richard when the earl was killed in 1489 at Blackmoor Edge near Thirsk during a rebellion against Henry VII over taxes.

Lady Margaret Beaufort gave up her own blood right to allow her son to succeed her. Elizabeth of York, summoned with her sisters and cousins from their home in the north, married Henry, uniting the two Houses of York and Lancaster with the birth of a male heir named Arthur in 1486. Like her predecessor, Elizabeth's role was perceived as a largely domestic one. Henry VII had no wish to remind his subjects that his wife had a better claim to the throne than he did himself. Anne and Isabel's aunt Margaret, the Countess of Oxford, was finally reunited with her husband and took her rightful place at court after years of poverty. It was perhaps because of her that Oxford helped to restore the widow of John Howard, Duke of Norfolk, to some of her estates. When Margaret died in 1506, Oxford married Elizabeth Scrope, the co-heiress of Sir Richard Scrope, but he chose to be buried beside Margaret at Colne Priory when he died in 1513.

Anne's extended family and the northern gentry needed to decide upon which side they would serve in the future. Lord Richard FitzHugh, Anne's cousin, received the lordships of Richmond, Middleham and Barnard Castle into his charge from King Henry. He was also required to obtain oaths of allegiance from influential members of the surrounding gentry before any of them could act as the king's commissioners.[2] Sir John Conyers transitioned from Plantagenet to Tudor in exactly the same way that he changed allegiance from Warwick to Gloucester, although his stewardship of Middleham was temporarily lost to him. It did not mean that popular support for Richard III had gone away, rather that the northern gentry, as well as Anne's extended family, were pragmatists who looked to securing their own futures under the Tudor monarchy. It helped that Henry Tudor was not only king but also the Earl of Richmond.

Sir Richard Huddleston, Anne's brother-in-law, was not listed amongst the dead at Bosworth. Margaret Huddleston was either pregnant with their second daughter who would be named Joan, or the infant was a babe in arms when the husband Warwick had selected for her died within 18 months of King Richard's defeat. Margaret's son, another Richard, was still a minor. He became a ward of the new king who handed control of the boy's inheritance to Sir Lancelot Threlkeld of Yanwath who became the boy's stepfather. Margaret's bloodline, and the value of her son as the future Lord of Millom, made her a desirable wife despite her base birth. There is no indication of how Margaret might have felt about the need to take a second husband who represented protection by the new regime and stability for the transfer of land to her son. Threlkeld was a loyal Lancastrian with ties of land and kinship to the Clifford affinity.[3] Threlkeld and Yanwath were both mesne manors held by the barons of Greystoke under the Cliffords. Threlkeld's first wife, Margaret Vescy, was the widow of John, Lord Clifford, who was killed at the Battle of Ferrybridge in 1461. It was Threlkeld who hid his two Clifford stepsons from the immediate vengeance of the Yorkists who held the boys' father responsible for the death of the young Earl of Rutland at the Battle of Wakefield in 1460. Threlkeld became Sheriff of Cumberland in 1492. Margaret died on 17 October 1499. Her son was still a minor so his stepfather continued to hold the lands and take its profits for another two years until Richard achieved his majority.[4] Four years later Threlkeld was granted a 'special pardon and release' from all matters connected with his office as sheriff as well as on the lands associated with Margaret's inheritance during her son's minority.[5] Margaret's second husband continued to serve the Tudor kings. He was created a Knight of the Bath on the marriage of Prince Arthur and was part of the retinue that escorted Princess Margaret to Scotland in 1503.

Countess Anne spent her final years at Sutton Coldfield Manor. Following Warwick's death at Barnet in 1471, the lordship passed to Duchess Isabel and then to her young son Edward. After Clarence's arrest and execution, it remained in Crown hands because of Edward's minority, but in 1487 the countess arrived at an accommodation with King Henry VII. Parliament revoked the decree that ignored her rights as though she was dead, as being, 'against all reason, conscience and course of nature, and contrary to the laws of God and man'.[6] On receiving her lands which included more than one hundred manors, the countess immediately gave them to the king and his heirs. In return Countess Anne received several manors sufficient for her lifetime. After her death in 1492, those estates reverted to the Crown rather than to her grandson who remained Henry's prisoner. Pragmatism prevailed.

Edward, Earl of Warwick, summoned from Sheriff Hutton together with his sister Margaret, was sent to live with Henry VII's mother, Lady Margaret Beaufort, as were the younger daughters of King Edward IV and Elizabeth Woodville. It is likely that Margaret knew the princesses from her time in Elizabeth Woodville's household. Also housed with them was Edward Stafford, whose father, the 2nd Duke of Buckingham, was executed in 1483. Stafford's mother, Katherine Woodville, would marry King Henry VII's uncle Jasper Tudor in November 1485. During 1485 Margaret and her brother were separated from one another once more. The young earl became a resident of the Tower while Margaret was permitted to take her place at court, as was King Richard's heir, John de la Pole, Earl of Lincoln. Initially Isabel's daughter and her cousin Lincoln played prominent roles in the new court. Lincoln assisted Cecily Plantagenet to carry Henry's son Prince Arthur during his christening ceremony and, in 1486, Lincoln accompanied Henry to Yorkshire to put down Francis Lovell's rebellion against the Tudor regime. Ashdown-Hill speculates that one of the reasons Isabel and Clarence's son was deemed a greater threat to the new regime than Lincoln was because Henry's uncle Jasper Tudor remembered the agreement made in Angers by Warwick; this recognised Clarence as the Lancastrian heir in the event of Edward of Westminster dying without heirs of his own. Under those terms, ignoring subsequent parliamentary acts passed by the Yorkist regime, the rightful king was not Henry Tudor but Isabel's son, Edward, Earl of Warwick.[7]

On 28 November 1499, Edward, Earl of Warwick, was beheaded on Tower Hill accused of treason. *The Great Chronicle of London* reported the execution and the fact that the body was placed in a coffin before being transported by barge to Bisham Abbey where Warwick was interred with his maternal grandfather.[8] If Edward Hall is to be believed, the execution of the young earl and the hanging, a week earlier, of the pretender Perkin Warbeck who claimed to be the younger of Edward IV's two sons, were in response to pressure from Ferdinand II of Aragon and Isabella of Castile, whose daughter Katherine of Aragon was to marry Henry's son Arthur Tudor. Hall would write of the ill-fated youth that being 'kept in the Tower from his tender age, that is to say from his first year of the king to this fifteenth year, out of all company of men and sight of beasts, in so much that he could not discern a goose from a capon'.⁹ The quote is often interpreted to mean that Warwick was simple-minded. It could simply have meant that he was naïve about the world. The Spanish ambassador, Rorigo de Puebla, claimed that all the doubtful royal blood in the kingdom was gone.

Whatever Warwick's sister Margaret may have thought about her brother's death, like her mother, aunt and grandmother before her, she knew how the political game was played. Margaret was too close to the throne to allow her to marry well, in case her husband and his supporters claimed the crown by right of her Plantagenet bloodline. Instead, Henry VII married her off to a distant relation of his own, Richard Pole, when she turned 14 in 1487. In time she would give her husband five children. Margaret became part of Katherine of Aragon's household and her friend. The fates of the two women were intertwined. When Katherine suffered poverty after the death of Prince Arthur in 1502, so did Margaret. In 1509, following Katherine's marriage to Arthur's younger brother King Henry VIII, fortune's wheel turned upwards and Margaret was once more in the ascendant. It appeared as though she had survived her grandfather, the Earl of Warwick's, dynastic ambitions. As well as being created Countess of Salisbury in her own right, she was restored to much of her inheritance making her one of the wealthiest women in the country.

But fate was not yet done with Isabel Neville's daughter. When Margaret's son Reginald, who had previously been shown great favour by his royal cousin, wrote against Henry's desire to annul his marriage to Katherine so that he could marry Anne Boleyn, Margaret's position deteriorated once more. She and her family were caught up in the so-called Exeter Conspiracy of 1538 whose purpose was to overthrow the king, replacing him with his cousin Henry Courtenay, Marquess of Exeter. It was claimed that Courtenay corresponded with Margaret's son Reginald. Thomas Cromwell's assertions were supported by the confession of Geoffrey Pole, another of Margaret's sons who incriminated his eldest brother, Henry. Evidence against Margaret was vague; even Cromwell wrote that there was nothing to convict her, but she and other members of her family were arrested in November on charges of treason. Their main offence was being related to Reginald. Geoffrey, who turned evidence against his own family, was released but Henry was executed. In 1539, aged 70, the countess was attainted of treason based on hearsay and evidence uncovered by a search conducted some six months after her belongings had originally been seized. She was sent to the Tower where her grandson Henry Pole, a child, was already incarcerated having been sent there with his father the previous year. The king's accounts show that he permitted £13 6s 8d per month for the purchase of food for the countess, her grandson and for Courtenay's son.[10] The countess was executed on 27 May 1541 without trial on the orders of her cousin, King Henry VIII. Eustace Chapuys, who served as the Holy Roman Emperor's ambassador from 1529 until 1545, wrote of her death:

> At first when the sentence of death was made known to her, she found the thing very strange, not knowing of what crime she was accused, nor how she had been sentenced.[11]

Even worse, if the stories are to be believed, the executioner was inexperienced and he ended the life of Isabel's daughter by 'hacking her head and shoulders to pieces in the most pitiful manner'.[12] Nothing more was heard of Henry Pole who, like his royal cousins King Edward V and Richard of Shrewsbury, disappeared into the Tower never to be seen again. Fortuna's wheel finally stopped turning for Countess Anne and her daughters.

> What fates impose, that men must needs abide;
> it boots not to resist both wind and tide.
>
> Henry VI, Part 3, 4.3.31–32

Appendix

Key Dates of the Wars of the Roses

1437
12 November — The minority of King Henry VI, now almost 16 years old, concludes. He succeeded to the crown before his first birthday, following the death on 31 August 1422 of his father King Henry V.

1443 — John Beaufort is created Duke of Somerset and Earl of Kendal. He is also appointed as Henry VI's Captain General of Guyenne. This, together with a payment from Henry VI's government of £25,000, results in an ongoing feud between the Beaufort family and Richard, Duke of York.

August 1443 — Somerset leads a military campaign in Gascony.

1444 — Death of the 1st Duke of Somerset. Beaufort's brother Edmund is later granted the dukedom of Somerset. Both Beauforts work with Henry's favourite, William de la Pole, Earl of Suffolk, to force the exclusion of the king's closest male relation and heir presumptive, Richard of York.

1445
23 April — King Henry VI marries Margaret of Anjou to cement the agreement made at the Treaty of Tours in 1444 by Suffolk, which includes a two-year truce with France as well as the surrender of any claim to Anjou and Maine.

30 May — The coronation of Margaret of Anjou who allies herself with Suffolk and the Beauforts, who support the strategy of a peace with France.

23 July — Richard Neville succeeds to the earldom of Warwick by right of his wife, Anne Beauchamp.

Key Dates of the Wars of the Roses

1447

September — York is sent as Lord Lieutenant to Ireland rather than being reappointed to his preferred role in France.

1449

21 October — George, later Duke of Clarence, born to Cecily, Duchess of York, in Dublin.

1450

26 January — Suffolk is impeached by Parliament for corruption and conspiracy with the French. Many of the charges are based on hearsay and suspicion.

17 March — King Henry VI uses his prerogative rights to banish Suffolk from his realm for five years rather than allow Parliament to imprison or execute his favourite.

30 April — Suffolk leaves the kingdom via Ipswich, but his vessel is intercepted at sea and he is murdered. His decapitated body is left on a beach near Dover for several days.

May — Jack Cade's rebellion begins in Kent based on the hypothesis that the people of Kent will be blamed by Margaret of Anjou for Suffolk's death. An army gathers and marches on London, camping at Blackheath. Cade's demands are rejected and orders are given to suppress the rising. As the violence escalates, the king and his court flee to Kenilworth Castle in Warwickshire and the Bishop of Salisbury, who officiated at the king's wedding, is murdered by his own congregation. There are rumours of York's complicity with the rebellion because of Cade's use of the name Mortimer; this is a name associated with York's maternal line and claim to the throne through his descent from Edward III's son Lionel of Antwerp.

2 July — Cade and his men enter London, but there is unrest, looting and execution of men identified by

	the rebels as evil counsellors, turning the capital's citizens against them.
5 July	Once order is restored London closes its gates against the rebels, but concludes negotiations that secure Cade and his men free pardons.
15 July	Cade is captured and his pardon, having been issued in the name of John Mortimer, is revoked. He dies from his wounds on the way back to London.

1451

5 September	Anne Beauchamp, Countess of Warwick, gives birth to Isabel Neville.

1452

9 January	York issues a statement of loyalty to the king, reinforcing a declaration given on 29 September 1450 in the aftermath of Cade's rebellion.
3 February	York takes up arms and marches on London with the intention of ending Somerset's dominance at court. He makes camp at Dartford.
2 March	The earls of Salisbury and Warwick are part of a group sent to negotiate with York. The matter is concluded when York makes an oath of public allegiance to Henry VI and is sent back to his home in Ludlow.

1453

Spring	Margaret of Anjou becomes pregnant after seven years of marriage.
July	A commission of oyer and terminer is appointed to look into the reginal Neville-Percy feud, but is unable to resolve the conflict. Warwick and Somerset clash over estates in South Wales, which both claim by right of their wives.
17 July	A French victory at the Battle of Castillon results in the death of the Earl of Shrewsbury and the loss of all English territories in France, except for Calais and its Pale.

August	King Henry VI suffers a mental breakdown when news of the English defeat arrives.
24 August	The Percy and Neville families come to blows at Heworth Moor, Yorkshire.
13 October	Margaret of Anjou gives birth to a son known as Edward of Westminster, or Edward of Lancaster. Somerset is named as a godparent, sparking the rumour that he is the prince's father rather than the king who is too ill to acknowledge his heir.
12 November	Parliament is summoned at Reading, but is prorogued until February to avoid revealing the extent of the king's illness.
23 November	Norfolk, an ally of York, blames Somerset for English losses in France. Somerset is arrested and sent to the Tower after York arrives in London supported by a large retinue.

1454

January	Margaret of Anjou asserts the rights of her infant son and makes a claim to the regency during her husband's illness.
13 February	The king's council nominates York as protector with limited rights and Parliament is summoned.
27 March	York is named protector until the king recovers, despite the queen's objections. He appoints Salisbury as his Lord Chancellor, Thomas Bourchier as Archbishop of Canterbury and John Tiptoft, Earl of Worcester as Treasurer. He takes over the captaincy of Calais from Somerset, but is unable to take possession of the office.
31 October	The Neville-Percy feud results in a clash at Stamford Bridge, Yorkshire
25 December	King Henry VI unexpectedly recovers from his illness.

1455

March	York, Salisbury and many of York's supporters are dismissed from their governmental roles by King

	Henry. Somerset is released from the Tower and reinstated as Constable of England and Captain of Calais. York, Salisbury and Warwick return to their own estates.
21 April	A council meeting is called at Leicester. York and Salisbury are excluded from the gathering and are both ordered to disband their retinues. The Yorkist faction believe they are in danger of arrest, while the Lancastrians believe that York craves his cousin's throne. Both sides gather their armies.
22 May	The First Battle of St Albans follows prolonged negotiations. The Lancastrian Earl of Northumberland is killed, as are the Duke of Somerset and Lord Clifford. Somerset's son Henry, who inherits his father's title, is wounded. York, Salisbury and Warwick are victorious and escort the king back to London where he is thought to suffer a second mental collapse.
25 May	Warwick is appointed Captain of Calais.
9 July	Parliament convenes in Westminster packed with York's supporters. By November, authority as Lord Protector is vested in York and the blame for the battle at St Albans is placed on Somerset and his faction.

1456

25 February	York resigns from the protectorate following King Henry's recovery. He is confirmed as Lieutenant of Ireland and Warwick retains the captaincy of Calais.
21 March	George Neville, Warwick's youngest brother, is appointed as Bishop of Exeter.
August	Margaret of Anjou establishes her court at Coventry closer to her supporters in the Midlands, taking the Tower's artillery with her.

1457

28 January	Lady Margaret Beaufort gives birth to her son, Henry Tudor, at Pembroke Castle. Her husband Edmund Tudor died on 3 November 1456.

1458

24 March — A reconciliation between the Lancastrian and Yorkist factions symbolised by a 'Love Day' is held in St Paul's Cathedral. York walks to the ceremony hand in hand with Margaret of Anjou.

1459

24 June — A council meeting is summoned in Coventry. York, Salisbury and Warwick fear that they will be arrested so they refuse to attend. They are indicted for treason.

23 September — The Battle of Blore Heath. Salisbury encounters a Lancastrian army, commanded by Lord Audley, on his way from Middleham to join York and Warwick at Ludlow. Salisbury is victorious. Warwick brings troops from Calais who are led by Sir Anthony Trollope.

12 October — King Henry VI's army arrives at Ludford Bridge with the king at its head. Trollope unexpectedly changes sides, taking Warwick's 600 men from Calais with him. During the night York and his second son, Edmund, Earl of Rutland, flee to Ireland. Salisbury, Warwick and York's eldest son, Edward, Earl of March, make their way to Calais, leaving their standards, armies and York's wife and younger children behind.

November — The so-called Parliament of Devils attaints the leaders of the Yorkist faction of treason. The Countess of Salisbury is also indicted. Cecily, Duchess of York, and her children are placed in the custody of her Lancastrian sister, Anne, Duchess of Buckingham.

1460

15 January — Warwick sends a force led by John Dinham to raid the port of Sandwich in Kent where Somerset is preparing a fleet to dislodge Warwick from Calais. The vessels are destroyed. Lord Rivers and his wife,

	Jacquetta of Luxembourg, are surprised in their bed and their eldest son Anthony is also captured. All three are taken to Calais where Lord Rivers is publicly attacked for marrying above his station.
26 June	Warwick, Salisbury and March land in Sandwich with approximately 2,000 men. Warwick passes via Canterbury to London recruiting more men for his army, entering the capital to popular acclaim on 2 July.
10 July	The Battle of Northampton. Warwick captures King Henry VI and gives the Great Seal of England to his brother George Neville, Bishop of Exeter. Margaret of Anjou flees to Harlech with her son before making her way to Scotland to gather support for her husband's cause. Warwick begins to run the country; the Duchess of York is released from her sister's custody and Parliament is called to reverse the attainder on the Yorkists passed the previous year.
September	York and his son Edmund, Earl of Rutland, return from Ireland and make a progress through the Welsh Marches with the Mortimer standard carried in front of them showing the royal arms.
10 October	York attempts to claim the throne, but has to be satisfied with the Act of Accord which identifies him as the king's heir bypassing Henry's son, Edward.
30 December	The Battle of Wakefield. York and his son Rutland are killed. A Lancastrian army under the command of Somerset is victorious.
31 December	The Earl of Salisbury is executed at Pontefract and his head is put on Micklegate Bar at York, along with those of York and Rutland.

1461

Despite the loss at Wakefield, Warwick continues to hold London and to run the country. Margaret of Anjou gathers an army of northerners and Scots. The Lancastrians advance south led by Somerset.

Key Dates of the Wars of the Roses

2 February	The Battle of Mortimer's Cross is fought close to the Welsh border. York's 18-year-old son Edward defeats a Lancastrian army led by Jasper Tudor, Earl of Pembroke, and his father Owen, who is captured and beheaded in Hereford by the Yorkists.
12 February	Warwick takes an army from London to prevent the Lancastrians from reaching the capital, taking King Henry VI with him.
17 February	The Second Battle of St Albans. Warwick is defeated by Somerset. Henry VI rejoins Margaret of Anjou. Hearing news of a Lancastrian victory, the Duchess of York sends her two younger sons, George and Richard, to their elder sister in Burgundy. Margaret of Anjou does not take the opportunity to enter London, preferring instead to return to Yorkshire.
4 March	Edward IV is proclaimed king at Westminster.
27 and 28 March	Yorkists, led by Warwick, attempting to cross the River Aire at Ferrybridge clash with Lancastrians, led by Lord Clifford and John, Lord Neville, the younger brother of the Lancastrian 2nd Earl of Westmorland. The Yorkists lose many men, Warwick is injured and his illegitimate half-brother is slain, but Warwick's uncle Lord Fauconberg fords the river and outflanks the Lancastrians. Lords Clifford and Neville are killed. The day ends with the Yorkist and Lancastrian armies encamped less than a mile from one another.
29 March	The Battle of Towton is fought during a snowstorm between a Lancastrian army commanded by Somerset and a smaller Yorkist force commanded by King Edward IV. The bitter fighting finishes with a decisive Yorkist victory. Henry VI and his family escape to Scotland where they raise support for their cause.
28 June	The coronation of King Edward IV.

1462 A Lancastrian force led by Jasper Tudor invades the north-east of England and captures Bamburgh Castle. By the end of the year, he is forced to surrender and takes a safe passage to Scotland before travelling to Brittany and France.

1464

25 April — The Battle of Hedgeley Moor near Alnwick between a Lancastrian army led by Somerset and a much larger Yorkist force led by Warwick's brother, John Neville, Lord Montagu. Most of the Lancastrians flee, leaving Sir Ralph Percy and other recently pardoned Lancastrians to be slaughtered.

1 May — King Edward IV secretly marries Elizabeth Woodville at Grafton.

15 May — Somerset attempts to advance into the Tyne Valley with King Henry VI at the head of his army. Montagu's men intercept the Lancastrians at Hexham and win the ensuing battle. Somerset is executed immediately after the battle, while other Lancastrian commanders are executed at Newcastle. Henry VI becomes a fugitive in his own realm. Following the second Lancastrian defeat within three weeks, the garrisons of Alnwick, Dunstanburgh and Bamburgh surrender. The Yorkist pacification in the north is complete.

29 September — King Edward announces his marriage to Elizabeth Woodville during a council meeting.

1465

Richard, Duke of Gloucester, enters the household of the Earl of Warwick.

13 July — King Henry VI, a fugitive since the Battle of Hexham in 1464, sheltering in various Lancastrian homes across the north of England, including Muncaster Castle, is captured while in hiding at Clitheroe.

1467

15 June	Death of Philip the Good, Duke of Burgundy; accession of Charles the Bold.

1468

3 July	Margaret of York, King Edward's sister, marries the Duke of Burgundy.
3 August	The English and Burgundians conclude an alliance.

1469

April–July	There are a series of rebellions in the north led by a shadowy captain known as Robin of Redesdale. The later stage of the rebellion is orchestrated by Warwick against the Woodvilles.
11 July	George, Duke of Clarence, marries Isabel Neville at Calais without the permission of King Edward IV before returning with Warwick to England to take up arms against the king.
26 July	William Herbert, Earl of Pembroke, and other Yorkist lords are defeated and executed by Warwick following the Battle of Edgecote Moor.
29 July	King Edward IV is deserted by his supporters and taken into custody. The kingdom is placed under Warwick's protection. The king is initially imprisoned in Warwick Castle before being moved to Middleham.
12 August	Richard Woodville, Earl Rivers, and his son Sir John Woodville are executed on Warwick's orders without trial at Coventry.
Circa 10 September	Warwick is forced to release Edward following rioting, unrest and the resurgence of Lancastrian resistance to Yorkist rule in the north.
October	King Edward IV enters London, regains control and pursues a policy of reconciliation with Warwick and Clarence, who remain dissatisfied with their role within government.

1470

12 March	Battle of Losecoat Field. King Edward IV defeats a rebellion led by Sir Robert Welles but directed by Warwick.
25 March	King Edward IV restores the Percy family to the earldom of Northumberland and makes Lord Montagu the Marquess of Montagu, granting him lands belonging to the Earl of Devon in recompense for the loss of Northumberland.
April	Clarence, Warwick and his family flee England.
Summer	There is rebellion in the north led by Lord Fitzhugh of Ravensworth on the orders of his brother-in-law, the Earl of Warwick. The Earl of Northumberland is unable to subdue the rebels. King Edward marches north.
22 July	The Angers Agreement completes an alliance between Richard Neville, Earl of Warwick, and Margaret of Anjou.
25 July	Anne Neville is formally betrothed to Margaret's son Edward.
15 September	Warwick and Clarence land in Weymouth with Jasper Tudor and proclaim their allegiance to King Henry VI.
29 September	Montagu declares his support for Warwick.
1 October	Elizabeth Woodville and her children claim sanctuary in Westminster Abbey.
2 October	King Edward, his brother Richard of Gloucester and his chamberlain Lord Hastings flee via King's Lynn to Burgundy.
6 October	Warwick arrives in London. The Readeption of King Henry VI begins.
2 November	Birth of Prince Edward of York in Westminster Abbey while his mother and sisters remain in sanctuary.
26 November	The Readeption Parliament confirms King Henry VI's crown and the succession through his son Prince Edward. In the event of Henry's line

	failing, his successor is named as George, Duke of Clarence.
13 December	Prince Edward of Lancaster marries Anne Neville at Amboise.

1471

14 March	King Edward lands at Ravenspur on the Humber Estuary, initially claiming only his father's dukedom of York. He is allowed to march south without being intercepted by the Earl of Northumberland and bypasses Pontefract without interference from Lord Montagu. By the end of the month, Edward is recruiting men in Nottingham.
3 April	Clarence deserts Warwick in favour of King Edward IV.
5 April	Rather than besiege Warwick at Coventry, Edward marches on London which he takes unopposed on 11 April despite Warwick's instructions to his brother George, Archbishop of York.
14 April	Battle of Barnet – King Edward wins a Yorkist victory. The Earl of Warwick and his brother, the Marquis of Montagu, are killed. Margaret of Anjou, Prince Edward and Anne Neville land at Weymouth, while the Countess of Warwick makes landfall at Southampton. Having learned of the defeat at Barnet, Margaret is persuaded by Somerset to travel to Wales to join with Jasper Tudor who is recruiting an army.
4 May	Battle of Tewkesbury – Somerset and other leading Lancastrians die on the battlefield or are executed on 6 May after being dragged from sanctuary in Tewkesbury Abbey. Prince Edward is killed on the battlefield or soon after his capture.
7 May	Margaret of Anjou and her ladies, including Anne Neville, are captured. They are taken first to Coventry and then to London.

21 May	King Edward enters London in triumph. King Henry VI is murdered that evening in the Tower of London.
2 June	Jasper Tudor, Earl of Pembroke, together with his nephew Henry Tudor flee to Brittany.
1472	
February	Clarence and Gloucester debate whether Gloucester should marry Anne Neville and the extent to which he should share the Neville inheritance.

Richard of Gloucester marries Anne Neville despite Clarence's opposition.

1474	
May	Parliament attempts to settle the dispute between Clarence and Gloucester about the share each will receive from Countess Anne and the Earl of Warwick's estates.
1475	
4 July	King Edward leads a military campaign against Louis XI.
29 August	An Anglo-French agreement is made by the Treaty of Picquigny following the failure of the Burgundian army to support Edward's campaign.
1476	
21 December	Death of Isabel Neville, Duchess of Clarence.
1477	
5 January	Death of Charles, Duke of Burgundy, ending England's hopes of an alliance with them against the French.
1478	
19 January	Parliament summoned for the trial of Clarence.
18 February	Execution of Clarence for treason.
1482	
29 August	Death of Margaret of Anjou in France.

1483

9 April	Death of King Edward IV; accession of Edward V.
9–16 April	The Council and dowager queen Elizabeth Woodville decide on 4 May as the date of King Edward V's coronation.
14 April	Edward V is informed at Ludlow of his father's death. Earl Rivers prepares to escort the new king to London.
20 April	Gloucester departs his family at Middleham for York.
23 April	Gloucester, forewarned by Lord Hastings of the Woodville faction's intentions to take control of the king and his council, leaves York having taken a solemn oath of loyalty to the king.
24 April	King Edward V leaves Ludlow accompanied by his half-brother Sir Richard Grey, his uncle Earl Rivers and an escort of 2,000 men.
29 April	Gloucester and the Duke of Buckingham await Edward V at Northampton. The royal party go further south to Stony Stratford. That evening Gloucester dines with Earl Rivers.
30 April	Rivers and Sir Richard Grey are arrested and sent north. Gloucester takes charge of Edward V and writes to the Lord Mayor and aldermen of London reassuring them.
1 May	Elizabeth Woodville seeks sanctuary in Westminster Abbey with her daughters, her younger son Richard, Duke of York, and her mother Jacquetta.
4 May	King Edward V arrives in London with Gloucester and cartloads of arms bearing the Woodville insignia. The coronation is delayed.
5 June	The Duchess of Gloucester arrives in London for the coronation of Edward V.
10 June	Gloucester writes to Yorkshire asking for armed men to be sent to London to assist him because the Woodville faction are plotting to murder him.

13 June	A council meeting is held in the Tower, but is interrupted by the arrest of several of the council members and is followed by the summary execution of William Hastings, Lord Hastings.
17 June	Richard, Duke of York, leaves sanctuary at Westminster Abbey and joins his elder brother Edward V in the Tower of London.
18 June	Troops loyal to Gloucester muster at Pontefract.
22 June	Dr Ralph Shaa preaches a public sermon claiming that King Edward IV and Elizabeth Woodville were not legally married, meaning that their children are illegitimate. He sets out Gloucester's claim to the throne.
25 June	Lord Rivers, his nephew Richard Grey and Edward V's tutor, Thomas Vaughan, are executed at Pontefract Castle.
26 June	A bill of petition is presented to Gloucester by Henry Stafford, Duke of Buckingham, setting out his title to the throne and asking that he should become king.
4 July	Gloucester and his wife move to the Tower in preparation for their coronation.
6 July	Coronation of Richard III and his wife Queen Anne.
30 August	Death of King Louis XI of France.
July–September	Probable deaths of Edward V and his brother Richard in the Tower of London.
10 October	Buckingham's rebellion, which involves Lady Margaret Beaufort, seeks to put Henry Tudor on the throne. The rising is planned for 18 October, but rebels in Kent rise too soon. Jasper and Henry Tudor attempt an invasion in support of Buckingham's rebellion, but their fleet is blown off course by a storm and they abort their mission once they realise that the rebellion is unsuccessful.
2 November	Execution of the Duke of Buckingham at Salisbury.

Key Dates of the Wars of the Roses

25 December	Henry Tudor announces his intention to marry Edward IV's daughter Elizabeth of York, which would unite the warring factions.
1484	
23 January	King Richard III's only Parliament meets to attaint Buckingham's rebels and to pass *Titulus Regius*.
1 March	Elizabeth Woodville and her daughters leave sanctuary in Westminster.
9 April	Death of Edward of Middleham.
1485	
16 March	Death of Anne Neville, queen of England.
30 March	Richard III publicly denies the rumour that he intends to marry his niece, Elizabeth of York.
7 August	Henry Tudor's invasion fleet lands at Milford Haven in Wales.
22 August	Battle of Bosworth – King Richard III is defeated and killed by Henry Tudor, who claims the crown for Lancaster by right of his mother Lady Margaret Beaufort. She is a descendant of John of Gaunt, the third surviving son of King Edward III. Henry Tudor's subsequent marriage to Edward IV's daughter Elizabeth of York in 1486 unites the Houses of York and Lancaster.
1486	
19 September	The birth of Prince Arthur, the son of King Henry VII and Elizabeth of York.
1487	
16 June	Battle of Stoke – A Yorkist rebellion to replace the Tudors with a pretender named Lambert Simnel is defeated. King Richard III's nephew and heir the Earl of Lincoln is killed.
1499	
29 November	Execution of Isabel and Clarence's son, Edward Plantagenet, Earl of Warwick.

Who's Who

Anne of York, Duchess of Exeter (1439–1476)
Eldest child of Richard, 3rd Duke of York and Cecily Neville. Her parents arranged for her to marry Henry Holland, 3rd Duke of Exeter, a Lancastrian commander. The couple had a daughter named Anne Holland. After the Battle of Towton in 1461, Exeter was attainted and fled to France. Anne received her husband's estates and in 1464 she formally separated from him. The marriage was annulled in 1472. In 1474 she married for a second time to Thomas St Leger. She died giving birth to St Leger's daughter.

Anne Beauchamp, 15th Countess of Warwick (1444–1449)
Daughter of Henry Beauchamp, Duke of Warwick and his wife Cecily Neville (d.1450). She inherited the earldom of Warwick when she was 2 years old but died before her sixth birthday, ending the direct line of the Beauchamp Earls of Warwick.

Anne Beauchamp, 16th Countess of Warwick (1426–1492)
Daughter of Richard Beauchamp, 13th Earl of Warwick and his second wife, Isabel Despenser. She married Richard Neville, the eldest son of the 5th Earl of Salisbury at the same time her brother Henry married Richard's sister Cecily. When her niece, the 15th Countess, Anne Beauchamp, died, Richard inherited the earldom of Warwick by right of Anne who was a full-blooded aunt to the last countess and considered more eligible than her elder half-sisters: Margaret, Eleanor and Elizabeth.

Eleanor Beauchamp, Duchess of Somerset (1408–1467)
Daughter of the 13th Earl of Warwick and his first wife, Elizabeth Berkeley. She married Edmund Beaufort, 2nd Duke of Somerset in an unlicensed marriage and was the mother to several children including the 3rd and 4th dukes of Somerset.

Elizabeth Beauchamp, Baroness Bergavenny (1415–1448)
Only child of Isabel Despenser from her first marriage to Richard Beauchamp, 2nd Baron Bergavenny and 1st Earl of Worcester. Elizabeth and her half-sister, Anne Beauchamp, were both entitled to a share of their mother's Despenser inheritance. She married Edward Neville who was a younger son of Ralph Neville, 1st Earl of Westmorland, and Joan Beaufort.

Elizabeth Beauchamp, Lady Latimer (1417–1480)
Daughter of the 13th Earl of Warwick and his first wife, Elizabeth Berkeley. She married George Neville, 1st Baron Latimer who was the fifth son of Ralph Neville, 1st Earl of Westmorland, and Joan Beaufort.

Margaret Beauchamp, Countess of Shrewsbury (1404–1467)
The eldest daughter of the 13th Earl of Warwick and his first wife, Elizabeth Berkeley. She married John Talbot, the noted military commander who fought during the campaigns of the Hundred Years War and was rewarded with the earldom of Shrewsbury.

Henry Beauchamp, 14th Earl and 1st Duke of Warwick (1425–1446)
Son of Richard Beauchamp, 13th Earl of Warwick, and Isabel Despenser. He was a childhood friend of Henry VI. He married Cecily Neville, a daughter of the 5th Earl of Salisbury. The couple had a daughter, named Anne, before Henry died unexpectedly.

Richard Beauchamp, 13th Earl of Warwick (1382–1439)
Richard was the eldest son of the 12th Earl of Warwick and his wife Margaret Ferrers of Groby. He continued a family tradition of military command, taking an important role in Henry V's campaigns in France. He was given responsibility for educating Henry VI. The earl married twice, firstly to Elizabeth Berkeley with whom he had three daughters: Margaret, Eleanor and Elizabeth. Beauchamp then married Isabel Despenser who gave him an heir, Henry, and a fourth daughter, Anne.

The Beaufort family
In 1396 John of Gaunt, the third surviving son of Edward III, married his long-term mistress, Katherine Swynford. Their four children, John

Beaufort, 1st Earl of Somerset; Cardinal Henry Beaufort; Thomas Beaufort, 1st Duke of Exeter; and Joan Beaufort, were legitimised by their cousin Richard II and by Pope Boniface IX. The Wars of the Roses divided the loyalties of John and Joan's descendants between Lancaster and York.

Edmund Beaufort, 2nd Duke of Somerset (1406–1455)
The fourth surviving son of John Beaufort, 1st Earl of Somerset, the eldest of the legitimised children of John of Gaunt and Katherine Swynford. Beaufort's command of the English army in France in 1431 escalated rivalries with his cousin by marriage Richard, Duke of York. In 1453 there were rumours that the duke was Margaret of Anjou's lover and the father of Prince Edward. Somerset was killed on 22 May 1455 at the First Battle of St Albans.

Edmund Beaufort (1439–1471)
Younger son of the 2nd Duke of Somerset styling himself Duke of Somerset after the execution, in 1465, of his brother Henry, 3rd Duke of Somerset. Beaufort commanded the Lancastrian army in 1471 following the death, on 14 April, of the 16th Earl of Warwick at the Battle of Barnet. He was executed on 6 May 1471.

Henry Beaufort, 3rd Duke of Somerset (1436–1464)
Henry was one of the Lancastrian commanders who won the Battle of Wakefield on 30 December 1460. He escaped from the battlefield at Towton on 29 March 1461, made his peace with Edward IV and was restored to his estates, only to turn his coat once more. He was captured soon after the Battle of Hexham on 15 May 1464 and was executed. He had no legitimate heirs.

Joan Beaufort, Countess of Westmorland (c.1379–1440)
Daughter of John of Gaunt and Katherine Swynford who married before the end of 1396 to Ralph Neville, 1st Earl of Westmorland, becoming his second wife. After Westmorland's death much of her husband's estates passed to her eldest son Richard, triggering a feud with the children of the earl's first wife, Margaret Stafford. Her children included Katherine Neville, Duchess of Norfolk; Eleanor, Countess of Northumberland;

Richard Neville, 5th Earl of Salisbury; Robert Neville, Bishop of Durham; William Neville, 1st Earl of Kent, more often identified as Lord Fauconberg; George Neville, 1st Baron Latimer; Anne, Duchess of Buckingham; Edward Neville, 3rd Baron Bergavenny; and Cecily, Duchess of York.

Margaret Beaufort, Countess of Richmond and Derby (1443–1509)
Daughter and sole heiress of John Beaufort, 1st Duke of Somerset, who married Edmund Tudor, Earl of Richmond, in 1455. The following year, aged 12 and already a widow, she gave birth to Henry Tudor, her only child. Margaret's second marriage was to Sir Henry Stafford, a younger son of the Duke of Buckingham and his wife Anne Neville. After Stafford's death in 1471 she married for a third time to Thomas Stanley, 2nd Baron Stanley, and secured the favour of Edward IV. After April 1483 she worked for her son Henry to become king by right of her own descent from John of Gaunt.

Cecily Bonville, 7th Baroness Harington, Marchioness of Dorset (1460–1529)
Only child and heiress of William Bonville, 6th Baron Harington, and his wife Katherine Neville. Cecily's father was killed at the Battle of Wakefield in 1460 and her grandfather, 1st Baron Bonville, was executed on 18 February 1461. The deaths of her father and grandfather made Cecily the wealthiest heiress in the country. In 1474 Cecily married Edward IV's stepson Thomas Grey, 1st Marquess of Dorset.

Thomas Bouchier, Cardinal, Archbishop of Canterbury (c.1404–1486)
Half-brother of Humphrey Stafford, 1st Duke of Buckingham. His promotion to the archbishopric of Canterbury was due to the influence of Richard, Duke of York.

Sir John Conyers of Hornby
Conyers, a member of the Yorkshire gentry who owed his allegiance to the Neville family, is thought to have assumed the persona of Robin of Redesdale in 1469 directed by Warwick to rise in rebellion against Edward IV. He was married to Alice Neville, one of Lord Fauconberg's daughters.

Isabel Despenser, Countess of Worcester and Warwick (1400–1439)
Sole heiress of Thomas Despenser, 1st Earl of Gloucester. She married first to Richard Beauchamp, 1st Earl of Worcester, and had one daughter, Elizabeth Beauchamp. After his death she married Richard Beauchamp, 13th Earl of Warwick. The two men were cousins. She gave her second husband two children – Henry and Anne.

Edmund, Earl of Rutland (1443–1460)
Second surviving son of Richard of York and Cecily Neville. He was slain as he fled the battlefield at Wakefield on 30 December 1460.

Edward IV (1442–1483)
Eldest surviving son of Richard of York and Cecily Neville. He was styled Earl of March before his father's death at the end of 1460 when he inherited his father's title. Following his victories at the Battles of Mortimer's Cross and Towton in 1461, he ascended the throne as King Edward IV. The king's marriage to Elizabeth Woodville in 1464 and the growing influence of the Woodville faction at court soured the relationship between him and his cousin Richard Neville, 16th Earl of Warwick.

Edward V (1470–1483) and his younger brother, Richard, Duke of York (1473–1483)
Edward was 12 years old when he became king. He, his brother Richard and their five surviving sisters were declared illegitimate on the grounds that their father Edward IV was precontracted to marry Lady Eleanor Butler before his marriage to their mother, Elizabeth Woodville. The last record of the princes was on 16 June 1483. Suspicions grew that they were murdered. What happened to the boys remains the subject of debate.

Edward of Middleham, Prince of Wales (c.1473 to 1476–1484)
The only child of Anne Neville and her husband Richard, Duke of Gloucester. He was born at Middleham Castle and was created Prince of Wales at York Minster on 8 September 1483. He died unexpectedly on 9 April 1484.

Edward of Westminster, Prince of Wales (1453–1471)
The only child of Henry VI and Margaret of Anjou, Edward is also known as Edward of Lancaster. In 1464 he fled with his mother to France. In December 1470 he married the 16th Earl of Warwick's daughter Anne Neville to cement an alliance between the royal House of Lancaster and the earl. On 4 May 1471 he was killed during the rout following the Battle of Tewkesbury or murdered soon afterwards.

Cecily of York (1469–1507)
Daughter of Edward IV and Elizabeth Woodville. Her first marriage, made by her uncle Richard III in about 1485 to Ralph Scrope, the younger brother of Baron Scrope of Masham, was annulled in 1486. In 1487, Henry VII arranged for her to marry his kinsman John Welles, 1st Viscount Welles.

Elizabeth of York, Duchess of Suffolk (1444–1503)
The third daughter of Richard, 3rd Duke of York and Cecily Neville. She was married to John de la Pole, 2nd Duke of Suffolk. She had eleven children including John de la Pole, 1st Earl of Lincoln; Edmund de la Pole, 3rd Duke of Norfolk; William de la Pole; and Richard de la Pole. Her descent from Richard, 3rd Duke of York, meant that her sons became Yorkist claimants to the throne during the reigns of Henry VII and Henry VIII.

Elizabeth of York, Queen of England (1466–1503)
The eldest child of Edward IV and Elizabeth Woodville. During the Christmas celebrations of 1483 Henry Tudor, the Lancastrian claimant to the throne, swore an oath to marry Elizabeth uniting the royal Houses of York and Lancaster. Elizabeth, who was part of Queen Anne's household at that time, was subject to the rumour that her uncle Richard III intended to marry her himself. Elizabeth and Henry VII married at the beginning of 1486.

Henry FitzHugh, 5th Baron FitzHugh of Ravensworth (d. 1472)
Married Alice Neville, a daughter of the 5th Earl of Salisbury and Alice Montagu. The FitzHugh family was an influential part of the Neville

affinity. The family transferred its allegiance to Richard, Duke of Gloucester, after Warwick's death.

George, Duke of Clarence (1449–1478)

George was his brother King Edward IV's heir from 1461 until the birth of Prince Edward in 1470. His relationship with his brother deteriorated after Edward's marriage to Elizabeth Woodville. When he was forbidden marriage with Isabel Neville, he rebelled against his brother. Having married Isabel at Calais in 1469, he changed sides once more and fought for Edward at the Battles of Barnet and Tewkesbury in 1471. He was arrested and tried for treason in 1478 before being found guilty and executed. For much of the 1470s, he and his brother Richard were involved in a dispute over the ownership of estates belonging to Anne Beauchamp, 16th Countess of Warwick.

Thomas Grey, Marquis of Dorset (1451–1501)

Eldest son of Elizabeth Woodville from her first marriage to John Grey of Groby. His mother arranged for him to marry Cecily Bonville in 1474; his first wife, the heiress Anne Holland, had died some time before. He fled into sanctuary with his mother in 1483 when Richard, Duke of Gloucester, seized control of Edward V. He escaped from England to join Henry Tudor in Brittany, having taken part in Buckingham's rebellion in October 1483.

William Hastings, Lord Hastings (c.1430–1483)

Friend and Lord Chamberlain of Edward IV. He was summarily executed by Richard, Duke of Gloucester, on 13 June 1483. He was married to Katherine Neville, the 16th Earl of Warwick's sister.

Henry VI (1421–1471)

Henry became king in 1422 during his infancy, following the death of his father Henry V. He married Margaret of Anjou to achieve peace between England and France. The couple's only son, Edward, was born in 1453 by which time the intermittent wars between the two countries had resumed. Henry was killed on 21 May 1471 at the Tower of London after the Lancastrian defeat on 4 May at the Battle of Tewkesbury and the death of his son Edward.

William Herbert, 1st Earl of Huntingdon and 2nd Earl of Pembroke (1451–1491)

William succeeded to the earldom of Pembroke, but was forced to surrender the title and its estates to Edward IV's heir. He was created Earl of Huntingdon as compensation for his loss. His first marriage was to Mary Woodville, a sister of Elizabeth Woodville. After her death he made a second marriage to Katherine Plantagenet, the illegitimate daughter of King Richard III.

William Herbert, 1st Earl of Pembroke (d. 1469)

Loyal to the House of York, Herbert was entrusted with the government of Wales by Edward IV. He and Jasper Tudor are regarded as key protagonists in Wales during the Wars of the Roses. Herbert secured Tudor's earldom of Pembroke and guardianship of Tudor's nephew Henry in 1468. Herbert intended to marry his ward to his daughter Maud but before this could take place, he came into conflict with the Earl of Warwick who sought some of Herbert's offices and estates to further his own ambitions. Herbert was defeated at the Battle of Edgcoat in 1469 and executed, together with his brother Richard, on Warwick's orders.

Anne Holland, Lady Astley (1461–before June 1474)

Anne was the only child of Anne of York and Henry Holland, 3rd Duke of Exeter. When her father was attainted, Anne's uncle Edward IV gave the bulk of Exeter's land to his sister Anne, but the remainder was given to Anne Holland. She was promised in marriage to Lord Montagu's son George Neville, but Elizabeth Woodville ensured that Anne became the wife of Thomas Grey (later Marquess of Dorset), her eldest son from her first marriage. Anne died without children.

John of Gloucester (c.1474–c.1499)

Illegitimate son of Richard III, also known as John of Pontefract. It is unknown whether or not John shared a mother with Richard's daughter Katherine Plantagenet.

Jacquetta of Luxembourg, Duchess of Bedford (d. 1472)

Mother of Elizabeth Woodville and thirteen other children through her second marriage to Richard Woodville.

Francis Lovell, 1st Viscount Lovell (c.1456–c.1487)
Friend and Lord Chamberlain of Richard III. Lovell became a ward of the 16th Earl of Warwick following his father's death in 1465. He was last recorded at the Battle of Stoke in 1487. He was married to Warwick's niece Anne FitzHugh of Ravensworth in Yorkshire by 1466.

Margaret of Anjou, Queen of England (1429–1482)
Married to Henry VI in 1445, the queen disliked her husband's heir, Richard, 3rd Duke of York. She preferred the advice of her own favourites including Edmund Beaufort, 2nd Duke of Somerset. She continued to wage war on the Yorkists following their victory at Towton on 29 March 1461, but was driven into exile in France in 1464. In 1470 she entered an unlikely alliance with the Earl of Warwick which was cemented by a marriage between her son, Edward of Lancaster, and the earl's younger daughter, Anne Neville. Defeated at the Battle of Tewkesbury on 4 May 1471 and captured soon after, she remained in captivity until 1475 when she was repatriated to France where she died in poverty.

Margaret of York, Duchess of Burgundy (1446–1503)
Daughter of Richard of York and Cecily Neville. In 1468 her brother Edward IV arranged for her to become the third wife of Charles the Bold, Duke of Burgundy.

Alice Montagu, 5th Countess of Salisbury (1407–1462)
Sole heiress of the 4th Earl of Salisbury, she was married in 1420 to Richard Neville, the eldest son of Ralph Neville, 1st Earl of Westmorland, and Joan Beaufort. She gave her husband six daughters and four sons including Richard Neville, 16th Earl of Warwick; John, 1st Marquess of Montagu; George, Archbishop of York; Joan, Countess of Arundel; Cecily, Duchess of Warwick; Alice, Baroness FitzHugh; Katherine, Baroness Hastings; Eleanor Neville, Baroness Stanley; and Margaret, Countess of Oxford.

Alice Neville, Baroness FitzHugh (d. 1503)
Daughter of Salisbury and Alice Montagu who was married to Henry FitzHugh, 5th Baron FitzHugh of Ravensworth in Yorkshire. She and

her daughter Elizabeth served as ladies-in-waiting to Queen Anne. Another daughter, Anne, married Francis Lovell.

Alice Neville (d. 1490)
Daughter of William Neville, Lord Fauconberg and his wife Joan Fauconberg. She was married to Sir John Conyers of Hornby in Yorkshire.

Anne Neville, Duchess of Buckingham (c.1408–1480)
Daughter of the 1st Earl of Westmorland and Joan Beaufort. She was an important landowner and patron of literature. In 1424 she married Humphrey Stafford, 1st Duke of Buckingham, a loyal Lancastrian. She was given custody of her sister Cecily, Duchess of York, and her younger children after the rout at Ludford Bridge on 12 October 1459. After Buckingham's death she married for a second time in 1467 to Walter Blount, 1st Baron Mountjoy, a supporter of King Edward IV.

Anne Neville, Duchess of Gloucester later Queen of England (1456–1485)
Younger daughter of the 16th Earl of Warwick and his wife Anne Beauchamp. She was married first to Edward of Lancaster, the only child of Henry VI and his wife Margaret of Anjou, and secondly to Richard, Duke of Gloucester, who ascended the throne as King Richard III in 1483.

Cecily Neville, Duchess of York (1415–1495)
The youngest daughter of Ralph Neville, 1st Earl of Westmorland, and Joan Beaufort. She married Richard, Duke of York, when she was 9 years old. She gave her husband twelve children, of whom seven survived to adulthood, including Edward IV; Edmund, Earl of Rutland; George, Duke of Clarence; Richard III; Anne, Duchess of Exeter; Elizabeth, Duchess of Suffolk; and Margaret, Duchess of Burgundy.

Cecily Neville, Duchess of Warwick and Countess of Worcester (d.1450)
Daughter of Richard Neville, 5th Earl of Salisbury and Alice Montagu. Married first to Henry Beauchamp and then to John Tiptoft. Her only child, Anne Beauchamp, was 15th Countess of Warwick in her own right.

Eleanor Neville, Baroness Stanley (d. before 1472)
Daughter of the 5th Earl of Salisbury and Alice Montagu, she was married to Thomas Stanley, 2nd Baron Stanley (later 1st Earl of Derby), in 1451. Her first surviving son George Stanley, 9th Baron Strange, was used by Richard III as a hostage at the Battle of Bosworth in 1485 in an attempt to ensure the support of his father and his uncle, William Stanley.

Elizabeth Neville (1435–1490)
Daughter of William Neville, Lord Fauconberg and his wife Joan. She was married before 1455 to Sir Richard Strangeways, the son of the Sheriff of Yorkshire and Chief Justice of Durham.

George Neville, Archbishop of York (1432–1476)
Younger son of the 5th Earl of Salisbury and Alice Montagu who was closely allied to his brother Richard Neville, the 16th Earl of Warwick. He was appointed Bishop of Exeter in 1458 but translated to the Archbishopric of York in 1465.

George Neville, 4th Baron Bergavenny (c.1440–1492)
The only child of Elizabeth Beauchamp (1415–1448) and Edward Neville, 3rd Baron Bergavenny. His wardship, and possession of his estates, were contested between the 16th Earl of Warwick and the 2nd Duke of Somerset.

George Neville, 1st Baron Latimer (d. 1469)
A younger son of Ralph Neville, 1st Earl of Westmorland, and Joan Beaufort. In 1430 he inherited the Latimer estates from his half-uncle, John Neville, whose mother was the heiress Elizabeth Latimer. George was married to Elizabeth Beauchamp, one of the 13th Earl of Warwick's daughters from his first marriage to Elizabeth Berkeley. In later years he was troubled by mental health problems which resulted in his lands being placed under the guardianship of the 16th Earl of Warwick, who was both his brother-in-law and nephew.

George Neville, Duke of Bedford (1465–1483)
Son of John Neville, Lord Montagu and Isabel Ingoldsthorpe. An agreement was made for him to marry an heiress, Anne Holland, but

in 1466 Elizabeth Woodville paid Anne's mother, Anne of York, to break the agreement. George was made Duke of Bedford in 1470 with the intention of a marriage to Edward IV's daughter, Elizabeth of York. When the 16th Earl of Warwick and Lord Montagu revolted against the Yorkist monarchy, the plan came to nothing. George was denied both his title and his rightful inheritance. He was a ward of Richard, Duke of Gloucester, who benefited from George's loss.

Sir Humphrey Neville of Brancepeth (d. 1469)
A descendant of Ralph Neville, 1st Earl of Westmorland, and his first wife Margaret Stafford. He sided with Lancaster and took part in Robin of Redesdale's uprising in 1469.

Isabel Neville, Duchess of Clarence (1451–1476)
Elder daughter of Richard Neville, 16th Earl of Warwick, and his wife Anne Beauchamp. She married George, Duke of Clarence, in 1469. She was the mother of Margaret, Countess of Salisbury, and Edward Plantagenet, 16th Earl of Warwick. She died soon after the birth of a short-lived second son named Richard. George, Duke of Clarence, came to believe that Isabel and their youngest son were both murdered.

Joan Neville, Countess of Arundel (c.1424–1462)
The eldest of the 5th Earl of Salisbury and his wife Alice Montagu's six daughters. She married William FitzAlan, 16th Earl of Arundel, sometime after 17 August 1438. They had four sons and one daughter. Her eldest son Thomas, Lord Maltravers, was present at the coronation of Richard III and Anne Neville.

John Neville, Marquess Montagu (c.1430–1471)
The third son of the 5th Earl of Salisbury and his wife Alice Montagu. He was a career soldier who fought with his father and Warwick. Following Edward IV's accession, he became Lord Montagu and in 1464 he was created Earl of Northumberland. He initially remained loyal to the king during Warwick's rebellion and exile in 1469 and the first half of 1470. However, Edward IV stripped him of his earldom making him Marquis of Montagu instead. Montagu joined with Warwick at the end of September 1470. He was killed on 14 April 1471 at the Battle of Barnet.

Katherine Neville, Duchess of Norfolk (c.1397–1483)

Eldest daughter of Ralph Neville and Joan Beaufort who was married four times. Her fourth marriage was to John Woodville, Elizabeth Woodville's brother. She was 65 and he was 19 years of age.

Katherine Neville, Lady Hastings (1442–1504)

Daughter of the Earl of Salisbury and Alice Montagu. She was married first to William Bonville who was executed in the aftermath of the Battle of Wakefield on 30 December 1460. She had one daughter, Cecily Bonville, with her first husband. In 1462 her brother, the 16th Earl of Warwick, arranged for her to marry William Hastings. The couple had six children.

Margaret Neville, Countess of Oxford (1442–1506)

Daughter of Richard Neville, Earl of Salisbury, and his wife Alice Montagu. Margaret's marriage to John de Vere, 13th Earl of Oxford, a Lancastrian loyalist, was arranged by her brother, the 16th Earl of Warwick.

Margaret Neville (c.1450–1498)

Illegitimate daughter of Richard Neville, 16th Earl of Warwick, by an unknown mistress. In 1464 Warwick arranged for her to marry Richard Huddleston of Millom whose family were part of the Neville affinity. After Huddleston's death Margaret married Lancelot Threlkeld, a descendant of the Clifford family and loyal Lancastrian.

Ralph Neville, 1st Earl of Westmorland (c.1364–1425)

Neville's support of Richard II against the Lords Appellant was rewarded by the creation of his earldom in 1397. In 1399 he chose to support his brother-in-law, Henry of Bolingbroke, who ascended the throne as King Henry IV. His first wife was Margaret Stafford and his second was Joan Beaufort. Between them they gave Westmorland a family of twenty-two children.

Richard Neville, 5th Earl of Salisbury (c.1400–1460)

Eldest son of the Earl of Westmorland's second marriage to Joan Beaufort. He became earl by right of his wife Alice Montagu. He was the father of

Warwick the Kingmaker and nine other legitimate children. He was a key supporter of his brother-in-law Richard, Duke of York.

Richard Neville, 16th Earl of Warwick, also known as Warwick the Kingmaker, (1428–1471)

The eldest son of the powerful northern Earl of Salisbury, Richard was married as a child to Anne Beauchamp, the youngest daughter of the 13th Earl of Warwick. When she inherited the bulk of her father's estates in 1449, Richard became Earl of Warwick by right of his wife. Known as 'the Kingmaker', Warwick's support for the Yorkists helped Edward IV to the throne. By switching sides in 1470 he also made it possible for the restoration of Henry VI. He arranged advantageous marriages for his daughters Isabel and Anne to further his ambitions.

Thomas Neville, Bastard of Fauconberg (d. 1471)

A cousin and supporter of Warwick, Neville was the illegitimate son of William Neville, Lord Fauconberg.

Thomas Neville, Lord Stanhope (c.1429–1460)

Second son of Salisbury and his wife Alice Montagu. His marriage to the heiress Maud Stanhope escalated the Neville-Percy feud. In 1460 he accompanied his father and Richard, Duke of York, into Yorkshire and was killed at the Battle of Wakefield.

William Neville, Lord Fauconberg and 1st Earl of Kent (d. 1463)

A younger brother of Salisbury and supporter of the Yorkist cause, William became Lord Fauconberg by right of his wife Joan Fauconberg. His three daughters – Elizabeth, Alice and Joan – were married into the Yorkshire-based Neville affinity to help bind the local gentry more closely to the Neville family.

Edward Plantagenet, Earl of Warwick (1475–1499)

Only surviving son of Isabel Neville and George, Duke of Clarence. Edward was a Yorkist claimant to the Crown despite being debarred by his father's attainder for treason in 1478. Soon after the Battle of Bosworth, Edward was moved to the Tower of London where he remained until his execution in 1499.

Katherine Plantagenet (died c.1487)
Acknowledged illegitimate daughter of Richard III. Her mother may have been Katherine Haute, a kinswoman of Elizabeth Woodville. Katherine married William Herbert, Earl of Huntingdon. In 1487 Herbert was described as a widower.

Margaret Plantagenet, Countess of Salisbury (1473–1541)
The only surviving daughter of Isabel Neville and George, Duke of Clarence. She was married by Henry VII, in 1487, to his kinsman Sir Richard Pole to ensure that her Plantagenet bloodline would not be a threat to his rule. She gave her husband five children. In 1512, Margaret was restored to the earldom of Salisbury in her own right. She was arrested for treason in November 1538 and executed after being held a prisoner in the Tower for more than two years.

Richard, Duke of Gloucester, later King Richard III (1452–1483)
The youngest son of Richard, 3rd Duke of York, and Cecily Neville. He became Duke of Gloucester when his eldest brother Edward became king in 1461. In 1472 he married Anne Neville despite opposition from his brother George. Richard was named as Lord Protector by King Edward IV in April 1483. In June 1483 he claimed the throne having declared his brother's children to be illegitimate. On 22 August 1485 Richard was killed during the Battle of Bosworth, bringing the rule of the Yorkist kings to an end.

Richard, 3rd Duke of York (1411–1460)
Son of Richard, Earl of Cambridge, and Anne Mortimer. Orphaned at the age of 4 and subsequently raised in the household of Ralph Neville, 1st Earl of Westmorland, and his second wife, Joan Beaufort. Richard married Cecily Neville, his guardian's youngest daughter.

Henry Stafford, 2nd Duke of Buckingham (c.1454–1483)
Henry became duke at the age of 4 in 1460. In 1466 he was married to Katherine Woodville, a sister of Elizabeth Woodville. He was executed for treason on 2 November 1484 at Salisbury.

Humphrey Stafford, 1st Duke of Buckingham (1402–1460)
Buckingham was married to Anne Neville, but disliked his brother-in-law Richard of York's ambition and remained loyal to Henry VI. He commanded the Lancastrian army at Northampton in 1460 and was killed defending his king. He was succeeded by his grandson.

Margaret Stafford, Countess of Westmorland (d. 1396)
A daughter of the 2nd Earl of Stafford and his wife Philippa Beauchamp, who was a daughter of the 11th Earl of Warwick. Margaret was the first wife of Ralph Neville, 1st Earl of Westmorland, giving him two sons and six daughters. Her grandson inherited Westmorland's earldom. Margaret's descendants supported the Lancastrian monarchy.

Thomas Stanley, 1st Earl of Derby (1435–1504)
He married Eleanor Neville, daughter of the 5th Earl of Salisbury and Alice Montagu, in 1451. By Eleanor he had eleven children. He married, secondly, Lady Margaret Beaufort. He is best known for his decisive intervention at the Battle of Bosworth to secure the victory of his stepson, Henry Tudor, over Richard III. He was created Earl of Derby on 27 October 1485.

John Tiptoft, Earl of Worcester (d. 1470)
Tiptoft was part of the extended Neville kinship network through his short-lived marriage to the 16th Earl of Warwick's sister Cecily Neville. In 1469 he remained loyal to Edward IV and condemned rebels siding with Warwick to death, earning the name 'butcher of England'. When Warwick forced Edward IV from the throne in 1470, Worcester was captured and executed.

Sir Andrew Trollope (d. 1461)
A commander of the Calais garrison under Warwick's command. Trollope came to England with the garrison to support Richard of York in 1459, but on 12 October 1459 he and other members of the garrison accepted Henry VI's offer of pardon at Ludford Bridge. He was part of the Lancastrian force at the Second Battle of St Albans in February 1461, but died on 29 March 1461 at the Battle of Towton.

Edmund Tudor, 1st Earl of Richmond (d. 1456)
Half-brother of Henry VI by their shared mother, Catherine of Valois. His father was Owen Tudor. The king raised both his half-brothers to the peerage and in 1455, Edmund married the 12-year-old heiress Margaret Beaufort. His son, Henry Tudor, was born posthumously.

Henry Tudor, later Henry VII (1457–1509)
The only child of Lady Margaret Beaufort and her first husband, Edmund Tudor. The deaths of Henry VI and his son Edward left Henry as the last Lancastrian male with a direct claim to the throne through his descent from the Beauforts.

Jasper Tudor, 1st Earl of Pembroke (1431–1495)
Younger half-brother of Henry VI. After Edmund Tudor's death, Jasper protected Margaret Beaufort and his young nephew. Jasper remained loyal to the Lancastrian cause throughout his life. He assumed guardianship of Henry when the boy was forced into exile, and after Edward of Lancaster's death he helped to put his nephew on the throne in 1485.

John de Vere, 13th Earl of Oxford (1443–1513)
De Vere was the second son of the 12th earl, but succeeded to the title after the executions of his father and elder brother. Warwick persuaded Edward IV to restore de Vere's lands after he arranged to marry the boy to his own sister Margaret Neville. De Vere maintained his Lancastrian sympathies, commanded the van of Warwick's army at the Battle of Barnet and fled to France after Edward IV's restoration. In 1473 he seized St Michael's Mount in Cornwall, was besieged for two months and then imprisoned at Hammes in Calais until 1484 when he escaped and returned to Henry Tudor in France. He commanded the right wing of Henry Tudor's army on 22 August 1485 at Bosworth.

Perkin Warbeck (1475–1499)
Pretender claiming to be Edward IV's younger son Richard. He was captured after he invaded Cornwall in 1497 and was confined to the Tower the following year. He was executed on 23 November 1499 to clear the way for an Anglo-Spanish marriage alliance between Henry VII and

Elizabeth of York's son Arthur and Catherine of Aragon, a daughter of Isabella I of Castile and Ferdinand II of Aragon.

Richard Welles, 7th Baron Welles (d. 1470)
A Lancastrian with family connections through his wife to the 16th Earl of Warwick. In February 1470 his only son Robert Welles attacked the home of Sir Thomas Burgh, Edward IV's Master of Horse. Richard and his brother-in-law Sir Thomas Dymmock were executed by Edward IV.

Robert Welles (d. 1470)
The only son of Sir Richard Welles. He led an uprising against Edward IV at the beginning of 1470, declaring for the 16th Earl of Warwick and George, Duke of Clarence. On 12 March 1470 he fought at the Battle of Losecoat Field and was executed soon afterwards.

John Wenlock, 1st Baron Wenlock (d. 1471)
Wenlock's relationship with the 16th Earl of Warwick led to him changing loyalty from Lancaster to York after the First Battle of St Albans in 1455. He served Edward IV as a soldier, a politician and a diplomat before switching sides in 1471 when Warwick came to terms with Margaret of Anjou. He commanded the middle of the Lancastrian line at the Battle of Tewkesbury on 4 May 1471 and died on the battlefield.

Anthony Woodville, 2nd Earl Rivers (d. 1483)
The eldest son of Richard Woodville and Jacquetta of Luxembourg. A leading member of the Woodville family, he advanced swiftly at court when his sister Elizabeth married Edward IV. In 1473, he was appointed governor of his nephew Prince Edward at Ludlow. On 29 April 1483, he met with Richard, Duke of Gloucester, at Stony Stratford and was placed under arrest the following morning, transported to Pontefract and executed on 25 June 1483.

Katherine Woodville (d. 1497)
Youngest sister of Elizabeth Woodville, married first to Henry Stafford, 2nd Duke of Buckingham, and secondly to Henry VII's uncle, Jasper Tudor. She made a third marriage to Sir Richard Wingfield sometime after 1495.

Elizabeth Woodville, Queen of England (c.1437–1492)
In 1464 Elizabeth, the widow of Lancastrian John Grey of Groby, entered into a secret marriage with Edward IV. She used her power as queen to the advantage of her large and ambitious family.

Sir John Woodville (d. 1469)
Fourth husband of Katherine Neville, Duchess of Norfolk. The marriage was arranged by Woodville's sister, Queen Elizabeth, in 1465. John Woodville was beheaded on 12 August 1469 on the orders of the 16th Earl of Warwick.

Richard Woodville, 1st Earl Rivers (d. 1469)
In 1437 Woodville married the Duke of Bedford's young widow, Jacquetta of Luxembourg, in a clandestine marriage that produced a family of fifteen children of whom only two died during infancy. He was created Baron Rivers in 1448 and Earl Rivers in 1466 by his son-in-law Edward IV. Regarded by the 16th Earl of Warwick as a social upstart, he and his son Sir John Woodville were captured after the Battle of Edgecote in July 1469 and executed on Warwick's orders.

Notes

Introduction
1. Mate, p.2
2. Kehler, p.102
3. Strickland, p.383
4. *Rous Roll*, no.62 cited in Licence:2013, p.72
5. Duffy, p.100; Sutton and Visser-Fuchs:1990, p.77

Chapter 1: A Noble Family and a Troublesome One
1. With grateful thanks to Dr Paul A. Fox for the information. Blockley, Sparks and Tatton-Brown, p.133
2. There are two versions of the roll. The first was made circa 1463 while the second, known as Copy A (British Library Add Ms. 48976), was completed circa 1483–1485. For a full account, see Crane.
3. British Library, Add. MS 48976
4. *Rous Roll*, no.62 cited in Hicks:2007, p.39
5. Page:1906, p.413 and Tillotson, n.29, p.38
6. Tillotson, p.4
7. Cressy, p.235
8. Banks, p.187
9. Goodman, pp.69–70
10. Gundy, pp.194–99
11. Despenser's mother was Isabella Beauchamp, the daughter of the 9th Earl of Warwick.
12. Hicks:1998, p.188
13. Poulson, p.403
14. Hicks:2007, p.37
15. Hicks:2012, p.17

Chapter 2: Childhood and Education
1. Rowland, pp.41–42
2. Ibid., pp.146–147
3. *Great Chronicle*, p.137
4. Royle, p.237
5. Gristwood, pp.17–25
6. *Croyland Chronicle*, p.418
7. Paston Letters, p.13
8. Green, pp.85–86 and pp.133–134
9. Ibid., pp.91–92
10. Rowland, pp.56–77

11. *Calendar of Papal Letters 1447–1455*, p.151 cited in Hicks:2007, p.47
12. Green, p.111
13. *London Chronicle*, p.139
14. Julian Calendar
15. Leyser, p.124
16. Orme, p.305
17. *London Chronicle*, p.139
18. *Rous Roll*, no.58 cited in Hicks:2007, p.48
19. By this time Rous was eager to win Henry VII's approbation.
20. York's sister Isabel of Cambridge married the archbishop's elder brother, Henry. Bourchier, 1st Earl of Essex
21. Bobrick, p.102
22. Rawcliffe, p.84
23. Nicholas, pp.356–357
24. *Rous Roll*, no.56
25. Philips, p.31

Chapter 3: Calais
1. Rose, p.75
2. Ibid., p.81
3. Vergil, p.120
4. Thornton, p.41
5. *Great Chronicle*, p.139
6. *Croyland Chronicle*, p.454
7. Grummit, p.12
8. https://nevillfeast.wordpress.com/category/the-nevills/alice-montacute-countess-of-salisbury/s
9. Lewis, chapter 2 for the rout at Ludford and its aftermath
10. Brut, p.529; Hicks:2007, p.51
11. Laynesmith, p.73

Chapter 4: A Northern Inheritance
1. *Waurin's Chronicle*, p.314
2. *Annales*, p.774
3. Ashdown-Hill:2018, p.97
4. Haigh, p.18
5. *Croyland Chronicle*, p.422
6. Ibid.
7. Ibid.
8. Ibid., p.424
9. *Notes and Queries*, p.218
10. Fritz, p.75
11. Woodward, pp.30–31

Chapter 5: The Marriage Market
1. Crane, p.1
2. Ibid., p.9
3. Hodder, p.19

4. Gunn, ODNB online
5. Ross:2011, pp.50–51
6. Strickland, p.243
7. *Croyland Chronicle*, p.440
8. Ibid.
9. Vergil, p.117
10. *Warkworth Chronicle*, p.3
11. Vergil, p.118
12. Hicks:2019, p.53
13. *Calendar of Inquisition Post Mortem, Henry VII*, series 2, volume 2, p.762
14. William of Worcester, p.783
15. Mancini, p.61, cited in Ashdown-Hill: 2014, p.82
16. Ashdown-Hill:2018, p.115
17. *Calendar of State Papers Milanese*, p.119

Chapter 6: Marrying a Prince
1. Baines, p.46
2. *The Lytille Childrenes Lytil Boke*, https://www.bl.uk/collection-items/the-lytille-childrenes-lytil-boke, BL, Egerton MS 1995
3. A tun is 252 gallons and a pipe is half a tun or 126 gallons.
4. A band running horizontally across the field.
5. Each arm of the cross is crossed to symbolise the fourfold mystery of the cross – sacrifice, forgiveness, love and victory.
6. *Croyland Chronicle*, p.444
7. Ibid., p.445
8. Ashdown-Hill:2014, p.95
9. Vergil, p.120
10. Ross:1983, p.117
11. Jacob, pp.552–553
12. Stevenson (ed.), *Letters and Papers*, p.788; Weightman, pp.16–17
13. *Croyland Chronicle*, p.445
14. Scofield, vol 1, pp.488–497; Ross:1983, pp.126–142, 439–440; Dockray:1983, pp.246–257
15. Dockray:1983, pp.246–257
16. Ross:1983, n.5, pp.120–121
17. *The Chronicle of John Stone*, p.109; Ashdown-Hill:2018, p.125
18. *Collection of Ordinances and Regulations for the Government of the Royal Household*, p.98
19. Hicks:2007, p.71

Chapter 7: The Wives and Daughters of Rebels
1. Married to Isabel and Anne's cousin Elizabeth FitzHugh by 1475. Parr brought a force of northerners to Edward IV at Doncaster in 1471 and fought against Warwick at Barnet. His brother was killed in the battle, fighting alongside the Duke of Gloucester. Parr was rewarded by Gloucester, but did not attend Richard's coronation and died soon after.
2. *Calendar of Close Rolls*, 1468–1476, vol 2, pp.85–87; Ross:1983, p.133
3. Mancini, p.75; Kendall, p.276

4. Ashdown-Hill:2014, p.103
5. Wagner, p.296
6. Kendall, p.291
7. Ross:1983, p.141
8. Fleming, p.24
9. Vergil, p.129
10. Commines, p.184
11. Tiptoft was Warwick's brother-in-law, having been Cecily Neville's second husband after the death of Henry Beauchamp, 1st Duke of Warwick, until her own death in 1450.
12. Scofield, I, pp.500–501; Weightman, pp.76–77
13. *Rous Roll*, no.58

Chapter 8: Anne – the Kingmaker's Bargain
1. Hicks:1998, p.289
2. *Calendar of State Papers Milan*, pp.134–145
3. Giles, p.232
4. Maurer, p.207
5. *Croyland Chronicle*, p.462
6. Ibid.
7. Commines, p.188
8. *Croyland Chronicle*, p.463
9. *Warkworth Chronicle*, p.14
10. Ross:2011, p.67

Chapter 9: Lancastrian Princess
1. *The Arrivall*, p.25
2. Marie's husband, Thomas Courtenay, the 14th Earl of Devon, was executed in the aftermath of the Battle of Towton in 1461.
3. Strickland, p.197
4. *The Arrivall* takes its information from a document written in French that came from Burgundy in 1471. This account was written by Nicholas Harpsifeld who was a clerk of the signet working for King Edward and was known to have been with the king on his return from exile and during the campaign that followed. *The Arrivall* is usually ascribed to him.
5. Masse, p.107
6. Hicks:2008, p.98
7. *The London Chronicle*, p.144
8. Ibid., p.19
9. Vergil, p.152
10. William Stanley is best known for turning coat at the Battle of Bosworth in 1485 and attacking the Yorkists, unlike his elder brother Lord Thomas Stanley, the husband of Lady Margaret Beaufort, who failed to commit his troops to either side. In 1495 William Stanley reverted to his Yorkist allegiance despite being well rewarded by King Henry VII for his assistance at Bosworth. He was beheaded for his part in the Perkin Warbeck rising.
11. *The Arrivall*, p.38
12. *The London Chronicle*, p.145

13. Hicks: 2008, p.93
14. Ross:2011, p.78
15. Wood, p.103
16. Ibid., p.104
17. Ibid.

Chapter 10: From Scullery Maid to Duchess
1. Pollard, pp.318–319
2. Dunn, pp.124–126
3. Hicks:2007, pp.130–134 and Barnfield, pp.84–89
4. Hall:1839, p.14
5. Mancini, p.63
6. Barnfield, p.88
7. *Calendar of the Patent Rolls*, p.455
8. Barnfield, p.88
9. Paston Letters, vol 3, p.18 and cited in Strickland, p.246
10. Pollard, p.320
11. Paston Letters, vol 3, p.30 and p.92
12. *Testamenta Eboracensia* volume 3 p.3

Chapter 11: The Duchess of Gloucester
1. *Warkworth Chronicle*, p.25
2. 1473, 1474 and 1476 are also cited as dates for Edward's birth.
3. For a full discussion see Hicks:1999
4. Cherry, p160
5. https://www.ancient-origins.net/news-history-archaeology/gold-bible-0016047
6. Spring, p.42
7. Laynesmith, p.141
8. Hilton, pp.465–466
9. *Calendar of Patent Rolls*, February 1478
10. Hicks:2007, p.157
11. Ibid.
12. Ibid.
13. D'Evelyn, Introduction
14. British Library, Harleian 433
15. See Walker for a full discussion on pets and pet ownership during the medieval period.
16. Hammond, p.48
17. Matthews, p.119
18. Cherry:1994, p.8
19. Hammond, Sutton and Visser-Fuchs, p.126
20. Hicks:2007, p.161
21. Baldwin, pp.119–120
22. Ibid., p.98
23. Emery, p.220
24. Hislop, p.30

Chapter 12: The Duchess of Clarence

1. *Collection of Ordinances*, p.100
2. Ibid., p.94
3. Ibid., pp.87–103
4. Ibid., p.146
5. *Visitation of Gloucester*, p.262
6. Ashdown-Hill:2018, p.144
7. Jackson, p.7
8. Jones and Olsan, p.409
9. Filippini, pp.79–80
10. Ibid., p.117
11. Leyser, p.130
12. Hammond, Sutton and Visser-Fuchs, p.126
13. Buckle, p.408
14. Ashdown-Hill:2018, p.154
15. Leyser, p.125
16. *Descriptive Calendar of the Ancient Manuscripts and Records in the Possession of the Corporation of Stratford-upon-Avon*, p.450

Chapter 13: Witchcraft, Murder and Treason

1. Ashdown-Hill:2014, pp.132–133, nn. 25 and 26
2. Ross:2011, p.187, n.3; Ashdown-Hill:2014, p.133
3. Mancini, pp.62–63
4. Hicks:2014, pp.124–135
5. He was caught up in the Duke of Buckingham's rebellion in 1483, but was subsequently pardoned and is believed to have fought on the side of the Tudors at Bosworth.
6. Ashdown-Hill:2014, p.141
7. Ibid., p.143
8. Ibid., p.154
9. Wroe, p.71
10. *Calendar State Papers Milan*, p.175 cited in Ross:2011, p.71
11. Ross:1983, pp.191–192; Ross:2011, p.71
12. Mancini, pp.62–63
13. *Christ Church Letters*, pp.36–37
14. *Calendar of Patent Rolls 1466–1488*, p.212
15. Higginbottom, p.7
16. Shakespeare, *Richard III* 1.4.887

Chapter 14: The Lord Protector's Wife

1. Davies, ODNB online
2. Hilton, p.454
3. *York House Books*, pp.282, 284–286, 712–17
4. More, p.39
5. Mancini, p.66
6. Mancini, pp.88–89
7. Commines, p.396–397
8. Dockray, Richard III, p.80
9. Hammond, Appendix II, p.62

Chapter 15: Queen Anne
1. Salter, p.66
2. Courtais, p.34
3. Hammond and Sutton, p.103
4. Ibid., p.31
5. Ibid., p.33 referencing the Great Wardrobe Accounts 9 April 1483–2 February 1484, PRO. LC9/50
6. Ibid., p.33
7. Ibid.
8. Sutton and Hammond, pp.167–168 and p.360

Chapter 16: A Royal Progress
1. *York House Books* cited in Hammond, p.45
2. More, p.41
3. Ashdown-Hill:2018, p.172
4. Pollard, p.345
5. Vergil, p.188–189
6. Johnson, p.58 and 64; Attreed, p.218
7. Tillot, pp.343–357
8. Attreed, p.218
9. *Croyland Chronicle*, p.161
10. *Rous Roll*, no.60 cited in Higginbottom, p.8
11. Raine, pp.218–219
12. Higginbottom, p.9
13. Pollard, p.345
14. Penn, p.92

Chapter 17: An Enigma – Piety and Patronage
1. Peters, p.10
2. Harris expands this view in *English Aristocratic Women and the Fabric of Piety, 1450–1550*. See also Harris's work on the fabric of piety as an expression of female aristocratic agency.
3. Chaucer, *The Wife of Bath's Tale*, lines 1044–1045
4. Ibid.
5. Charlotte D'Evelyn (ed.), *Peter Idley's Instructions to his Son*, EETS (London, 1935), lines 1227–1229, p.101.
6. Crouch:2000, p.30
7. *Calendar of Patent Rolls 1476–85*, no.464
8. Hicks:2007, p.164
9. Ross:1983, p.130
10. Cosman, Madeleine Pelner and Jones, Linda Gale, *Handbook to Life in the Medieval World*, 3-volume set. Infobase Publishing, 2009; p.765
11. Hurlock, p.18
12. Vergil, p.192
13. *Victoria County History*, pp.478–485
14. Bell, p.743
15. Lambeth Palace Library, MS 474
16. Tudor-Craig, p.27

17. Hughes, p106
18. British Library, MS Egerton 2006
19. Yoshikawa, p.27
20. British Library, Royal MS 18 A XII, f.1re

Chapter 18: Sudden Grief
1. Pollard, A.J. 'One Summer at Middleham', *The Worlds of Richard III*. Tempus, 2001; p.143
2. *Croyland Chronicle*, p.497
3. Ibid.
4. Sutton, Visser-Fuchs and Kleineke, pp.31–32
5. Ibid., pp.32–33 and Higginbottom, p.9
6. Horrox:2004 ODNB and Ashdown-Hill, p.66
7. Gunn, ODNB
8. *Henry V*, 3.3.27

Chapter 19: Christmas 1484
1. *Croyland Chronicle*, p.498 cited in Weir:1992, p.203
2. Discussed in Barnfield, p.92
3. Weir:1992, p.202
4. Vergil, p.211
5. Ibid.
6. *Rous Roll*, no.63
7. Hanham, pp.118–124
8. *Croyland Chronicle*, p.499
9. Sutton and Visser-Fuchs, pp.71–72

Chapter 20: Afterwards
1. *York House Books*, vol 1., pp.368–369
2. Pollard, p.370
3. Ibid., p.307
4. *Inquisition Postmortem Chancery Series*, 19 Henry VII, no.86.
5. *Patent Rolls*, 21 Henry VII, Part 3., mem. 22.
6. Wolffe, p.216
7. Ashdown-Hill, pp.66–67
8. Thomas, *Great Chronicle*, p.292 and Ashdown-Hill:2015, pp.176–177
9. *Hall's Chronicle*, p.490
10. *Calendar of State Papers, Spain*, vol 6. (1), p.166
11. Higginbottom, p.165
12. Ibid, p.1

Bibliography

Primary sources

A Chronicle of London, from 1089 to 1483 Written in the 15th Century, and for the First Time Printed from Mss. in the British Museum, ed. Harris, Nicolas (London: Longman, Rees, Orme, Brown and Green, 1827)

A Descriptive Calendar of the Ancient Manuscripts and Records in the Possession of the Corporation of Stratford-upon-Avon, ed. Halliwell, J.O. (Stratford-upon-Avon, 1863)

Attreed, Lorraine, C., (ed.), *The York House Books 1461–1490*, (Stamford: Paul Watkins, 1991)

Bowyer, Robert, et al, *An Exact Abridgement of the Records in the Tower of London: From the Reign of King Edward the Second, Unto King Richard the Third, of All the Parliaments Holden in Each Kings Reign, and the Several Acts in Every Parliament: Together with the Names and Titles of All the Dukes, Marquesses, Earls, Viscounts, and Barons, Summoned to Every of the Said Parliaments*, (William Leake, stationer, at the Crown in Fleetstreet, between the two Temple gates, 1657)

Bennett, J., *The History of Tewkesbury*, (Tewkesbury: 1830)

Bruce, John, (ed.), *Historie of the Arrivall of Edward IV in England and the Finall Recoverye of His Kingdomes From Henry VI. A.D. M.CCCC.LXXI* (London: The Camden Society, 1838)

Calendar of Close Rolls, Edward IV: Volume 2, 1468–1476, ed. Bird, W.H. and Leedward, K.H. (London, 1953)

Calendar of Papal Letters (1447–1455), Volume 10, ed. Twemlow, J.A. (London: HMSO, 1915)

Calendar of the Patent Rolls preserved in the Public Record Office: Edward IV, Henry VI, 1467–1477, (London: HMSO, 1900; reprinted 1971)

Calendar of State Papers, Milanese, ed. Hinds, A.B., (London: HMSO, 1912)

Calendar of State Papers, Spain, 1538–1541, ed. Gayangos (London: HMSO, 1890)

Documents Relating to the Foundation and Antiquities of the Collegiate Church of Middleham, in the County of York, ed. Atthill, William (London: The Camden Society, 1847)

Calendars of Inquisitions Post Mortem, xxii–xxvi, ed. Carpenter, Christine (Woodbridge: The Boydell Press, 2003–11) accessed via https://inquisitionspostmortem.ac.uk

Camden, William, et al, *The Visitation of the County of Gloucester: Taken in the Year 1623*, (London: Harleian Society Publications, 1885)

Commines, Philippe de, *The Memoirs for the Reign of Louis XI, 1481–1483*, ed. Jones, M. (London: Harmondsworth, 1972)

Courthope, W.H., (ed.), *The Rows Rolls* (1859)

Davis, N. (ed.), *Paston Letters and Papers of the Fifteenth Century*, 2 vols. (Oxford: Oxford University Press, 1971–1976)

Edwards, Rhoda, *The Itinerary of King Richard III 1483–1485* (London: Richard III Society, 1983)

Fabyan, Robert, *The New Chronicles of England and France*, ed. Ellis, Henry (London: Rivington, 1811)

Foster, Joseph (ed.), *Visitation Pedigrees of Cumberland and Westmorland Recorded by Richard St George 1615 and William Dugdale in 1666* (1891; reprinted Whitehaven: Michael Moon, 2010)

Gairdner, James (ed.), *The Historical Collections of a Citizen of London*, old series, volume 17 (London: Camden Record Society, 1876) – also known as *Gregory's Chronicle*

Gairdner, James (ed.), *The Paston Letters, AD 1422–1509*, 6 volumes (London, 1904)

Giles, J.A. (ed.), *The Chronicles of the White Rose of York* (London, 1845)

Green, Monica (ed.), *The Trotula: An English Translation of the Medieval Compendium of Women's Medicine (The Middle Ages Series)*, (Philadelphia: PENN University of Pennsylvania Press, 2002)

Hall, Edward, *Hall's Chronicle, Containing the History of England During the Reign of Henry IV and the Succeeding Monarchs to the end of the Reign of Henry VIII*, ed. Ellis, Henry (London, 1809)

Hammond, P.W., and Sutton, A.F., *The Coronation of Richard III: The Extant Documents* (Gloucester: Alan Sutton, 1983)

Harvey, J.H. (ed.), *William Worcestre Itineraries* (Oxford: OUP, 1969)

Holinshed, *Chronicles of England, Scotland and Ireland*, 6 vols. (London, 1807–1808)

Horrox, Rosemary and Hammond, Peter, (eds), *British Library Harleian Manuscript 433*. 4 vols. (Stroud: Sutton for the Richard III Society, 1979–1983)

Idley, Peter, *Peter Idley's Instructions to his Son*, ed. D'Evelyn, Charlotte (London: Early English Text Society, 1935)

Jackson, J.E., *A Guide to Farleigh Hungerford, Co. Somerset, Illustrated with Ground Plans and Plates of Arms, and an Appendix of Ancient Manorial and Ecclesiastical Deeds* (1879)

Mancini, Dominic, *The Usurpation of Richard III, Dominic Mancini*, ed. Armstrong, C.A.J. (Stroud: Sutton, 1989)

Maskelyne and Lyte, H.C. Maxwell, 'Inquisitions Post Mortem, Henry VII, Entries 751–800', in *Calendar of Inquisitions Post Mortem: Series 2, Volume 2, Henry VII* (London: 1915), pp.486–508

Molinet, Jean, *Chroniques de Jean Molinet*, 3 vols, ed. by Doutrepont, G.D. (Brussels: Académie Royale de Belgique, 1935–37)

More, Sir Thomas, *The History of Richard III*, student's edition, (thomasmorestudies.org, 2020)

Myers, A.R. (ed.) *English Historical Documents 1327–1485*, (London: Eyre & Spottiswoode, 1969)

Myers, A.R., (ed), *The Household of Edward IV: The Black Book and the Ordinance of 1478*, (Manchester: Manchester University Press, 1959)

Proceedings and Ordinances of the Privy Council of England, 7 vols, volume 6, ed. by Nicholas, N.H., (1834–37)

Raine, James (ed.), 'The Statutes Ordained by Richard Duke of Gloucester for the College of Middleham,' Dated July 4, 18 EDW. IV. (1478), *Archaeological Journal*. 14, 1857, pp.160–170

Riley, Henry Thomas (ed.), *Ingulph's Chronicle of the Abbey of Croyland with the Continuations by Peter of Blois and Anonymous Writers* (London: Bohn, 1854)

Sheppard, J.B. (ed.), *Christ Church Letters*, Camden Series (London, 1877)

Sinclair, A. (ed.), *The Beauchamp Pageant* (Donnington: Richard III and Yorkist History Trust, 2003)

Society of Antiquaries, *A Collection of Ordinances and Regulations for the Government of the Royal Household made in Divers Reigns* (London: John Nichols, 1790)
Stevenson, J. (ed.), *Annales Rerum Anglicarum: Letters and Papers Illustrative of the Wars of the English in France*, vol. 2, part 2, Rolls Series (London: 1864), pp.774–775
Stevenson, J.S. (ed.), 'William of Worcester's Collections' (*Annales Rerum Anglicarum*), *Letters and Papers illustrative of the Wars of the English in France*, no 22, vol. 2, pat.2 (4 vols, Rolls Series, 1864)
Stone, John, *Christ Church, Canterbury: The Chronicle of John Stone, Monk of Christ Church, 1415–1471*, volume 1, ed. by Searle, W.G., (Cambridge: Cambridge Antiquarian Society, 1902)
Sylvester, R.S. (ed), *The History of King Richard III* written by Sir Thomas More, (New Haven, 1976)
The boke of curesy beginning 'Litylle chyldrynne here may y elere', British Library, Egerton MS 1995, https://www.bl.uk/collection-items/the-lytille-childrenes-lytil-boke
The Brut of England or The Chronicles of England, Part 1–2, ed. Brie, F.W.D. (London: Kegan Paul, 1906)
The Fabric Rolls of York with an Appendix of Illustrative Documents, ed. Raine, James (Durham: Surtees, 1859)
The Holinshed Project, *Holinshed's Chronicles*, http://english.nsms.ox.ac.uk/holinshed/ (Oxford University)
Thomas, A.H. and Thornley, I.D. (eds), *The Great Chronicle of London* (London: 1938; Gloucester: reprinted 1983)
Vergil, Polydore, *Three Books of Polydore Vergil's English History, Comprising the Reigns of Henry VI, Edward IV and Richard III: From an Early Translation Preserved Among the MSS. of the British Museum*, ed. Ellis, Henry (London: Camden Society, 1844)
Warkworth, John, *Chronicle of the First Thirteen Years of the Reign of King Edward IV*, ed. Halliwell, J.O. (London: Camden Society, 1839)
Waurin, Jean de, *Recueil des Chroniques et Anchienne Istories de la Grant Bretaigne, à Present Nommé Engleterre*, volume 5, ed. Hardy, W. and Hardy, E.L.C.P. (1891; Cambridge: reprinted 2012)
Whethamsteade, John, *Registrum abbatiae Johannis Whetamstede*, 2 vols., ed. Riley, Henry T., Rolls Series (1872–1873)
Wood, Mary Anne Everett, *Letters of Royal and Illustrious Ladies of Great Britain*, Volume 1 (London: Henry Colburn, 1846)

Secondary Sources
Anon., *Notes and Queries*, 186/10 (6 May 1944), p.218
Amundsen, Darrel W., and Diers, Carol Jean, 'The Age of Menopause in Medieval Europe', *Human Biology*, 45/4 (1973), pp.605–612
Archer, R.E., 'Rich Old Ladies: The Problem of Late Medieval Dowagers' in Pollard, A.J. (ed.), *Property and Politics: Essays in Later Medieval English History* (Stroud: Sutton, 1984), pp.15–35
Ashdown-Hill, John, *The Third Plantagenet: George Duke of Clarence, Richard III's brother* (Stroud: The History Press, 2014)
Ashdown-Hill, John, *The Dublin King: The True Story of Edward, Earl of Warwick, Lambert Simnel and the 'Princes in the Tower'* (Stroud: The History Press, 2015)
Ashdown-Hill, John, *Cecily Neville: The Mother of Richard III* (Barnsley: Pen and Sword, 2018)

Baines, Thomas, *A History and a Description of the Three Ridings of the Great County of York, from the Earliest Ages to the Year 1870; with an Account of Its Manufactures, Commerce, and Civil and Mechanical Engineering*, Volume 3 (London: Mackenzie, 1870)

Banks, Thomas Christopher, *The Dormant and Extinct Baronage of England* (London: J. White, 1808)

Barnfield, Marie, 'Diriment Impediments, Dispensations and Divorce: Richard III and Matrimony', *The Ricardian*, 17 (2007), pp.84–98

Barwell, A. 'The Healing Arts and Social Capital: The Paston Women of Fifteenth-Century England', *Canadian Bulletin of Medical History*, 35/1, (Spring 2018), pp.137–159

Blockley, Kevin, Sparks, Margaret and Tatton-Brown, Tim, *Canterbury Cathedral Nave: Archaeology, History and Architecture* (Canterbury: Dean and Chapter of Canterbury Cathedral and Canterbury Archaeological Trust, 1997)

Bobrick, B., *The Fated Sky: Astrology in History* (London: Simon & Schuster, 2005)

Breverton, Terry, *Richard III: The King in the Car Park* (Stroud: Amberley Publishing, 2015)

Buck, George, *The History of King Richard III*, (ed.) Kinkaid, A.N. (Gloucester: Alan Sutton, 1979)

Buckle, Alexandra, '"Fit for a King": music and iconography in Richard Beauchamp's chantry chapel', *Early Music*, 38/1 (2010), pp.3–20

Cherry, John, *The Middleham Jewel and Ring* (York: The Yorkshire Museum, 1994)

Cherry, John, 'Healing Through Faith: The Continuation of Medieval Attitudes to Jewellery into the Renaissance', *Renaissance Studies*, 15/2 (2001), pp.154–71

Clark, David, *Barnet - 1471: Death of a Kingmaker* (Barnsley: Pen and Sword, 2007)

Clark, K.L., *The Nevills of Middleham: England's Most Powerful Family in the Wars of the Roses* (Stroud: The History Press, 2016)

Clark, Linda, (ed.), *The Fifteenth Century XIV: Essays presented to Michael Hicks* (Woodbridge: The Boydell Press, 2015)

Clarke, P.D., 'English Royal Marriages and the Papal Penitentiary in the Fifteenth Century', *English Historical Review*, 120/488, (2005) pp.1014–1029

Cokayne, G.E., with Gibbs, Vicary, Doubleday, H.A., White, Geoffrey H., Warrand, Duncan, and Lord Howard de Walden, (eds), *The Complete Peerage of England, Scotland, Ireland, Great Britain and the United Kingdom, Extant, Extinct or Dormant, new ed.*, (1910–1959; reprint in 6 volumes, Stroud: Alan Sutton Publishing, 2000), volume IX. Hereinafter cited as *The Complete Peerage*.

Courtais, Georgine de, *Women's Hats, Headdresses and Hairstyles: With 453 Illustrations, Medieval to Modern* (New York: Dover Publications, 2013)

Crane, Susan, 'Representations of Courtship and Marriage in the Salisbury Rolls', *The Coat of Arms 3rd series*, 6/1 (2010), pp.1–15

Crawford, A, 'Victims of attainder: the Howard and de Vere women in the late fifteenth century', *Reading Medieval Studies*, 15 (1989), pp.59–74

Cressy, David, *Birth, Marriage and Death: Ritual, Religion, and the Life-Cycle in Tudor and Stuart England* (Oxford: Oxford University Press, 1999)

Crosswhite, Anastasia, B., 'Women and Land: Aristocratic Ownership of Property in Early Modern England', *New York University Law Review*, 77/4, (October 2002), pp.1119–1156

Davies, C.S.L., 'Stafford, Henry, second Duke of Buckingham (1455–1483)', *Oxford Dictionary of National Biography* (2004; online edition, 2011)

Davies, Robert (ed.), *Extracts from the Municipal Records of the City of York during the Reigns of Edward IV, Edward V and Richard III with Notes illustrative and explanatory* (London: B. Nichols and Son, 1843)

Dobson, R. Barrie, 'Politics and the Church in the Fifteenth Century North,' in Pollard, Anthony (ed.), *The North of England in the Age of Richard III* (Stroud: Sutton Publishing, 1996), pp.1–18

Dobson, R. Barrie, *Church and Society in the Medieval North of England* (London: Hambledon Press, 1996)

Dockray, Keith, 'The Yorkshire Rebellions of 1469,' *The Ricardian*, 6/83 (December 1983), pp.246–257

Dowden, John, 'Note on the Foundation of Richard Duke of Gloucester, at Queens College Cambridge (1477)', *Transactions of the Scottish Ecclesiological Society*, 1, (1904–1905): pp.156–158

Duffy, Eamon, *Marking the Hours: English People and their Prayers* (New Haven and London: Yale University Press, 2011)

Dunn, Caroline, *Stolen Women in Medieval England* (Cambridge: Cambridge University Press, 2013)

Emery, Anthony, *Great Medieval Houses of England and Wales*, Vol 2 (Cambridge: Cambridge University Press, 2000)

Filippini, Nadia Maria, *Pregnancy, Delivery, Childbirth: A Gender and Cultural History from Antiquity to the Test Tube in Europe* (London: Routledge, 2021)

Fritz, P.S., 'From "Public" to "Private": the Royal Funerals in England 1500–1830', in Whaley, J., (ed.), *Mirrors of Mortality* (New York: Routledge, 1981; republished 2012)

Given-Wilson, Chris, *The English Nobility in the Late Middle Ages: The Fourteenth-Century Political Community* (London: Routledge, 1996)

Gee, Eric, 'The Topography of Altars, Chantries and Shrines in York Minster', *Antiquaries Journal*, 64 (1984), pp.337–335

Gristwood, Sarah, *Blood Sisters: The Women Behind the Wars of the Roses* (New York: Basic Books, 2013)

Grummitt, David, 'The Defence of Calais and the Development of Gunpowder Weaponry in England in the Late Fifteenth Century', *War in History*, 7/3 (2000), pp.253–72

Goodman, Anthony, *Loyal Conspiracy: The Lords Appellant Under Richard II* (London: Routledge, 1971)

Gundy, A.K., *Richard II and the Rebel Earl* (Cambridge: Cambridge University Press, 2013)

Gunn, S.J., 'Vere, John de, thirteenth Earl of Oxford (1442–1513), *Oxford Dictionary of National Biography*, (September 2004; online edition, January 2008)

Haigh, Philip A., *The Battle of Wakefield 1460* (Stroud: Sutton Publishing, 1996)

Hall, George, *The History of Chesterfield* (London: Whittaker & Co, 1839)

Hammond, P.W. and Sutton, Anne F., *Richard III: The Road to Bosworth Field* (London: Constable, 1985)

Hammond, P.W., Sutton, Anne F. and Visser-Fuchs, Livia, *The Reburial of Richard, Duke of York, 21–30 July 1476* (London: Richard III Society, 1996)

Hanawalt, Barbara, et al. (eds), *City and Spectacle in Medieval Europe* (Minnesota: University of Minnesota Press, 1994)

Harris, Barbara J., *English Aristocratic Women and the Fabric of Piety, 1450–1550* (Oxford: Oxford University Press, 2002)

Hicks, Michael, 'Anne (née Anne Neville) (1456–1485)', *Oxford Dictionary of National Biography*, (2004; online edition, 2006)
Hicks, Michael, *Anne Neville: Queen to Richard III* (Stroud: The History Press, 2007)
Hicks, Michael, *English Political Culture in the Fifteenth Century* (London: Taylor & Francis, 2003)
Hicks, Michael, 'Neville (Fauconberg), Thomas (called the Bastard of Fauconberg) (d.1471)', *Oxford Dictionary of National Biography*, (2004; online edition, 2004)
Hicks, Michael, *Richard III and His Rivals: Magnates and their Motives in the Wars of the Roses* (London: Bloomsbury Academic, 1991)
Hicks, Michael, *Richard III: The Self-Made King* (New Haven and London: Yale University Press, 2019)
Hicks, Michael, *The Fifteenth-Century Inquisitions Post Mortem: A Companion* (Woodbridge: Boydell Press, 2012)
Hicks, Michael, 'The Neville earldom of Salisbury, 1429–71', *Wiltshire Archaeological Magazine*, 72 (1977–1981), pp.141–147
Hicks, Michael, 'What might have been: George Neville Duke of Bedford 1465–83 – his identity and significance', *The Ricardian*, 7/95 (December 1986), pp.321–326
Higginbotham, Susan, *Margaret Pole: The Countess in the Tower* (Stroud: Amberley Publishing, 2016)
Hilton, Lisa, *Queens Consort: England's Medieval Queens* (London: Orion Books, 2008)
Hislop, Malcolm, *Barnard Castle, Bowes Castle and Egglestone Abbey* (London: English Heritage, 2019)
Hodder, Sarah J., *Cecily Bonville-Grey Marchioness of Dorset from Riches to Royalty* (Winchester: Chronos Books, 2022)
Horrox, Rosemary, *Richard III: A Study of Service* (Cambridge: Cambridge University Press, 1989)
Horrox, Rosemary, 'Conyers Family (per. c.1375–c.1525)', *Oxford Dictionary of National Biography*, (2004; online edition, 2004)
Horrox, Rosemary, 'Pole John De la, earl of Lincoln (1464–?1487)', *Oxford Dictionary of National Biography*, (2004; online edition, 2004)
Hughes, D.W., et al., 'The History of Halley's Comet [and Discussion],' *Philosophical Transactions of the Royal Society of London. Series A, Mathematical and Physical Sciences*, vol. 323, no. 1572, 1987, pp.349–67
Hughes, Jonathan, *The Religious Life of Richard III* (Stroud: Sutton, 1997)
Hurlock, Kathryn, *Medieval Welsh Pilgrimage, c.1100–1500* (London: Palgrave MacMillan, 2018)
Jacob, E.F., *The Fifteenth Century 1399–1485* (Oxford: Oxford University Press, 1969)
Jackson, W., 'The Threlkelds of Threlkeld, Yanwath and Crosby Ravensworth', *Transactions of the Cumberland & Westmorland Antiquarian & Archaeological Society*, 9/1 (1866), pp.311–312
Jones, P.M. and Olsan, L.T., 'Performative Rituals for Conception and Childbirth in England, 900–1500, *Bulletin of the History of Medicine*, 89/3 (Fall 2015), pp.406–433
Kehler, Dorothea, *Shakespeare's Widows* (London: Palgrave Macmillan, 2009)
Kendal, Paul Murray, *Warwick the Kingmaker* (London: Phoenix Press, 2002)
Lander, J.R., *Crown and Nobility 1450–1509* (London: Edward Arnold, 1976)
Langley, Philippa and Jones, Michael, *The King's Grave: The Search for Richard III* (London, John Murray, 2013)
Laynesmith, J.L., *Cecily Duchess of York* (London: Bloomsbury Academic, 2019)

Laynesmith, J.L., *The Last Medieval Queens: English Queenship 1445–1503* (Oxford: Oxford University Press, 2004)
Lewis, Matthew, *Richard III: Loyalty Binds Me* (Stroud: Amberley Publishing, 2018)
Leyser, Henrietta, *Medieval Women: A Social History of Women in England 450–1500* (London: Weidenfeld & Nicolson, 1995)
Licence, Amy, *Anne Neville: Richard III's Tragic Queen* (Stroud: Amberley Publishing, 2013)
Licence, Amy, *Edward IV & Elizabeth Woodville: A True Romance* (Stroud: Amberley Publishing, 2016)
Licence, Amy, *The Lost Kings* (Stroud: The History Press, 2017)
McGill, Pat and Jones, Jonathan, *Standards, Badges & Livery Colours of the Wars of the Roses* (Lincoln: Freezywater Publications, 1992)
Masse, H.J.L.J., *The Abbey Church of Tewkesbury with Some Account of the Priory Church of Deerhurst Gloucestershire* (London: George Bell and Sons, 1900)
Mate, Mavis, *Women in Medieval English Society* (Cambridge: Cambridge University Press, 1999)
Matthews, Helen, *The Legitimacy of Bastards* (Barnsley: Pen and Sword, 2019)
Maurer, Helen E., *Margaret of Anjou: Queenship and Power in Late Medieval England* (Woodbridge: Boydell Press, 2005)
Orme, Nicholas, *Going to Church in Medieval England*, (London: Yale University Press, 2021)
O'Regan, Mary, 'Richard III and the Monks of Durham', *The Ricardian*, 4/60 (March 1978, pp.19–22
Page, William (ed.), 'Hospitals: St John the Baptist, Lechlade', in *A History of the County of Gloucester*, Volume 2 (London: Victoria County History, 1907), pp.125–126
Page, William (ed.), 'The priory of Shouldham', in *A History of the County of Norfolk*, Volume 2 (London: Victoria County History, 1906), pp.412–414
Page, William, and Ditchfield, P.H., (eds), 'Parishes: Stanford in the Vale', in *A History of the County of Berkshire: Volume 4* (London: Victoria County History, 1924), pp.478–485
Peters, Christine, *Patterns of Piety: Women, Gender and Religion in Late Medieval and Reformation England* (Cambridge: Cambridge University Press, 2003)
Petre, James, 'The Nevills of Brancepeth and Raby 1425–1499. Part 1 1425–1469: Nevill v Nevill', *The Ricardian*, 5/75, (1981), pp.418–435
Philips, Kim M., *Medieval Maidens: Young Women and Gender in England, c.1270–c.1540* (Manchester: Manchester University Press, 2003)
Pollard, A.J., 'Neville, Richard, fifth Earl of Salisbury (1400–1460)', *Oxford Dictionary of National Biography*, (2004; online edition, 2008)
Pollard, Anthony, 'St Cuthbert and the Hog: Richard III and the County Palatinate of Durham, 1471–85', in Griffiths, Ralph (ed.), *Kings and Nobles in the Later Middle Ages*, (Gloucester: Sherbourne, 1986) pp.109–129
Pollard, A.J., *North Eastern England During the Wars of the Roses: Lay Society, War, and Politics, 1450–1500*, (Oxford: Clarendon Press, 1990)
Poulson, George, *The History and Antiquities of the Seigniory of Holderness, in the East Riding of the County of York*, Volume 1 (Hull: R. Brown, 1840)
Rawcliffe, C., *Medicine and Society in Later Medieval England* (Stroud: Sutton Publishing, 1995)

Roach, J.P.C. (ed.), 'The colleges and halls: Queens'', in *A History of the County of Cambridge and the Isle of Ely: Volume 3, the City and University of Cambridge*, (London, 1959), pp.408–415

Rose, Susan, *Calais: An English Town in France, 1347–1558* (Woodbridge: Boydell Press, 2008)

Ross, Charles, *Edward IV* (London: Methuen, 1983)

Ross, James, *John de Vere, Thirteenth Earl of Oxford (1442–1513): 'the Foremost Man of the Kingdom'* (Woodbridge: Boydell Press, 2011)

Royle, Trevor, *The Road to Bosworth Field* (London: Little Brown, 2009)

St John Hope, W.H., 'The Discovery of the Remains of King Henry VI in St George's Chapel, Windsor Castle', *Archaeologia*, (1911)

Salter, Elisabeth, *Six Renaissance Men and Women: Innovation, Biography and Cultural Creativity in Tudor England, c.1450–1560* (Farnham, Surrey: Ashgate, 2007)

Scofield, Cora L., *The Life and Reign of Edward IV*, 3 volumes (London: Green & Co., 1923)

Searle, William George, *The History of the Queens' College of St Margaret and St Bernard in the University of Cambridge* (London: Deighton, Bell & Company, 1867)

Spring, Peter, *Sir John Tiptoft: 'Butcher of England'* (Barnsley: Pen and Sword, 2018)

Strickland, Elisabeth and Strickland, Agnes, *Lives of the Queens of England: From the Norman Conquest*, vol. 2, (London: H. Colburn, 1851)

Sutton, Anne, 'The Coronation Robes of Richard III and Anne Neville', *Costume: the Journal of the Costume Society*, 13/1, (1979), pp.8–16

Sutton, Anne and Hammond, Rodney (eds), *The Coronation of Richard III: The Extant Documents* (Gloucester: Alan Sutton, 1984)

Sutton, Anne, and Visser-Fuchs, Livia, *Richard III's Books* (Stroud: Sutton Publishing, 1997)

Sutton, Anne and Visser-Fuchs, Livia, *The Hours of Richard III* (Stroud: Sutton Publishing, 1990)

Sutton, Anne, Visser-Fuchs, Livia, and Kleineke, Hannes, 'The Children in the Care of Richard III: New References. A Lawsuit between Peter Courteys, Keeper of Richard III's Great Wardrobe, and Thomas Lynom, Solicitor of Richard III, 1495–1501', *The Ricardian*, 24/4 (2014), pp.31–62

Swallow, Henry James, *De Nova Villa: or, The house of Nevill in sunshine and shade*, (Newcastle Upon Tyne: Andrew Reid, 1885)

Thornton, Tim, *The Channel Islands, 1370–1640: Between England and Normandy*, (Woodbridge: Boydell Press, 2012)

Tillot, P.M., (ed.) 'Worship in the Minster', in *A History of the County of York: The City of York* (London: Victoria County History, 1961) pp.343–357

Tillotson, John H., *Marrick Priory: A Nunnery in Late Medieval Yorkshire* (York: University of York, 1989)

Trow, M.J., *Richard III in the North* (Barnsley: Pen and Sword, 2020)

Wagner, John A. and Wagner, Edward, *Encyclopaedia of the Wars of the Roses*, (ABC-CLIO, 2001)

Walker-Meikle, Kathleen, *Medieval Pets*, (Woodbridge: Boydell Press, 2012)

Wedgwood, Josiah Clement and Holt, Anne D., *History of Parliament. Biographies of the Members of the Commons House 1439–1509* (London: HMSO, 1936)

Weightman, Christine, *Margaret of York: The Diabolical Duchess* (Stroud: Amberley Publishing, 2009)

Weir, Alison, *The Princes in the Tower* (London: Pimlico, 1997)
Willers, Andrea, *Richard, the Man Behind the Myth* (AuthorHouse UK, 2014)
Wolffe, B.P., *Crown Lands, 1461–1536: An Aspect of Yorkist and Early Tudor Government* (London: Routledge, 1970; reprinted 2021)
Woodward, Jennifer, *The Theatre of Death: The Ritual Management of Royal Funerals in Renaissance England, 1570–1625* (Woodbridge: Boydell Press, 1997)
Wroe, Ann, *Perkin: A Story of Deception* (London: Jonathan Cape, 2003)

Index

abduction, xviii, xxii, 4, 106, 131
Abergavenny, Wales, 14, 15
Abingdon, Oxon, 96
Accord, Act of, 48–50, 51, 186
adultery, xvii, 143, 156
affinity, 5, 6, 11, 18, 24, 36, 43, 51, 60, 66, 72, 73, 77, 90, 107, 111, 112, 116, 131, 184, 155, 166, 176, 202, 208, 209
Aire-sur-la-Lys, France, 74
alms giving, 55, 125
Alnwick Castle, Northumbria, 54, 62, 188
Amboise, France, 88, 91, 191
amulet, 19, 114, 124
Angers, France, 87, 88
Angers Agreement (1470), 88, 177, 190
Anglo-Burgundian alliance, 68, 69, 78, 189, 192
Anglo-French alliance, 61, 68, 69, 70, 192
Anglo-Portuguese alliance, 168, 172
Anglo-Spanish alliance, 178–179, 212
Anne of York, Duchess of Exeter, 63, 196
Arrivall of Edward IV, 97, 98, 99
artillery, 43, 49–50, 83, 96, 98, 160, 184
Ashton family, 148
Ashton, Sir Ralph, 112
astrology, 32–33, 101, 133
attainder, 30, 44, 45, 47, 62, 102, 105, 135, 137, 186, 209
Audley, Margaret, 4

Bainbridge, Yorkshire, 11
Bamburgh Castle, Northumbria, 54, 79, 188
Banbury, Oxon, 77, 93
Bannockburn, Battle of, (1314) 7
baptism, 31–32, 84–85, 108, 125
Barnard Castle, Co Durham, 11, 16, 109, 120, 175
   St Mary's Church, 159, 160, 172
Barnet, Battle of (1471), xvii, 93, 96, 101, 110, 149, 191

Basset, Ralph, 3
bastard feudalism, 7
Bastard of Fauconberg, *see* Neville, Thomas
bastardy, *see* illegitimacy
Baynard's Castle, London, 52, 81, 142
Beauchamp family, xiii, 1, 2, 8, 38, 67, 132
   arms, 1, 68, 138
   chapel, *see* Collegiate Church of St. Mary's, Warwick
   inheritance, 8, 102, 10
   motto, 47
Beauchamp, Anne, 15th Countess of Warwick (d.1449), 8, 196, 205
Beauchamp, Anne, 16th Countess of Warwick, xvii, xviii, xx, xxiii, 7, 9, 14–15, 18–20, 25, 26–28, 30–31, 32, 33, 34, 35, 36, 39,42–44, 47, 49, 57, 59, 68, 73, 74, 77, 78, 81, 83, 84–85, 91, 93, 95, 103, 108–109, 111, 113–114, 115, 153, 163, 176–177, 182, 196, 202, 205, 207, 209
   legal death of, 109, 110, 137
   suo jure rights, 102–103, 106–107
Beauchamp, Eleanor, Duchess of Somerset, 6, 9, 30, 196
Beauchamp, Elizabeth, Baroness Bergavenny, 9, 197, 206
Beauchamp, Elizabeth, Lady Latimer, 12–13, 197
Beauchamp, Elizabeth, nun, 2
Beauchamp, Guy, 2
Beauchamp, Henry, 1st Duke of Warwick, xx, 7, 8, 16, 38, 197, 205
Beauchamp, Joan, 3
Beauchamp, Joan, Lady Abergavenny, 14
Beauchamp, Katherine, nun, 2–3
Beauchamp, Margaret, Countess of Shrewsbury, 6, 8, 9, 22, 197
Beauchamp, Maud, Lady Clifford, 3
Beauchamp Pageant, The, xxiii, 28, 38

Beauchamp, Philippa, Countess of
  Stafford, 3, 4, 211
Beauchamp, Richard, 2nd Baron, 133
Beauchamp, Richard, 13th Earl of
  Warwick, 4–5, 6–7, 38, 160, 197
  tomb, 28–29
Beauchamp, Richard, 1st Earl of
  Worcester, 8, 13, 197, 200
Beauchamp, Sir Richard, 96
Beauchamp, Thomas, 11th Earl of
  Warwick, 2, 3, 28
Beauchamp, Thomas, 12th Earl of
  Warwick, 2, 4–5
Beauchamp Tower, 5
Beauchamp, William, 1
Beaufort faction, 21, 22, 23, 24, 182, 204
Beaufort family, 10, 197–198
Beaufort, Edmund, 2nd Duke of Somerset,
  9, 20–21, 22, 23, 25, 29, 30, 182, 183,
  184, 185, 186, 187, 188, 196, 198, 204,
  206
Beaufort, Edmund, self-styled 4th Duke of
  Somerset, 94, 95, 96, 98, 99, 191, 196,
  198
Beaufort, Henry, 3rd Duke of Somerset,
  41, 42, 43, 46, 49, 50, 51, 52, 54, 68, 196,
  198
Beaufort, Joan, Countess of Westmorland,
  xv, xvi, 10, 11, 12, 13, 71, 88, 115, 118,
  162, 166, 197, 198–199
Beaufort, John, 1st Duke of Somerset, 14,
  180, 199
Beaufort, Margaret, Countess of Richmond
  and Derby, xviii, xxi, 14, 15, 17, 37, 63,
  99, 101, 149, 150, 151, 155, 162, 175,
  177, 184, 194, 195, 199, 211, 212
Beaulieu Abbey, Hants, 95, 102, 103, 110
Beaumont, Margaret de, 7th Countess of
  Warwick, 2
Beaumont, Thomas de, 6th Earl of
  Warwick. 2–3
Berkeley Castle, Gloucestershire, 96
Berkeley family, 3, 6
Berkeley, Elizabeth de, Countess of
  Warwick, 5, 6, 196, 197, 206
Bettini, Sforza, Milanese ambassador in
  France, 64, 78, 86, 87, 101, 135, 136
Birtsmorton Court, Worcestershire, 97
Bisham Abbey, Berks, xxiii, 55, 94, 126,
  128, 177

Black, Thomas, 133
Blackheath, Kent, 181
Blackmoor Edge, Thirsk, Yorkshire, 175
Blaybourne, archer, 78
Blennerhasset, Cumbria, 62
Blore Heath, Battle of (1459), 42, 45, 49,
  185
Blount, Walter, 1st Baron Mountjoy, 13,
  205
Blyth Priory, Northumbria, 113
Boleyn, Anne, 178
Bolingbroke, Roger, astrologer, 33, 133
Bona of Savoy, 61, 68
Boniface IX, Pope, 10, 198
Bonville, Cecily, Marchioness of Dorset,
  58, 199, 202, 208
Bonville, William, 6th Baron Harington,
  58, 199, 208
Bonville, William, 1st Baron, 58, 199
Book of Hours, 22, 35, 37
books, xx, 36, 27, 29 37, 38, 116, 117, 122,
  162–163, 172
Bosworth, Battle of (1485), 174, 195, 206,
  210, 211, 212
Bourchier, Thomas, Archbishop of
  Canterbury, 33, 47, 48, 71, 183
Brancepeth, Co. Durham, 11
Brandon, Henry, 174
breast feeding, 34
Bristol, 82, 96
Brittany, 21, 155, 156, 188, 192, 202
Buck, George, 171
Buckingham Rebellion (1483), 155–156,
  194, 195, 202, 210
Burdett, Thomas, servant, 133–134, 136
Burford, Oxfordshire, 93
Burgh, Alice, possible mother of John of
  Gloucester, 116
Burgh family, 116
Burgh, Henry, 115
Burgh, Isabel, wet nurse, 115
Burgh, Sir Thomas, Master of Horse, 80,
  213
Burgundy, 52, 90, 130, 187, 190
Burgundy, Antoine, Bastard of, 69
Burgundy, Charles I, Duke of, 68, 69, 71,
  74, 84, 92, 126, 130, 189, 192, 204
Burgundy, Philip II, Duke of, 189
Butcher of England, *see* Tiptoft, John
Butler, Lady Eleanor, 144, 148, 200

Cade's Rebellion (1450), 19, 21, 181–182
Cade, Jack, 21, 182
Caister Castle, Norfolk, 79
Calais, France, 23, 37, 39–47, 53, 71, 72, 73, 74, 75, 84, 89, 112, 135, 149, 182, 185, 186, 189
    captaincy, 34, 53, 68, 69, 70, 83, 183, 184, 211
    Pale, 49, 103, 113, 134, 166, 212
    staple, 66
Caldewgate, Carlisle, Cumbria, 62
calendar, medieval, 28, 32, 54, 163
Cambridge, 52, 70
    King's College, 161
    Queen's College, 108, 161
canon laws of marriage, 4, 14–15, 71, 88, 89, 91, 108, 166, 167, 170
canonical hours, 122
Canterbury, Kent, 47, 53, 74, 76, 77, 186
    cathedral, 1
Cardiff Castle, Wales, 23
Carlisle, Cumbria, 18, 54, 62
Carminow, Margaret, wife of Sir Hugh Courtenay, 97
Castillon, Battle of (1453), 22, 182
Catesby, John, 5
Catesby, William, 143
Catherine of Valois, 9, 212
Catour, William, servant, 111
Caversham, Oxfordshire, 7
Cawood, Yorkshire, 66
Cecily of York, 166, 177, 201
Cerne Abbey, Dorset, 95
Chancellor of England, *see* Beaufort, Henry; Neville, George; Stillington, Robert
Channel Islands, 40
Chantries, xx, 157, 158, 172
    Lechlade Church, Gloucestershire, 123
    St Mary's Church, Ricall, Yorkshire, 159
    Shrewsbury Abbey, 160
    Tewkesbury Abbey, 16, 129, 130, 136
    York, 154, 161, 165, 171, 172
Chapuys, Eustace, ambassador to the Holy Roman Empire, 179
Charles VII, King of France, 22
Charles, Count of Charolais, *see* Burgundy, Charles I, Duke of
Chaucer, Alice, Duchess of Suffolk, 56, 66
Chaucer, Geoffrey, 56
    Canterbury Tales, 117, 155
    Troilus and Creseyde, 37
Chertsey Abbey, Surrey, 101
Chester, 48
Chesterfield, Derbyshire, 82, 108
childbirth and lying in, 19, 26, 31, 35, 82–83, 84–85, 114–115, 123, 127–128
Christmas, 50, 54, 55, 71, 80, 101, 117, 122, 164
    Christmas 1484, 167–173
churching of women, 125
Cirencester, Gloucesterhire, 96, 131
claims to the throne, 77
    Edward IV, 51, 92, 145, 186
    Elizabeth of York, 172, 175
    Edward Plantagenet, 17th Earl of Warwick, 154
    Henry IV, 6, 24
    George, 2nd Duke of Buckingham, 141
    George, Duke of Clarence, 88, 134
    Lady Margaret Beaufort, 101
    Richard of York, 48, 49, 51, 52
    Richard III, 144–145, 156, 194
    Henry VIII, 168
Clare, Eleanor de, 7
Clare, Gilbert de, 8th Earl of Gloucester, 7
Clarence's ordinances, 121, 122
Claver, Alice, silkwoman, 146
Clifford family, 4, 11, 62, 176, 208
Clifford, John, 9th Baron, 50, 52, 187
Clifford, Roger, 5th Baron, 3
Clifford, Thomas, 8th Baron, 30, 184
Clitheroe, Lancashire, 72, 199
clothing, 5, 26, 36, 119, 121, 124, 137, 145, 146, 147, 148, 165, 167
Cobham, Eleanor, Duchess of Gloucester, 33, 133
Colchester, Essex, 70
College of Arms, 55
Collins, Jane, servant, 116
comet, 33, 101
    Halley's comet, 32
Commines, Philip de, 83, 84, 89, 136, 139, 143, 144
Company of the Staple, 39, 40, 43, 47, 66
consanguinity, 88, 107, 167, 170
Constance of York, 6
Constanza of Castile, 10
consummation, 14–15, 17, 91

Conyers, Sir John, 73, 111, 112, 148, 175, 199, 205
Cooper, Agnes, servant, 116
Coppini, Francesco, papal legate, 47
coronation
    Anne Neville and Richard III, xxii, 13, 18, 146, 148–151
    Edward II and Isabella of France, 146
    Edward IV, 52, 53, 54
    Edward V, 140, 141, 142, 143–144
    Elizabeth Woodville, 64
Corpus Christi Guild, York, 153, 158, 163
Courtenay, Henry, 72
Courtenay, Henry, Marquess of Exeter, 178, 179
Courtenay, Sir Hugh, 97
Courtney, Earls of Devon, 82
Courteys, Peter, Keeper of the Great Wardrobe, 146, 166, 230
Coventry, Warwickshire, 22, 42, 45, 71, 74, 75, 77, 81, 92, 100, 163, 184, 185, 189, 191
Coverham Abbey, Yorkshire, 114, 145, 164
Cromwell, Lord, 24
Cromwell, Thomas, 178
Crosby Place, Bishopgate, London, 142, 143
Croyland Abbey, 51
Croyland Chronicle, 25, 51, 52, 61, 68, 69, 87, 90, 92, 105, 106, 110, 118, 128, 133, 134, 136, 139, 144, 154, 164, 167

Dartford, Kent, 22, 182
Dartmouth, Devon, 83, 90
De re militari, 163
Delalynde, Elizabeth, 132
Delalynde, Thomas, 132
Despenser family, 1, 6, 107, 129
    inheritance, 7, 8, 9, 102, 108, 197
Despenser, Hugh, 1st Baron, 7
Despenser, Isabel, Countess of Worcester and Warwick, 8, 9, 13, 14, 16, 38, 40, 160, 162, 196, 197 200
Despenser, Thomas, 1st Earl of Gloucester, 5, 6
diet, 27, 28, 67, 121, 122
Dintingdale, Yorkshire, 52
dogs, 117
Doket, Andrew, 161

dower/dowry/dowries, xix, 5, 10, 16, 44, 46, 51, 62, 88, 103, 110
Dublin, 21, 181
Dunstable, Bedfordshire, 51
Dunstanburgh Castle, Northumbria, 54, 188
Durham, 11
    bishop, 109, 111, 199
    cathedral, 11, 158
    Sisterhood of Durham Cathedral Priory, 158
Dymmock, Sir Thomas, 81, 213
Dynham, Sir John, 48

Edgecote, Battle of (1469), 77, 149, 189, 214
Edward I, King of England, 4, 109
Edward II, King of England, 7, 75, 142
Edward III, King of England, 3
    descent from, xii, 7, 21, 33, 48, 155, 181
Edward IV, King of England, xxi, 21, 42, 43, 44, 46, 58, 59, 63, 65, 66, 69, 70, 72, 93, 94, 96, 97, 98, 100, 101, 103, 104, 105, 107, 110, 112, 127, 133, 149, 159, 160, 185, 187, 190, 192, 199, 200, 202, 203, 209, 211, 213
    accession, 51, 52, 53, 150
    bigamy, 143–144, 145, 148, 200
    Clarence trial and execution, 132, 134, 135, 136
    death, 139, 140, 193
    foreign policy, 69, 71, 73, 74, 75, 77, 78, 79, 80, 81, 82, 84, 86, 89, 118, 125–126, 130, 189
    household ordinances, 102
    marriage, 61, 64, 188, 214
    mistresses xvii, xxii, 143, 156
    paternity, 64, 134, 144
Edward of Lancaster, Prince of Wales, 92, 95, 97, 107, 108, 186, 201
    birth and paternity, 78, 183, 198
    death, 98–99
    marriage, 49, 88, 90, 91, 191, 204
Edward of Middleham, Prince of Wales, 113, 200, 116–117, 119–120, 152, 153, 154, 159, 163, 164–165, 195, 200
Edward of Westminster, *see* Edward of Lancaster, Prince of Wales
Edward V, 102, 140, 141, 142, 144, 145, 147, 155, 194, 200

Edward, Earl of March, *see* Edward IV
Elizabeth of York, Duchess of Suffolk, 66, 149, 201
Elizabeth of York, Queen of England, 63, 90, 142, 162, 175, 193
   marriage negotiations, 126, 168, 195, 201
   relationship with Anne Neville, 167
   rumours of relationship with Richard III, 167–168, 172
embroidery and sewing, 36, 103, 157
Empingham, Battle of, *see* Losecoat
English Chronicle, The, 50
entertainment, 54, 69, 67, 117, 153, 158
Essex, 90, 100, 112
Eton College, 97
Evesham Abbey, 97
execution, xx, 4, 51, 58, 83, 132, 134, 136, 149, 177, 179, 181, 192, 194, 195
Exeter, 82, 83, 96
Exeter Conspiracy (1538), 178

fasting, 28
Farleigh Hungerford Castle, Somerset, 123
Fauconberg, Joan, 12, 205, 206, 209
Feast of Holy Innocents, 54
feasting, 14, 31, 54–55, 66–67, 127, 151
Ferrers family, 4
Ferrers, Elizabeth de, nun, 5
Ferrers, Margaret de, Countess of Warwick, 4–5, 197
Ferrers, William de, 4
Ferrybridge, Battle of (1471), 52, 176, 187
FitzAlan, Thomas, 7th Baron Maltravers, 63, 149–150
FitzAlan, William, 16th Earl of Arundel, 204, 207
FitzHugh family, 148
FitzHugh, Alice, 60
FitzHugh, Anne, Viscountess Lovell, 60, 204
FitzHugh, Sir Henry, 73
FitzHugh, Henry, 5th Baron, 60, 190, 201
FitzHugh, Richard, 6th Baron, 175
FitzMaldred, Robert, 10
FitzRanulph, Mary, 11
Fleetwood's Chronicle, 100
Fontenailles, Matthew, 89
Forest of Wensleydale, Yorkhire, 11
Formigny, Battle of (1450), 20

Fortescue, Sir John, 87
Fotheringhay, Northamptonshire, 21, 119, 126, 127
Franke, Geoffrey, 116

Galen's principle of the four humours, 27
Gascony, 22, 180
Gate, Sir Geoffrey, 83
Goddard, Dr John, 136
godparents, 31–32, 108, 183
Goldwell, Dr James, 71
Great Chronicle of London, 21, 22, 30, 42, 53, 60, 72, 73, 75, 98, 101, 118, 147, 177
Great North Road, 49, 50, 81, 126
Great Seal of England, 47, 61, 69, 186
Greenwich, 60, 162
Grey, Dorothy, 137
Grey, Sir John, 202, 214
Grey, Sir Richard, 140, 145, 193, 194
Grey, Thomas, Marquess of Dorset, 131, 137, 141, 145, 199, 202, 203
guardian/guardianship, xviii, 3, 8, 14, 15, 58, 104, 106, 203, 206
Guernsey, Channel Islands, 40, 43
guilds, 117, 130, 153, 158, 163
Gupshill, Gloucestershire, 96
Guy of Warwick, 67–68, 125

Hall's Chronicle, 50, 135, 139, 177
Hammes, Frances, 43, 103, 113, 166, 174, 212
Hanley Castle, Worcestershire, 8
Harewell, Roger, 135
Harlech, Wales, 186
Hastings family, 58
Hastings, William, 1st Baron Hastings, 37, 56, 58, 77, 79, 90, 93, 126, 139, 143, 149, 190, 193, 194, 202
Haute, Katherine, potential mother of Katherine Plantagenet, 118, 210
Hawkeston, Ankarette, *see* Twynyho, Ankarette
Hawling family, 137
Hedgley Moor, Battle of (1464), 188
heiresses, xviii, xx, 2, 4, 6, 7, 8, 9, 10, 11, 12, 14, 16, 17, 24, 57, 58, 59, 60, 62, 69, 70, 104, 130, 137, 142, 175, 199, 200, 202, 204, 206–207, 209, 212
Henry IV, King of England, 6, 11, 24

Henry of Bolingbroke, Earl of Derby, *see* Henry IV
Henry VI, King of England, 8, 15, 17, 38, 41, 42, 47, 48, 51, 58, 72, 75, 79, 86, 93, 97, 149
  fugitive, 52, 54
  mental breakdown, 23, 25, 30
  murder, 101, 161
  potential successor, 49, 88, 133
  Readeption, 90–91, 136
Henry VII, King of England, 17, 63, 101, 124, 146, 155, 156, 162, 166, 168, 176, 178, 195, 212
Henry VIII, King of England, 178–179
heraldry, 1, 57, 68, 138, 163
Herbert, Richard, 77
Herbert, William, Earl of Huntingdon, 165, 203, 210
Herbert, William, 1st Earl of Pembroke, 75, 77, 189
Hereford, 51, 187
Heworth Moor, Battle of (1453), 24, 183
Hexham, Battle of (1464), 68, 72, 188, 198
Hildegard of Bingen, 169
History of King Richard III, xxi, 135, 137
Holland, Anne, Lady Astley, 63, 203, 202, 206
Holland, Eleanor, 12
Holland, Henry, 3rd Duke of Exeter, 92, 93, 94, 196
Holland, Thomas, 1st Duke of Surrey, 5
Holy Helpers, 159
Honfleur, Normandy, 69, 86, 93
horoscopes, 33, 133
Hospital of St John, London, 171, 172
hot trod, 18
Hours of Richard III, 172
housewifery and household management, xix, xxi, 15, 35–36, 55, 60, 121, 122
Howard, Elizabeth, Countess of Oxford, 59, 110
Howard, John, 1st Duke of Norfolk, 70, 171, 175
Huddlestons of Millom, 62, 111
Huddleston, Joan, 175
Huddleston, Margaret, xxii, 17, 18, 62, 111, 112, 115, 148, 175–176, 208
Huddleston, Sir Richard, 62, 147, 175
Huddleston, Richard, 176
Huddleston, William, 111

Hugford, John, Justice, 132
Hundred Years War, 3, 7, 11, 197
Hungerford, Robert, 3rd Baron, 68, 72
Hungerford, Thomas, 72
Hyde, Richard, servant, 131

Idley, Anne, Mistress of the Nursery, 116, 117
Idley, Peter, author, 116, 117, 158
Idley, William, 117
illegitimacy, 10, 17, 18, 64, 78, 118, 144, 166, 194, 200
infancy, 30, 31, 32, 34, 125
infirmary, 127
infertility, 26, 115, 170
Ingoldsthorpe, Isabel, 142, 206
inheritance rights, xviii, 2, 3, 5, 8, 9, 12, 17–18, 19, 20 103
Invasion of France (1475), 118, 132, 192
Ireland, 5, 22, 43, 45, 46, 47, 48, 131, 135, 185, 186
Isle of Man, 5

Jacquetta of Luxembourg, Duchess of Bedford, xxii, 46, 78, 90, 105, 186, 193, 203, 213, 214
Jersey, Channel Islands, 40
Jervaulx Abbey, Yorks, 145, 164
Joanna of Aviz, 168, 172
John of Gaunt, Duke of Lancaster, 5, 6, 10, 11, 48, 88, 118, 139, 195, 197, 198, 199
John of Gloucester, illegitimate son of Richard III, 117, 154
John of Pontefract, *see* John of Gloucester
jointure rights, xix, 5, 10, 46, 51, 88, 94, 104, 107

Katherine of Aragon, 177, 178
Keeper of the Narrow Seas, 40–41
Kendal, John, Richard III's secretary, 153
Kenilworth Castle, Warwickshire, 181
Kent, 16, 40, 74, 90, 100, 106, 155, 181, 185, 194
  support for Warwick, 43, 47, 76, 77
Keyford, Frome, Somerset, 123, 131
King's Lynn, Norfolk, 90, 190
Kyriel, Sir Thomas, 58

L'Erber, London, 18, 60, 102
La Guerche, Brittany, 21

La Hogue, Normandy, 90
Lancaster, House of, xii, 10, 101
   and affinity, 6, 11, 46
   Duchy of, 64, 105, 110
   and alliance with the Earl of Warwick, 87, 88, 91
Last Judgement, 129
Leicester, 25, 29, 30, 153, 156, 174, 184
Lieutenant of the North, 118
Lincoln, 155
Lincolnshire rebellion, 73, 80–81
Lionel of Antwerp, 21, 48, 181
literacy, 37
Little Malvern Priory, Worcestershire, 97
livery, 121
   badges, 23, 24, 40, 94, 108, 119, 153
   bear and ragged staff, 16, 40, 43, 47, 50, 138
   collars, 56
   colours, 40
London, xxii, 16, 22, 29, 39, 41, 47, 48, 49, 51, 52, 53, 60, 69, 70, 72, 77, 79, 80, 81, 90, 93, 100, 101, 102, 119, 137, 139, 140, 141, 142, 145, 146, 153, 154, 155, 160, 164, 172, 181, 182, 183, 184, 186, 197, 189, 190, 191, 192, 193
Lords Appellant, 4, 208
Lord Lieutenant of Ireland, 21, 91, 152, 166, 181, 184
Lordship of Glamorgan, 7, 23, 25, 40, 109
Losecoat Field, Battle of (1470), 82, 190, 213
Louis XI, King of France, 65, 68, 69, 73, 78, 86, 87, 89, 91, 101, 126, 130, 135–136, 192, 194
love day, London (1458), 41, 185
Lovell, Frances, 1st Viscount Lovell, 59, 60, 150, 171, 177, 204, 205
Low Countries, 52, 70, 90, 92
Lucy, Margaret, 53, 82–83
Ludford Bridge, Battle of (1459), 42, 84, 185, 205, 211
Ludlow, Shropshire, 22, 42, 139, 140, 141, 182, 185, 193, 213
Lynom, Thomas, 165

Manchester, Lancashire, 82
Mancini, Dominic, 84, 119, 135, 136, 139, 141, 143, 144
manners, 10, 38, 60, 66, 116, 117, 152

Margaret of Anjou, Queen of England, xvii, 21, 22, 23, 25, 29, 33, 39, 41, 42, 46, 47, 49, 51, 52, 54, 58, 59, 68, 72, 86–87, 88–89, 91–92, 93, 95–97, 100–101, 126, 157, 180, 181, 182, 183, 184, 185, 186, 187, 190, 191, 192, 198, 201, 202, 204
Margaret of York, Duchess of Burgundy, 42, 52, 60, 61, 69, 71, 74, 89, 93, 130, 189, 204, 205
Margaret, Neville, Countess of Oxford, 36, 44, 59, 94, 102–103, 175, 208
Margate, Kent, 71
Marie of Anjou, Countess of Devon, 97
marriage, xix, xx, 1, 2, 3, 4, 5, 6, 7, 11, 13, 15, 17, 25, 44, 53, 57, 58, 59, 60, 61, 62, 63, 64, 82, 87–88, 91, 106, 107, 119, 130, 138, 157, 160, 168
   child marriage, 8, 10, 14, 15
   clandestine *see* secret
   and consummation, 14–15
   and prohibited degrees, 71, 73, 89, 108, 166, 167, 170
   secret marriage, xxii, 75, 135, 144–145, 188, 214
Mary of Burgundy, 64, 68, 130, 135
Mauduit, Isabel de, 1
Mauduit, William de, 8th Earl of Warwick, 2
Mechtild of Hackborn, 163
medicine, xviii, 26, 27, 30, 32, 34, 83, 122
Middleham Jewel, 114, 115
Middleham, Yorkshire, 11, 15, 18, 41, 45, 59, 60, 70, 72, 78, 110, 111, 113, 117, 140, 143, 145, 153, 164, 175, 185, 189, 193, 200
   castle, 53–54, 165
   Church of St Mary and St Alkelda, 159–160, 172
Midlands, the, 2, 3, 5, 7, 9, 16, 39, 41, 42, 58, 77, 80, 81, 90, 155, 184
Milford Haven, Wales, 195
Minster Lovell, Oxfordshire, 152
Montagu family, Earls of Salisbury, 57
Montagu, Alice, Countess of Salisbury, xxiii, 12, 15, 44, 45, 55, 56, 108, 118, 128, 201, 204, 205, 206, 207, 208, 209, 211
Montagu, John, 3rd Earl of Salisbury, 5
Montagu, Thomas, 4th Earl of Salisbury, 12

Index   239

moon, 19, 33, 171
Moor Park, Rickmansworth, Hertfordshire, 172
More, Sir Thomas, xxi, 135, 136, 137, 143, 152
Mortimer, Anne, 210
Mortimer, Edmund, 5th Earl of March, 13
Mortimer, John, *see* Cade, Jack
Mortimer's Cross, Battle of (1461), 51, 58, 187, 200
Morton, Cardinal John, 142, 155
mourning, 55–56, 100, 119, 126–127, 136
Mowbray family, Dukes of Norfolk, 7
Mowbray, Ann, 159
Mowbray, John, Duke of Norfolk, 13, 29, 183
mummers' plays, 117
Muncaster Castle, Cumbria, 188
murder, xxii, 128, 131, 132, 170
Myton, Warwickshire, 132

Nanfan, Jane, 98
Nanfan, Sir John, 40–41, 97–98
Nanfan, Sir Richard, 98
Naworth Castle, Cumbria, 54
Neville affinity, xxii, 10, 11, 18, 54, 59, 199, 211
Neville, Alice, 73, 205
Neville, Alice, Baroness FitzHugh, 201
Neville, Anne, Duchess of Buckingham, 13, 32, 37, 42, 199, 205, 211
Neville, Anne, Duchess of Gloucester, Queen of England, 33–37, 38, 44, 55, 59, 66, 80, 83, 91, 93, 95, 96, 97, 100, 101–102, 104, 106, 110, 111, 113, 117, 118, 119, 120, 152, 153, 154, 156, 157, 161, 163, 164, 166, 205
 astrology, 32, 171
 birth, 30–31
 burial, 171–172
 coat of arms, 1
 coronation, 146–151
 disguised as a scullery maid, 104–105, 106
 illness and death, 128, 165, 168–171, 195
 marriage to Edward of Lancaster, 87–89, 91, 190, 191, 201, 204
 marriage to Richard of Gloucester xix–xx, xxi, 60, 104–108, 192, 210
 piety, 158–160
 pregnancy and children, 113, 115, 116, 119, 200
 relations with Elizabeth of York, 167
Neville, Cecily, Countess of Warwick and Worcester, xx, 8, 9, 14, 15, 16, 19, 82, 197, 211
Neville, Cecily, Duchess of York, xxiii, 13, 21, 24, 26, 33, 37, 42, 45–46, 52, 64, 74, 75, 78, 89, 108, 115, 122, 123, 125, 127, 144, 151, 160, 163, 174, 181, 185, 196, 199, 200, 201, 204, 205, 210
Neville, Edward, Lord Bergavenny, 8, 12, 25, 197
Neville, Eleanor, Baroness Stanley, 206
Neville, Eleanor, Duchess of Northumberland, 13
Neville, Elizabeth, 206
Neville, Elizabeth, Baroness Scrope of Masham, 111, 149
Neville family, Earls of Westmorland, xiv, xv, xvi, 10–12
Neville, George, Bishop of Exeter, later Archbishop of York, 33, 52, 59, 66, 69, 104, 126, 184, 186, 206
Neville, George, Duke of Bedford, 58, 63, 105, 109, 141–142, 203, 206–207
Neville, George, 4th Baron Bergavenny, 8–9, 23, 206
Neville, George, 1st Baron Latimer, 12, 197, 206
Neville, Sir Henry, 73
Neville, Sir Humphrey, 79–80, 207
Neville, Isabel, Duchess of Clarence, xx, 19–20, 33–37, 38, 44, 53, 55, 59, 60, 66, 77, 80, 88, 89, 102, 113, 121, 130, 134, 137, 182, 207, 210
 death, 127–128, 131
 funeral, 128–129
 household, 121–122
 marriage to George, Duke of Clarence, 64–65, 68, 70, 71, 74–76, 189, 202
 pregnancy and birth of her children, 78, 81, 82, 83–84, 115, 122, 123–125, 126, 127–128
 tomb, 129, 137–138
Neville, Isabella de, 10–11
Neville, Joan, Countess of Arundel, 149–150, 204, 207
Neville, John, Baron Neville (d.1461), 50, 187

Neville, John, Marquess of Montagu and Earl of Northumberland, 49, 54, 55, 67, 72–7, 79, 82, 90, 92, 93, 94, 188, 207
Neville, Katherine, Duchess of Norfolk, 13, 64, 78, 138, 198, 208, 214
Neville, Katherine, Lady Hastings, 37, 58, 199, 202, 208
Neville, Margaret, Countess of Oxford, xxiii, 36, 44, 59, 102–103, 175, 208, 212
Neville, Margaret, illegitimate sister of Anne and Isobel Neville, *see* Huddleston, Margaret
Neville-Percy feud, 23, 25, 49, 62, 182, 183, 209
Neville, Ralph, 1st Earl of Westmorland, 4, 6, 11–12, 26, 197, 198, 208, 211
Neville, Ralph, 2nd Earl of Westmorland, 12, 187
Neville, Richard, 16th Earl of Warwick, 'The Kingmaker', xvii, xviii, xx, 8, 10, 14–16, 17, 19, 20, 30, 33, 39–40, 41, 42–43, 46–47, 48, 49, 53, 54, 59, 61–63, 65, 66, 67, 68–70, 71–73, 74, 77, 78–79, 81, 82, 83, 84, 85, 86–87, 90–91, 92–93, 94, 101, 180, 200, 209
Neville, Richard, 5th Earl of Salisbury, 11, 13, 18, 19, 30, 33, 41–42, 43, 46, 49–50, 55, 56, 57, 105, 199, 204, 208–209
Neville, Richard, Lord Latimer, 142
Neville, Sir Humphrey of Brancepeth, 79, 207
Neville, Thomas, Lord Stanhope, 24, 49, 209
Neville, Thomas, 'The Bastard of Fauconberg', 18, 44, 86, 100, 106, 209
Neville, William, Lord Fauconberg, 1st Earl of Kent, 12, 43–44, 46, 52, 61, 73, 187, 199, 205, 206, 209
Newark, Nottinghamshire, 74, 75, 92
Northampton, 140, 193
Northampton, Battle of (1460), 13, 47, 53, 77, 186, 211
Nottingham, 75, 77, 92, 93, 153, 164, 191
nursery management, 20, 34, 115, 116–117, 124, 125

Ockwells Manor, Berkshire, 98
omens and predictions, 32, 33, 101, 68
Order of the Garter, 3
original sin, xviii, 26, 31, 84, 123

oyer and terminer, commission of, 133, 182

papal dispensation, 5, 27, 28, 71, 73, 89, 90, 107, 108, 170
Parliament, xix, xxii–xxiii, 9, 10, 30, 39, 40, 43, 44–45, 48, 49, 54, 78–79, 97, 102, 108, 109, 135, 137, 141, 176, 177, 181, 183, 184, 185, 186, 190, 192, 195
Parr, Sir William, 77
Paston family, 36, 79
Paston, John, 43, 103, 106, 110, 111
Paston, Margaret, 26, 43
Paul II, Pope, 66, 71
Pembroke Castle, Wales, 184
penance, xxii, 143
Pennines, 82
Penrith, Cumbria, 18, 62, 105
   castle, 120
Percy family, Earls of Northumberland, 11, 24, 72, 190
Percy, Henry, 1st Earl of Northumberland, 24
Percy, Henry, 4th Earl of Northumberland, 82, 174, 175
Percy, Henry 'Hotspur', 24
Percy, Joyce, 150
Percy, Sir Ralph, 54, 188
Percy, Sir Robert, 59, 150
Percy, Thomas, Lord Egremont, 24, 47
Péronne, Treaty of (1468), 86
pets, 117
Picquigny, Treaty of (1475), 126, 192
piety, 36, 37, 114, 122, 154, 157–163
pilgrimage, 26, 71, 74, 75, 80, 157
piracy, 40, 41, 60, 74, 86
plants, 36
   betony, 36
   doctrine of signatures, 189
Plantagenet Edmund, Earl of Rutland, 49, 50, 126, 176, 185, 186, 200, 205
Plantagenet, Edward, 17th Earl of Warwick, xxiii, 125, 135, 143, 154, 163, 165, 176, 177 195, 207, 209
Plantagenet, George, Duke of Clarence xx, xxii, 56, 60, 64, 65, 68, 69, 70, 71, 73–75, 77, 78, 79, 80, 81, 82, 88, 89, 90, 91, 92, 93, 98, 99, 102, 103, 104, 105–107, 108, 109, 110, 111, 113, 119, 121–122, 123, 124, 126, 127, 128, 130–138, 144, 152,

Index 241

181, 189, 190, 191, 192, 202, 205, 207, 210, 213
Plantagenet, Katherine, illegitimate daughter of Richard III, 165, 203, 210
Plantagenet, Margaret, Countess of Salisbury xxiii, 124–125, 136, 137, 138, 154, 165, 177, 178–179, 207, 210
Plantagenet, Richard (d.1477), 127–128
Plantagenet, Richard, Duke of Gloucester, *see* King Richard III
Plantagenet, Richard, Duke of York, son of Edward IV
Plantagenet, Richard, Duke of York, 13, 20–22, 23, 25, 29, 30, 33, 39, 41, 42, 43, 44, 45, 46, 47, 48–50, 51, 83, 119, 144, 180, 181, 182, 183, 184, 185, 186, 187, 196, 200, 201, 204, 209, 210, 211
Plantagenet, John, 1st Duke of Bedford, 21, 214
Pole Geoffrey, 178
Pole, Cardinal Reginald, 178
Pole, Edmund de la, 3rd Duke of Norfolk, 201
Pole, Henry, 179
Pole, John de la, 2nd Duke of Suffolk, 8, 15, 66, 201
Pole, John de la, Earl of Lincoln, 166, 177
Pole, Margaret, Countess of Salisbury, *see* Plantagenet, Margaret
Pole, Richard, 178, 201
Pole, William de la, 201
Pole, William de la, 1st Duke of Suffolk, 8, 56, 66, 149, 180
Pontefract, Yorkshire, 50, 52, 55, 80, 92, 116, 126, 140, 142, 153, 155, 165, 186, 191, 194, 203, 213
Priory of St John, 119
Poor Clares Without Aldgate, London, 5
pregnancy, 17, 19, 23, 25, 27, 28, 30, 33–34, 57, 66, 78, 81, 82, 83, 104, 113, 114–115, 119, 122, 123, 126, 128, 167, 175, 182
Puebla Rorigo de, Spanish ambassador, 178
Purfrey, Thomas, 5
Purgatory, 129, 158, 171

queens, xvii–xviii, 9, 147, 157, 161–162

Raby, County Durham, 10, 11
raptus laws, xviii, 106
Ratcliffe, Sir Richard, 142, 145
Ravenspur, Yorkshire, 6, 24, 92, 191
Readeption, 90–92, 112, 135, 136, 190
reburial
  Henry VI, 101
  Richard Neville, 5th Earl of Salisbury, 55–56
  Thomas Beauchamp, Earl of Warwick, 28
  Richard of York, 126–127
religious observance, 14, 26, 36, 37, 55, 84, 114, 116, 119, 122, 125, 127, 129, 130, 136, 147, 150, 151, 153, 158, 159, 160, 162, 172
Richard II, King of England, 4, 5, 6, 11, 75, 139
Richard III, King of England, xxi, 21, 32–33, 42, 52, 53, 60, 66, 90, 93, 101, 103, 112, 117, 119, 126, 135, 139, 140, 142, 143, 144, 145, 146, 150–151, 152–163, 165, 166, 169, 171, 172, 174, 175, 187, 188, 195, 204, 205, 206, 207, 210
  illegitimate children and mistresses, 116, 118, 210
  marriage to Anne Neville, xix, xxi, 1, 70, 99, 104–110, 192
  marriage negotiations with Portugal, 168
  proposed marriage to Elizabeth of York, 167–168, 195
  and Shakespeare, xviii, xxi, 170
Richard, Duke of York (d.1483), 122, 141, 147, 194, 212
Richmond, Yorkshire, lordship of, 17, 105, 109, 175
Robin of Redesdale, 74, 75, 77, 79, 81, 111, 112, 189, 199, 207
Robson, Henry, 110
Rotherham, Thomas, Archbishop of York, 168
Rouen, Normandy, 16, 22, 28, 160
Rous Roll, xxiii, 1, 31, 38, 166, 170
Rous, John, xxi, 32–33, 36, 38, 67, 84, 111, 152, 163, 164, 170
royal progress (1483), xxii, 152–156, 169

Salisbury, 23, 156, 89, 156
Salisbury Cathedral, 33, 123
Salisbury Rolls of Arms, 1, 57
salvation, 31, 129, 158
sanctuary, xxi, xxiii, 81, 90, 94, 95, 99, 102, 106, 111, 141, 156, 166, 175, 190, 191, 193, 194, 105, 202

Sandal Castle, Yorkshire, 49, 50, 165, 166
Sandwich, Kent, 40, 46, 47, 69, 74, 100, 185, 186
Scales, Elizabeth, 69
Scales, Thomas, 7th Baron, 47
Scarborough Castle, Yorkshire, 108
scoliosis, 142
Scotland, 62
  borders, 1
  campaigns into Scotland, 3, 11, 111, 141
  support for Lancastrians, 49, 51, 53, 54, 64, 186, 187, 188
Scrope family, 11, 148, 166
Scrope, Elizabeth, Countess of Oxford, 175
Scrope, Ralph, 166, 201
Scrope, Sir Richard, 175
Scrope, Thomas, 6th Baron of Masham, 111
servants, xxi, 34, 35, 36, 117, 121, 122, 137
Shaa, Dr Ralph, 144, 194
Shakespeare, William
  and Anne Neville, xviii, xx, xxi, 170
  and Clarence, 137
  and Margaret of Anjou, xvii–xvii
  and Richard III, 137
Sheriff Hutton, Yorkshire, 11, 18, 79, 105, 114, 140, 142, 177
  St Helen and Holy Cross Church, 164, 165
Shore, Jane (Elizabeth), xxii, 143
Shouldham Priory, Norfolk, 2
shrines
  Coverham Priory; 145
  Fountains Abbey, 145
  Jervaulx Abbey, 145
  St Edward's, Westminster, 15
  St Mary, Sudbury, 70
  St Mary, Walsingham, 26
  St Thomas Cantelupe, Hereford, 26
  St Winifred's, Shrewsbury, 160
  Thomas Becket, Canterbury, 71, 74, 80
Simnel, Lambert, 195
Skelton Castle, Cleveland, 12
South Wales, 18, 40, 42, 80, 109, 182
Southampton Plot, 13
Southampton, Hampshire, 40, 83, 91, 95, 191
Spencer, William, Mayor of Bristol, 82
St Albans, First Battle of (1455), 29–30, 39, 41, 42, 161

St Albans, Second Battle of (1461), 51, 58
St Martin-le-Grand, London, xxi, 102, 106
St Mary's Church, Ricall, Yorkshire, 159
St Mary's Collegiate Church, Warwickshire, 7, 28, 31, 36, 126
St Mary's Priory, Deerhurst, Gloucestershire, 97
St Michael's Mount, Cornwall, 112, 212
St Paul's Cathedral, 22, 41, 52, 90, 94, 136, 144, 185
Stacy, John, 133
Stafford, Edward, 177
Stafford, Sir Henry, 101, 149, 199
Stafford, Henry, 2nd Duke of Buckingham, 63, 136, 140–141, 145, 146, 155–156, 194, 210, 213
Stafford, Hugh, 2nd Earl of Stafford, 3
Stafford, Humphrey, 1st Duke of Buckingham, 13, 29–30, 46, 47, 205, 211
Stafford, Humphrey, 1st Earl of Devon, 75, 78
Stafford, Margaret, Countess of Westmorland, xiv, 4, 12, 79, 198, 207, 208
Stafford, Ralph, 1st Earl of Stafford, 3
Stafford, Sir John, 53
Stamford, Lincolnshire, 51, 81, 183
Stanford in the Vale, Berkshire, 108
  St Deny's Church, 108, 162
Stanhope, Maud, 24, 209
Stanley, George, 9th Baron Strange, 206
Stanley, Thomas, 1st Earl of Derby, 82, 99–100, 101, 127, 149, 174, 199, 206, 211
Stanley, Lord William, 206
Stillington, Robert, Bishop of Bath and Wells, 69, 144, 150
Stoke by Nayland, Suffolk, 70
Stoke, Battle of (1487), 195, 204
Stony Stratford, Buckinghamshire, 140, 141, 193, 213
Strangeways, Sir James, 54
Strangeways, Sir Richard, 206
Stratford at Bow Nunnery, 110
Stratford-upon-Avon, 132
  Guild of the Holy Cross, Stratford-upon-Avon, 130
Strensham, John, Abbot of Tewkesbury, 97, 125, 129, 135
Strugge, Roger, servant, 131
subtleties, 67

succession to the throne, 22, 23, 65, 75, 102, 133, 137, 142, 154, 177, 180, 190
sumptuary laws, 119
Sutton Coldfield, 176
Swynford, Katherine, Duchess of Lancaster, 10, 88, 118, 197, 198

Talbot, Eleanor, *see* Butler, Lady Eleanor
Talbot, Elizabeth, Duchess of Norfolk, 148
Talbot, John, 1st Earl of Shrewsbury, 9, 22, 29, 197
Taylor, John, servant, 135
Tewkesbury, xxi, 96, 128, 131, 152
   Abbey xx, 7, 16, 19, 97, 127, 136, 138
   Abbey Chronicle, 14, 113, 129
   Battle of (1471), 98–99, 100, 101, 147, 191, 201, 202, 204, 213
Threlkeld, Sir Lancelot, 176
Thursby, John, servant, 131, 132
Tiptoft, John, 1st Earl of Worcester, 8, 9, 19, 38, 56, 82, 83, 91, 114, 183, 205, 211, 218
Titulus Regius, 172, 195
Tocotes, Sir Roger, 132
Topcliffe, Yorkshire, 24, 62
Tower of London, 5, 25, 47, 72, 74, 86, 90, 93, 101, 104, 112, 113, 134, 136, 137, 141, 142, 143, 144, 146, 152, 154, 177, 179, 183, 184, 192, 194, 202, 209, 210, 212
Towton, Battle of (1461), 9, 52, 53, 82, 126, 149, 187, 196, 198, 200, 204, 211
Trinity, the, 74, 83
Trollope, Sir Andrew, 41, 42, 43, 50, 185, 211
Trotula, the, 20, 27, 28
tuberculosis, 115, 128, 164, 165, 168, 169
tuberculous endometritis, 115
Tuchet, James, 5th Baron Audley, 42, 185
Tuchet, John, 6th Baron Audley, 46, 47
Tudor dynasty, xviii
Tudor, Arthur, 175, 176, 177, 178, 195, 213
Tudor, Edmund, 1st Earl of Richmond, 15, 17, 105, 149, 184, 199, 212
Tudor, Henry, *see* Henry VII
Tudor, Jasper, 1st Earl of Pembroke, 51, 87, 89, 90, 91, 94, 95, 96, 101, 177, 187, 188, 190, 191, 192, 203, 213
Tudor, Owen, 51, 212

Tutbury Castle, Staffordshire, 39, 60, 64, 110
Twynyho, Ankarette, xxii, 123, 131–134
Twynyho, John, 123, 131
Twynyho, William, 123
Tyrell, Sir James, 111, 152, 153

Upmanby, Cumbria, 62

Valognes, Normandy, 86
Vaughan, Thomas, 140, 145, 194
Vaux, Lady Katherine, 97, 101
Vere, Aubrey de, 58
Vere, John de, 13th Earl of Oxford, 59, 110, 166, 208, 212
Vere, John de, 12th Earl of Oxford, 58–59
Vergil, Polydore, 10, 22, 40, 61, 62, 65, 70, 73, 100, 113, 136, 140, 145, 149, 153, 161, 165, 167, 170
Vernon, Sir Henry, 92
Vescy, Margaret, Lady Clifford, 176

Wake, Thomas, 78, 82
Wakefield, Battle of (1460), 50–51, 55, 58, 176, 186, 198, 199, 200, 208, 209
Wales, 75, 80, 90, 94, 96, 100, 109, 155, 191
   flight of Margaret of Anjou, 47, 49
   Somerset-Warwick dispute, 20, 23, 182
Warbeck, Perkin, 177, 212
wardenry of the Scottish Marches, 11, 39, 53
   East March, 79
   West March, 18, 82, 110, 118
wards, 3, 8, 13–14, 15, 23, 58, 59, 104, 137, 154, 176
Warkworth Chronicle, 61, 98, 99
Warwick Castle, 6, 7, 15, 19, 20, 40, 49, 53, 78, 125, 127, 128, 131, 132, 137, 152
Warwick-Lancaster alliance, 86–87, 88, 91, 190, 201, 204
Waurin, Jean de, 71
Waurin's Chronicle, 47, 48, 50, 64, 70, 74, 80, 107
Welles, John, 1st Viscount, 201
Welles, Richard, 7th Baron, 80–81
Welles, Sir Robert, 81–82, 190
Wells, Somerset, 96
Welsh Marches, 9, 49, 166, 187

Wenlock, John, Lord Wenlock, 71, 72, 84, 89, 92, 98, 161, 213
Westminster Abbey, xxii, 8, 90, 93, 94, 95, 113, 141, 143, 146, 147
 Hall, 145, 151
 Palace of, 23, 41, 48, 52, 134, 150, 171
wet nursing, 20, 34, 115, 124
Weymouth, Dorset, 93, 190, 191
William of Worcester, 64
Wilberfoss nunnery, Yorkshire, 160
wills, xx, 37, 162, 171
Windsor Castle, 69, 96, 112, 152
 St George's Chapel, 101
witchcraft, xxii, 33, 36, 78, 90, 131, 133, 142
women, xvii, xviii, xx, xxii, xxiii, 25, 26, 27, 34, 35, 36, 37, 38, 58, 83, 84, 116, 122, 127, 138, 158, 162
 femme covert, 44
 femme sole, xviii
 in law, legal rights of inheritance, 3, 44
 mortality, 19, 128
 nuns, 3
 and sin, 31
 widows, xviii, xix, 10, 13, 53, 58, 102, 103, 104, 107, 108, 157, 158, 172
Woodville faction, 62, 63, 68, 69, 75, 79, 102, 118, 131, 133, 135, 139, 143, 156, 189
Woodville plot, 141, 193

Woodville, Anthony, Lord Scales, later 2nd Earl Rivers, v, 69, 83, 139, 140, 213
Woodville, Eleanor, 63
Woodville, Elizabeth, Queen of England, xviii, xxii, 61, 63, 64, 68, 72, 95, 109, 122, 127, 134, 135, 140, 141, 142, 143–144, 145, 148, 151, 155, 157, 161, 166, 174, 177, 188, 190, 193, 194, 195, 200, 201, 202, 207, 214
Woodville, Sir John, 64, 78, 79, 208, 214
Woodville, Katherine, 177, 213
Woodville, Margaret, 63, 150
Woodville, Mary, 63, 203
Woodville, Richard, 1st Earl Rivers, 46, 78, 214
Worcester, 100
 bishop of, 129
Worksop, Nottinghamshire, 50
Wressle, Yorkshire, 24

York, city of;
 Corpus Christi Guild, 153, 158, 163
 House Books, 142
 Micklegate Bar, 50, 153, 186
 Minster, 126, 153–154, 157, 164, 172
 St William's College, 161
 Trinity Guild, 153
York, House of, xii, 63, 87, 94, 127, 149, 174, 175, 195, 201, 203
York, Sir Richard, Sheriff of York, 66